D1691983

CLASSIC SAILS
THE RATSEY & LAPTHORN STORY

George & Maureen

Not for Sale

CLASSIC SAILS

THE RATSEY & LAPTHORN STORY

William Collier

RATSEY & LAPTHORN
SAILS

First published in 1998 in the UK by Ratsey & Lapthorn Ltd.
The Sail Loft, Medina Road, Cowes, Isle of Wight PO21 7BY
Tel: +44 (0) 1983 294051   Fax: +44 (0) 1983 294053
E-mail: ratseysails@ratsey.com
Internet: http://www.ratsey.com/ratseysails.

Photography copyright
© Franco Pace 1998, © Rosenfeld Collection,
© Mystic Seaport Museum Inc., © Beken of Cowes

Text copyright © Ratsey & Lapthorn Ltd.

Design by FRANCO PACE Studio

ISBN 0 9534603 0 4   All rights reserved. No part of this publication
may be reproduced in any form or by any means - graphic, electronic or mechanical,
including photocopying, recording, taping or information storage and retrieval systems -
without the prior permission in writing of the publishers.

Printed and bound in Italy

Front cover: *Mariette*
© Franco Pace

**THERE IS TO BE ONLY
ONE STANDARD OF WORK IN THIS LOFT
AND THAT IS THE BEST**

Author's Preface

Ratsey & Lapthorn's name has a universality in yachting. Amidst endless trends that favour one particular designer or builder's yachts over another's, yacht owners have been unequivocal in their choice of sailmaker. From the earliest origins of yachting on the Solent Ratsey & Lapthorn played a leading role in its development. In transatlantic competitions, Britain's repeatedly frustrated attempts to win back the America's Cup dented the prestige of her designers and builders but not that of her sailmakers. Just as British yachtsmen had encouraged the development of Ratsey & Lapthorn on the Solent, their American counterparts invited the firm to establish a loft in New York.

Until the 1960s every British challenger for the America's Cup was equipped with Ratsey & Lapthorn sails and from 1903 all American defenders set the firm's canvas. This long period at the forefront of technological development eclipses the relatively short-term contributions of even the most long-lived yacht designers. But, as many sailmakers have commented, their contribution to successful yachts is that which is most frequently overlooked. The sheer scale of Ratsey & Lapthorn's dominance of their market may have fostered this apparent indifference. Quality yachts were invariably equipped with Ratsey & Lapthorn sails and sustained excellence stifled debates such as those that have helped document the careers of the leading yacht designers.

For over two centuries the success of Ratsey & Lapthorn has been driven by far seeing individuals. The alliance between the two families accounts in large part for the firm's longevity. This said, relations between Ratseys and Lapthorns and even within the families were frequently difficult and the predictable pattern of father-to-son handovers was interrupted by war. Remarkably, these and other difficulties acted to challenge the individuals within the firm, hardening their resolve to make outstanding sails and so prove their worth.

The wartime bombing of the Ratsey & Lapthorn's eighteenth century lofts in Cowes and Gosport reduced what was once the greatest archive of yacht sailmaking in the world to mere fragments. As interest in the firm's history grew fact was increasingly mingled with legend and hearsay. In late 1996 Ratsey & Lapthorn's offices were destroyed by fire inflicting yet further damage on the few archives that remained. The frustration caused by these compounded losses led Peter Woodd of Ratsey & Lapthorn to the conclusion that whilst historians would never have access to a complete archive, this should not be the excuse for further delay; now was the time to assemble the fragments and write the history of Ratsey & Lapthorn. I gladly accepted the commission to research and write this book.

The evidence presented in this book draws on a wide range of material including in-house, official, and published sources. These have been supplemented with interviews and the surviving papers of the many firms that collaborated with Ratsey & Lapthorn. The research process has been valedictory inasmuch as members of both the Ratsey and Lapthorn families have occasionally recorded segments of their stories, underlining a belief that they were a part of something important. Equally the mere process of research has helped identify the archival information that remains and ensure its future preservation.

I was fortunate in being able draw on a myriad of diverse documents conserved by archivists, museum curators, informed individuals and enthusiasts who had all been motivated by a sense of the firm's great importance and a long-term desire to gain a better idea of Ratsey & Lapthorn's history. I hope this book goes some way towards easing the frustration felt by all those seeking knowledge of the company's history.

In preparing this book I have received invaluable help. At Ratsey & Lapthorn's Peter Woodd, Mark Ratsey-Woodroffe and Andy Cassell did all they could to assist me. Now retired, James F. Lapthorn and Franklin Ratsey-Woodroffe welcomed my intrusions into their long memories. Less tangible but equally invaluable, Harry Spencer's account of his family's long association with the firm gave me confidence in my interpretation of some of the key characters and their motivations. Harold Ratsey, who as boy sat on the knees of Michael Ratsey, who built the first America's Cup challengers in the 1870s, underlined the proximity of what often seemed lost in the opacity of poor information.

At the Cowes Library and Maritime Museum Kathleen Harrison and Martin Crowther gave me invaluable assistance and Ian Edleman at the Gosport Museum did likewise. Cindy Olden of the Association of British Sailmakers kindly trawled through her files to my greater gain. Family historians and Ratsey family descendants Fred and Sheila Atkey generously shared the fruits of their long interest in the Ratsey family.

Far more archival information survives in America than in England and Llewellyn Howland III generously shared the results of his long interest in the firm. Equally A. Walter Stubner kindly gave me a copy of his unpublished notes. At Mystic Seaport Museum, where the archives of Ratsey & Lapthorn's New York loft are held, I received great assistance from Douglas Stein in the manuscript library and Georgia W. York in the registrar's office.

I am particularly pleased that it has been possible to include so many outstanding illustrations and this would not have been possible without the generous open house attitude at Beken of Cowes where Keith and Ken Beken, Peter Mumford and Jean Musson made my trips to Cowes pleasant and fruitful. The generosity of Major Robin Rising and the members of the Royal Yacht Squadron has allowed the reproduction of paintings from their outstanding collection. At Mystic Seaport's Rosenfeld Collection Victoria Sharps' happy efficiency rewarded my all too brief visits and long distance enquiries. Franco Pace's enthusiasm for this project has brought not only his photographs but his expertise in turning my manuscript into this book. David Ryder-Turner proof read the manuscript in record time and contributed a number of valuable suggestions. Many others too numerous to mention have helped and their contributions are none the less appreciated.

William Collier
Hamble, October 1998

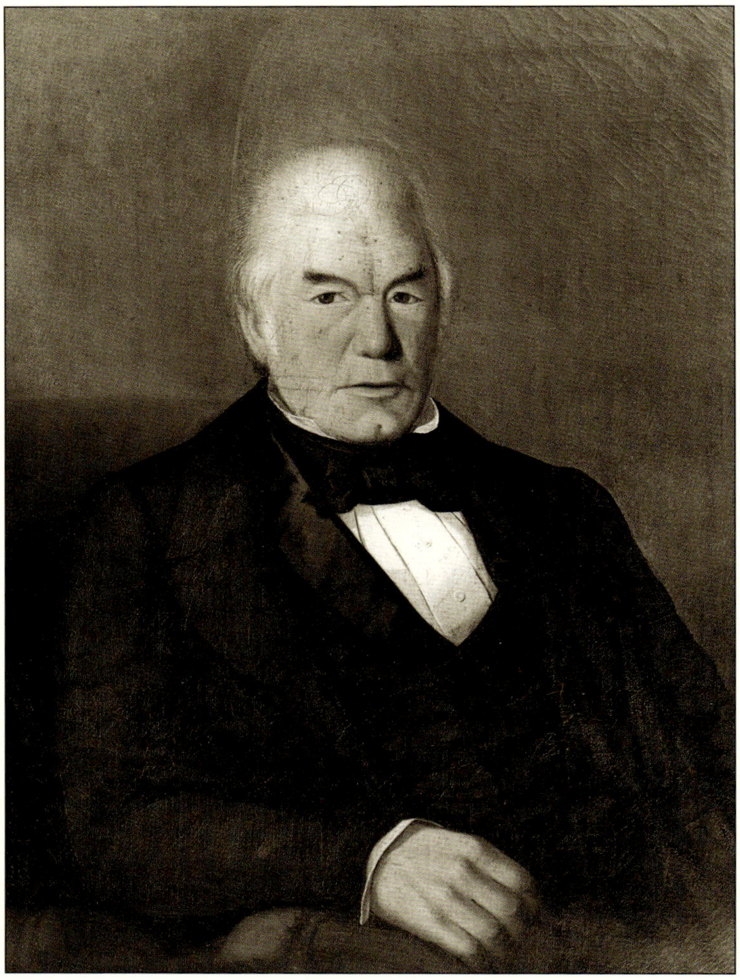

The Ratsey family have lived on the Isle of Wight for upwards of 500 years and throughout that period have had close seafaring connections. The Ratsey's sail making firm was established by George Rogers Ratsey who was born in 1769 and remained a relative landlubber when compared to his brothers. All six of his brothers who survived into adulthood followed their father into the British Royal Navy. The late eighteenth and early nineteenth centuries were dominated by the Napoleonic wars and at various times up to a dozen Ratsey brothers and cousins were scattered through the Mediterranean, Atlantic and even the Pacific serving aboard various naval ships. George's father and three of his brothers fought at the battle of the Glorious First of June in 1794 when the British successfully broke the French blockade complete with its implications of food shortages and possible starvation. With so many family members away from home in high risk occupations, the Ratsey family tradition which says that George Rogers Ratsey was merely obeying his father's instructions in staying ashore is certainly credible. His role was to care and provide for the wives and possible widows of his naval brothers. This said, he did join the Cowes Militia Volunteers when French invasion threatened.

Initially George's business was general trading between Cowes and the mainland. Coal was a staple cargo for his in-bound vessels as was Isle of Wight-grown wheat for those returning from Cowes to Southampton and other ports along the Solent. He owned shares in a number of small trading wherries and as early as 1814, when the British were briefly at peace with the French, he was engaged in importing wheat from France.[1] In parallel with this legitimate trade Ratsey was implicated in smuggling which his son, Charles, would later describe as being '*most extensively carried on at this port.*'[2] In 1814 the smack *Lord Wellington* of which he was part-owner was seized by customs officers when they discovered '*spirits in small jars concealed.*'[3] Sailmaking was a relatively late addition to Ratsey's diverse and generally opportunistic activities. His uncle John Ratsey had worked as a sailmaker in other lofts from as early as 1772 and in 1790 he joined his nephew initiating the diversification of the latter's business.

There is no evidence to suggest that the new sail making enterprise was particularly large-scale. Rather, it most probably provided sails for a variety of small vessels built in, and trading out of, Cowes and this continued after John Ratsey's retirement in 1797. Certainly in 1813, the year from which the earliest archives survive, the firm was supplying sails to the owners of smacks, pilot cutters and even the Excise Board, begging the possibility that these served in the arrest of the Ratsey-owned *Lord Wellington*. Incongruous amongst the various clients listed are Lords Nugent and Kilcommie whose requirements may have been linked to yachting.[4] Although unsubstantiated, this would make these the first patrons for the type of sails for which the firm would gain renown. If these sails were for yachts, such early yachting activity was certainly unusual given that the great rise of British yachting on the Solent occurred following the close of the Napoleonic wars in 1815 and the formation of The Yacht Club, later better known as the Royal Yacht Club or Royal Yacht Squadron.

The establishment of the Royal Yacht Squadron in Cowes did not go hand in hand with any but the vaguest of objectives and it was ten years or so before racing by its members became organised. Lacking a stated purpose, the most active squadron members divided their attentions between building large cutters derived from the smuggling type or naval style brigs. Those who built brigs did so in a bid to improve the admiralty's standards of naval architecture. Consequently their yachts were fully armed and to the uninformed, largely indistinguishable from the naval equivalent. It was the activities of the so called naval-imitators that brought the Squadron to national prominence and the activities of its members were greeted as highly patriotic. In 1826 a Southampton newspaper commented that:

> If, however, there is among the introductions of modern times, any one species of sport that deserves to be dignified with the name and character of patriotic, it must be the Royal Yacht Club; for not only has science been greatly increased by the various experiments pursued by those wealthy individuals in the building and equipment of their vessels, but as a nursery for able seamen and an auxiliary source of employment to a class of artisans, the shipwright, who in time of peace requires some such aid, it cannot be too highly applauded nor too generally acknowledged. To approve this, is to promote every new member of the Royal Yacht Club, who must be considered a national benefactor.[5]

Opposite: George Rogers Ratsey (1793-1851) founded the Cowes loft in 1790. / *Mystic Seaport Museum*

Just like the sailors and shipwrights, all those involved in the maritime trades benefited from the activities of the yacht building élite and Cowes became the centre of the new pursuit. The yachtsmen were responsible for initiating a new trade, the building and equipping of yachts and it was Ratsey whom they turned to for their sails. Moreover, Ratsey soon gained the role of advisor to the early yachtsmen who relied on his judgement at a time when neither hull length or sail area were yet taken into account by the owners of competing yachts. Few descriptions of these first yacht races survive but amongst the best are those written by George Rogers Ratsey's son Charles. Born in 1812, Charles Ratsey, joined his father's firm circa 1830 and not only recorded his father's role in early yacht racing but also described these from first hand experience:

> In 1826 Mr Joseph Weld challenged the Marquis of Anglesey to sail the *Arrow* against the *Pearl* for £500. The Marquis at that time had the *Pearl* and a smaller vessel of 40 tons, called the *Liberty*, whilst Mr Weld had the *Arrow* and the *Julia* of 40 tons. It was arranged that the *Arrow* should sail against the *Pearl*, and the *Liberty* against the *Julia*; and as the *Pearl* won her match, and the *Julia* hers, no money passed. Lord Anglesey in accepting the challenge, said, '*If the Arrow should beat the Pearl, I will burn her as soon as we get back*'; as it was the *Pearl* won by a fluke. Lord Belfast at the time had a cutter named *Elizabeth* which he sold, and employed Joseph White, of Cowes, to build the *Harriet*. He later sailed several times against the *Arrow*, but not very successfully and it was thought the fault lay with the sailing master. Lord Belfast consulted Geo. R. Ratsey (the sailmaker) on the subject, and asked him if it would do to challenge the owner of *Arrow* for a hundred, and Ratsey said '*Yes*'. Edward Corke, the pilot, was sent for to know if he would take charge, and he did. The challenge was given, and Mr Weld accepted it, to sail over the King's Cup course. They started to the westward under four sails, a stiff breeze blowing from the southward. Edward Corke, as soon as he rounded the vessel off Yarmouth, got the topmast on deck as the wind backed easterly and freshened. In the end *Harriet* won the prize by twenty two and a half minutes. After that Lord Belfast had the *Therese*, 140 tons, built also by Joseph White, but she was of no great account. Next he had the *Louisa* built, of about 150 tons, but being too full forward was lengthened the next year by the bow, and made 165 tons. I sailed

in her on several occasions against the *Alarm*, Mr Weld; *Menai*, Mr Assheton Smith; *Arundel*, Duke of Norfolk; and *Mirande*, Mr Maxse; all large cutters. The *Alarm* was generally the winning vessel, and Lord Belfast came to Ratsey's sail loft rather disappointed, and said to him, '*It is very evident we can do nothing with the Alarm inside the island, what do you say to challenging her for a thousand round the Owers?*' Ratsey replied, '*Yes, do it by all means.*' The challenge was given at once, and immediately accepted. The day appointed was in September, 1831. They started from Spithead at six in the morning, wind E. Stations were tossed for on *Louisa's* deck, and Mr Weld won the choice. The *Alarm* at the time was on the starboard weather bow of the *Louisa* both vessels heading towards Southsea. Mr Weld immediately went forward and let go his foresheet. Several attempts were made to get the *Louisa* clear of *Alarm's* lee quarter, but Corke could not succeed. The yachts tacked under Southsea, and in standing out on the port tack *Louisa* held her own. As soon as they got into a little lump of a sea it was very evident what the result would be, as the *Louisa* sailed right through the *Alarm's* lee, and then gradually soaked away from her. It was very visible on that day that *Alarm's* bow was most unsuitable for a sea, and when the sea struck her under her hollow run the mainsail was of little use to her, as it made the sail shake all over. A mark vessel called the *Sons of Commerce* was sent the night before up to the Owers, which mark vessel the yachts had to round. In beating up to the Owers it was a matter of speculation as where this vessel would be, and a watch was kept on the cross-trees to look out for her; at last the vessel was seen, but *Louisa* could not fetch her on the tack (port) she was on. The flood tide was drawing to a close, and the wind gradually lessening, and *Louisa* was put about. Michael Corke said to his brother Edward who was sailing the Louisa, '*We must run a little hazard today. Don't go about until I*

Opposite: The cutter *Harriet* built by Joseph White of Cowes for the Earl of Belfast in 1825. This painting was commissioned by Belfast from William John Huggins in 1827 but the ensign was added later to record the granting of the White Ensign to the Royal Yacht Squadron in 1829. / *Royal Yacht Squadron*

Above: The Earl of Belfast's cutter *Louisa* painted by William John Huggins in 1832. Louisa's 1831 victory over the *Arrow* allowed Belfast to claim ownership of the fastest cutter afloat before he set out to challenge the Royal Navy with his brig *Waterwitch*. / *Royal Yacht Squadron*

tell you, the ebbtide is now just beginning to come down hard; and if we don't fetch round next time we shan't get round at all, as the wind is falling light.' When *Louisa* put about for the last time I could see the rocks underneath the *Louisa's* bottom, and by standing in so far over the rocks, for weathering distance, *Louisa* just fetched round on her next port tack; the *Alarm* was about two miles under *Louisa's* lee at the time, and it was evident that they were faint-hearted on board, as she did not reach in so far as *Louisa* did, and in reaching off the port tack they could not fetch the mark; that settled the *Alarm* and they gave up the race. The wind gradually dropped, and *Louisa* did not reach the mark vessel off Cowes Castle until four o'clock next morning. Lord Belfast then said to G. R. Ratsey (my father), '*I have proved to the world that I possess the fastest cutter afloat, I will now see what I can do with a square rigger.*'[6]

When the Earl of Belfast graduated from cutter sailing and decided to try his hand at building a better brig than any other, he set his eye on the navy's *HMS Pantaloon* as the ship to beat. When Belfast's *Waterwitch* was launched from Joseph White's yard in East Cowes in 1832 and fitted out with all the guns and equipment of a man-of-war it was widely understood that if she could beat the *Pantaloon*, the British government would buy her. At the time *Pantaloon* was away from Portsmouth but not to be put off Belfast set off in search of her with his sailmaker, George Rogers Ratsey, numbering amongst his 70 crew. When eventually the two ships met off the coast of Portugal, *Waterwitch* proved superior on all points of sailing. After a brief return to Cowes, Belfast set out to cruise with the navy's Channel Squadron and it was from *Waterwitch* that the ever present Ratsey was summoned aboard the flagship *HMS Donegal* by Admiral Sir Pultney Malcolm. The Admiral met him at the gangway demanding to know what it was about his sails that made them '*so far superior to those in all the fleet.*' Ratsey's response is not recorded but shortly after *The Times* reported that:[7]

Above: The Royal Yacht Squadron fleet off Spithead during their 1832 voyage to Cherbourg. To the left the cutter *Pearl* owned by the Marquis of Anglesey, right the Earl of Belfast's brig *Waterwitch*. In the centre the brig *Falcon* owned by Royal Yacht Squadron Commodore the Earl of Yarborough. / *Author's Collection*

The Board of Admiralty having expressed its very great admiration of the beautiful symmetry and standing of the sails of the *Waterwitch* yacht, made by Mr Ratsey, of Cowes, have ordered that the sails of the men-of-war shall in future be cut in a similar manner.[8]

Before finally selling *Waterwitch* to the Admiralty, Belfast sought further victories and challenged the owner of any square rigger afloat to race his ship from Cowes round the Eddystone light house and back for a £1,000 stake. With no competitors immediately forthcoming, Belfast was eventually forced to take on the schooner yacht *Galatea* in 1834. On the day of the race, the weather was so violent that the commissioners of Portsmouth Dockyard who were due to start them would not venture out of the harbour leaving the yachts to do their best alone. The race instructions included no specific direction for rounding the Eddystone and the yachts met each other going in opposite directions as they rounded; Charles Ratsey on board the eventually victorious *Waterwitch* recorded the scene:

The Eddystone was rounded by *Waterwitch* at two o'clock in the morning, it being very dark and blowing a gale, breakers coming aboard. After rounding, and to our surprise, there was the *Galatea* within a hail on out port side, both vessels then being before the wind, *Waterwitch's* boom being on the starboard, and *Galatea's* on the port. The *Galatea* closed so near that [captain] Corke hailed him, 'Starboard your helm, or otherwise we must go ashore on the rocks or sink you!' They then starboarded, and the vessels parted company, the *Galatea* shipping a sea, as we afterwards heard, which split the forestay-sail from clew to head.[9]

Within 10 years of this race Charles Ratsey succeeded his father at the head of the firm.

Below: The schooner *Galatea* temporarily ahead of the Earl of Belfast's brig *Waterwitch* at the start of their celebrated race around the Eddystone lighthouse in September 1834. Charles Ratsey raced aboard *Waterwitch*. / *Author's Collection*

Over: William John Huggins' commemorative portrait of the Earl of Belfast's yachts. *Waterwitch* is in the centre with the cutters *Harriet* and *Louisa* to either side. The yachts in the background may be the those of his rivals whilst the diminutive brigantine to the left of *Waterwitch* is the experimental *Emily* of 1830. / *Royal Yacht Squadron*

14

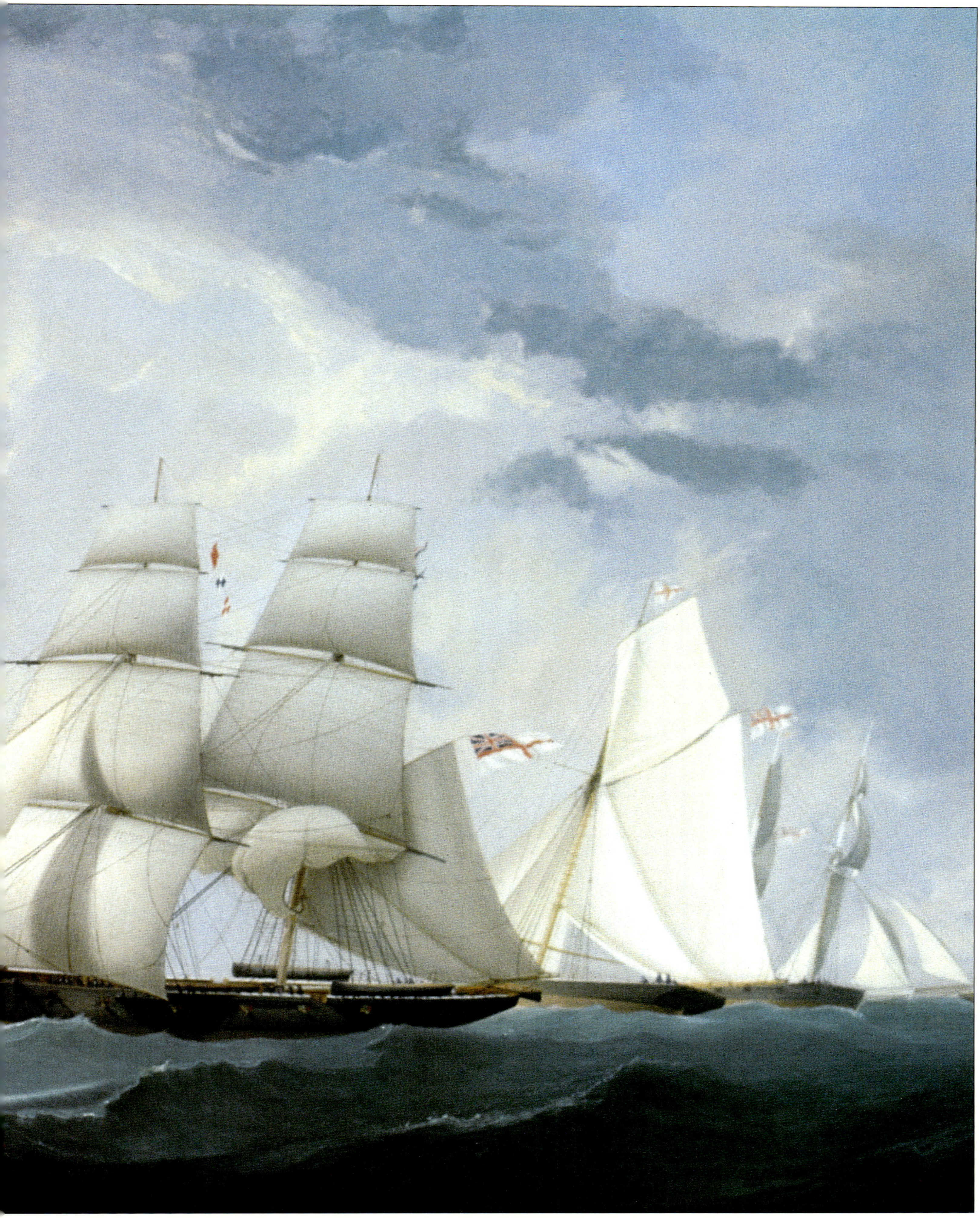

The specialised infrastructure that emerged to service yachting on the Solent first appeared in Cowes but it soon spread to the mainland. In Lymington, Joseph Inman's yacht building yard was established in 1821 and William Camper, who took over the Amos yard in Gosport in 1824, was clearly involved in yacht maintenance long before he built his first yacht in 1836. Like Cowes, Gosport suffered from recession with the close of the French wars; essentially a satellite town to Portsmouth, its economic welfare was inextricably linked to the navy. Amongst the naval suppliers who suffered was William Battershall from whose sail loft, adjacent to Camper's yard, naval ships were supplied throughout the hostilities. By the 1820's the Battershall sail loft was in decline and eventually closed down altogether. Conversely, in 1825 a new sailmaker arrived in Gosport and flourished. James Lapthorn was a descendant of a well-established family of sail makers from Portlemouth, Devon but having quarrelled with his brothers he had moved to London. In the capital he met Royal Yacht Squadron member Capt. Lyon who gave him the financial backing he needed to establish himself as a specialised yacht sailmaker in Gosport.

It was Lyon's brother, James, who commissioned Camper's first yacht *Osprey* and together with other members of his family, they proved to be the most important early patrons of Gosport yachting interests. By the mid-1840s Lapthorn had taken over Battershall's premises and his interests became directly aligned with those of his yacht-building neighbour. Beyond yachting, the two entrepreneurs were active members in a number of Gosport-based ship owning syndicates through the 1840's. With exception of coal dealing, the Lapthorn business was initially very similar to that of their Ratsey rivals and certainly sailmaking extended to the manufacture of flags, bunting and other accoutrements of yachting. Like Ratsey, Lapthorn was joined by his sons, but where these made great contributions to the growth of the Lapthorn loft, Charles Ratsey presided over a decline in his firm's fortunes.

Below: Portsmouth harbour in 1828 seen from the site of William Camper's Gosport yard in a painting by M. Yarwood. William Battershall's (spellings vary) sailmaking business had close associations with the Royal Navy but suffered after the close of the Napoleonic wars and his loft was taken over by James Lapthorn. The proximity of these yacht building and sail making businesses established Gosport as a major yachting centre. / *The Dean and Chapter of Chichester Cathedral*

After taking over a successful firm in 1844, Charles Ratsey's business environment was shaken through the 1850's by a series of events which acted to alienate him from his traditional yachting business. Not only did the death of his father in 1851 sever links with still emergent yachting but two months later the New York Yacht Club schooner *America* inflicted a stunning defeat on a fleet of British yachts, which challenged contemporary wisdom in British yacht building and sailmaking. A year after the death of his first wife in 1847, Charles Ratsey married Elizabeth White, daughter of Joseph White, the doyen of Cowes yacht builders. Any business benefits that such an alliance might have brought were soon ended when the Crimean War (1854 to 1856) brought about a virtual cessation of yachting with White amongst the first bankrupts. From this period and until the 1870s Ratsey's firm was clearly in trouble and he appears to have returned to such staples as coal trading to ensure an income. His earliest surviving gore book is for 1866 and this reveals the wide variety of sailmaking work he was forced to take on. Sails for commercial ships feature prominently alongside orders for yacht sails suggesting the possibility of a strategic shift away from yachting as a core business. But, this market area was already being eroded by the ever increasing use of steam propulsion and in the 1860s the firm was even chasing orders for awnings and boat covers.

In 1866 Charles took his 15 year old son from his second marriage, Thomas White Ratsey, out of school and set him to work in his sail loft with the words '*Get me out of debt Tom.*' Certainly, the family firm could not support both Charles' sons and within two years George Rogers Ratsey II, his eldest son from his first marriage, was forced to leave Cowes and take employment with London sailmakers Lane & Neeve. In London George R. Ratsey II seems to have done his fair share of moonlighting, visiting Ratsey clients after hours, liaising with other coal dealers and seeking out details of the Lapthorn's sail cloth suppliers. In these difficult years for the firm Tom Ratsey evidently learnt his trade fast and within 3 years of joining the firm he had cut and sewn his first suit of sails; the earliest identified being for the auxiliary steam yacht *Cervantes*.

Below: In 1868, two years after joining his father's business, the 17 year old Tom Ratsey (1851-1935) posed on the roof of the firm's original Cowes sail loft. The grocer's premises in the background were later converted into a residence by Uffa Fox. / *Franklin Ratsey-Woodroffe*

Right: Charles Ratsey (1812-1897) was the second of the family to head the sail making business. Although a prominent Cowes businessman, he was unable to sustain the firm's position which was only revived when he was joined by his son Thomas W. Ratsey. / *Mystic Seaport Museum*

In Gosport, the Lapthorn loft benefited from a very different situation; the key to this was its proximity to the Camper's prospering yard. James Lapthorn and William Camper's careers spanned similar eras. Whilst Lapthorn was joined by his sons James II and Edwin, Camper had no direct successors, but by passing his business on to Ben Nicholson with the consequent formation of Camper & Nicholson in 1863, he ensured the future of the Gosport yard. It was the Nicholson-designed schooner *Aline* of 1860 which offered the first genuinely innovative British response to the challenge of *America* and as result the Camper & Nicholson yard dominated large sailing yacht construction in Britain for over twenty years. Through a generous system of commissions, the Lapthorns ensured a virtual monopoly over Camper & Nicholson's output. As early as 1863, James Lapthorn II had been able to commission his own yacht from Nicholson, the 7 ton TM *Snowdrop*. The families grew close and intermarried. In 1888 Edwin Lapthorn's twin sons Edwin W. and Thomas H. F. both married Nicholson daughters in a double wedding celebrated on their birthday. For Gosport this was a significant event, '*flags and bunting were displayed about the town*', the yachts in the harbour dressed over all and '*hundreds of people eager to see the happy couples were assembled.*' Additionally, the newspaper report recorded the significance of brides' and grooms' fathers as the largest employers in the town.[10]

The only surviving Lapthorn gore book of the period (for 1874-75) proves the great importance of the connection with the Camper & Nicholson yard. It features details of the sails the Lapthorn's built for many of the largest sailing and auxiliary yachts built in Britain, including those for the Camper &

Right: Ben Nicholson (1828-1906) was apprenticed to William Camper in 1842 and rose to become one of the most significant yacht designers and builders of the Victorian era. In 1863 he became sole owner of the Camper & Nicholson yard. / *Author's Collection*
Below: On 1 June 1888 the twins Edwin W. and Thomas H. F. Lapthorn married Ben Nicholson's daughters Louisa Jane and Elsie May sealing a strong alliance between the sailmaking and yacht building families. Edwin Lapthorn is seen to the left of his wife Eliza, who stands between the brides whilst Edwin W. is to the left of his father and Thomas H. F. to the right of his mother. Ben Nicholson and his wife Sarah Anne are to the right of Thomas H. F. Lapthorn. Charles E. Nicholson who had yet to find fame as a yacht designer is second from right. / *Carey Blake*

Above: The 1860 Ben Nicholson-designed schooner *Aline* was the first genuinely innovative response to the *America's* challenge British yachting supremacy. This yacht later owned by Edward, Prince of Wales established her designer's leading position. / *Beken of Cowes*

Over: Schooner racing died out in the 1880's and Ben Nicholson's *Amphitrite* of 1887 was the last of the type to be built. Flying her full up-wind wardrobe of Lapthorn-made sails *Amphitrite* is seen leading the M. E. Ratsey-designed schooner *Cetonia*. / *Beken of Cowes*

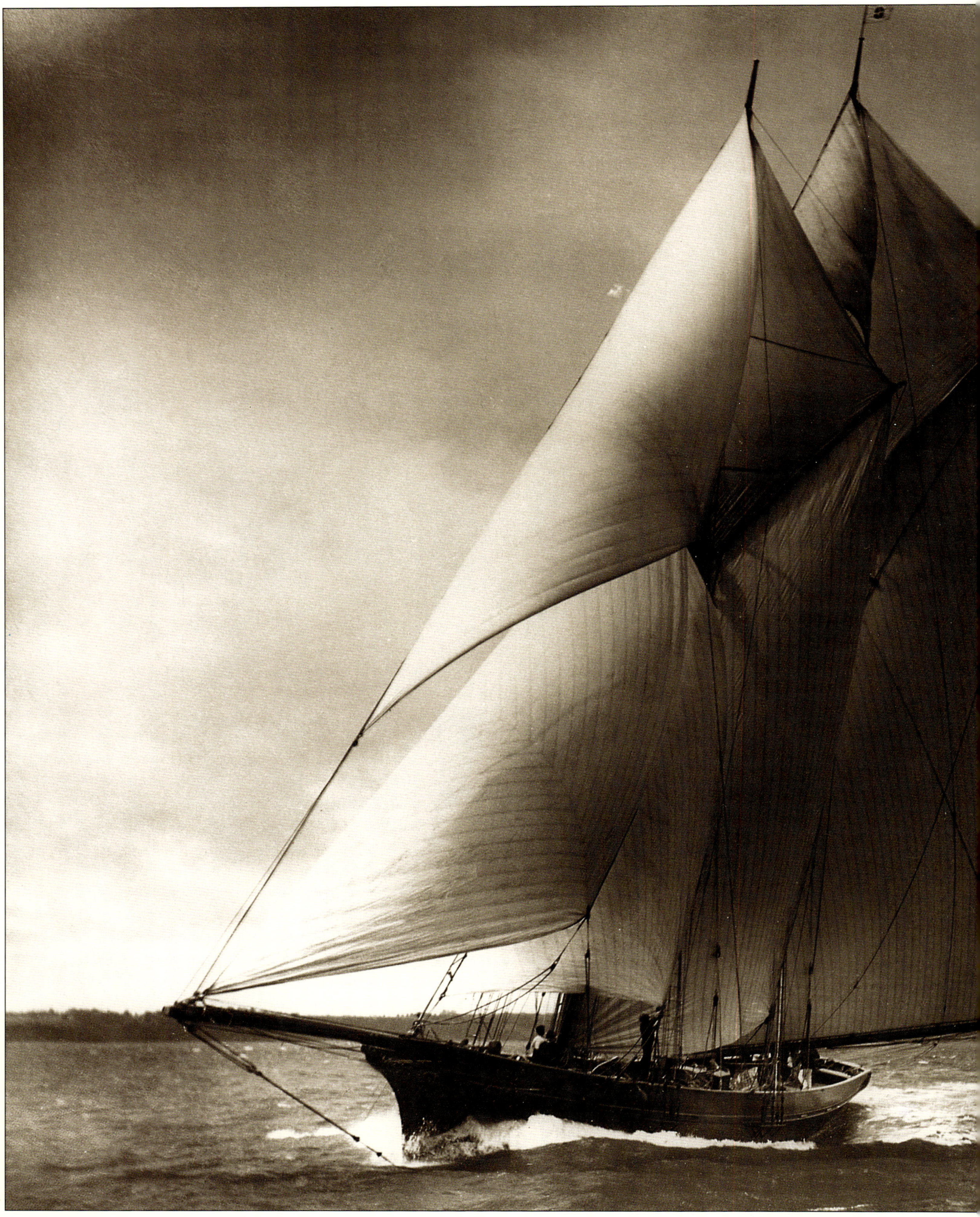

Nicholson-built *Bodicea* which remains the largest pure sailing yacht ever built in Britain. Moreover, in the 20 years from 1860 Camper & Nicholson led large sailing yacht construction, building more than 30 vessels of 100 feet or more. Furthermore, at a time when British yacht building was split between centres on the Solent, in Essex and on the Clyde in Scotland, the Lapthorns had forged strong business connections with the yacht building yards in all these areas; a sharp contrast to the Ratseys purely local market. The Lapthorns contributed sails to many of the larger Fife and other Scottish-built yachts from the mid-1860's onwards. Similarly on the East coast they collaborated with the now largely forgotten builder John Harvey, most notably providing sails for his 1875 rule cheater *Jullanar*.

In the aftermath of the 1850's crisis in yacht building, two Cowes yards emerged as particularly significant. Of these Charles Hansen's never grew to rival that of Michael Ratsey who succeeded Joseph White as the foremost Cowes yacht builder. Michael was the son of Lynn Ratsey who built the *Leopard* in 1807, one of the earliest documented Cowes-built yachts. Despite their shared name and similarity of business areas the yacht building and sailmaking Ratseys acknowledged no family relationship. They were related but only by dint of a common ancestor, Matthew Ratsey born in 1650, a fact they had no cause to be aware of. Retiring in 1865, Michael Ratsey was succeeded by his son Michael Edward who ran the firm until it eventually closed in 1878. His name is indelibly associated with the first two British challengers for the America's Cup which he designed and built for James Ashbury.

The schooner *Cambria* was launched in 1868 and it was only after her success against the visiting American schooner *Sappho* and Ashbury's suggestion that English yacht owners should make a return visit to New York, complete with a transatlantic race, that the New York Yacht Club informed him that the cup won by *America* in 1851 had been available for international challenge since 1857. Immediately Ashbury set about organising his challenge but this was eventually delayed until 1870 since he had previously committed himself to being present at the opening of the Suez canal. By the time *Cambria* returned from this Mediterranean diversion the American schooner *Dauntless* had arrived in Cowes with a view to repeating *America*'s achievement. Ashbury seized the opportunity to challenge

Dauntless to the first international ocean race and combined this with his inaugural challenge for the America's Cup. After winning the trans-Atlantic race by a mere hour and 45 minutes, the unsuccessful America's Cup race against a fleet of N. Y. Y. C. yachts was an unsatisfactory event. Not to be put off, Ashbury challenged again and returned to New York in 1871 with a new schooner, the *Livonia*.

To build his new yacht, Ashbury again chose M. E. Ratsey but having had Lapthorn-made sails on *Cambria*, for *Livonia* he opted for Ratsey sails. The securing of this order was the first significant sign that the Ratsey loft was on the up again. The America's Cup as a contest had been established and Ratsey's were the sailmakers of choice. The surviving 1871 to 1874 gore book records the details of all 19 sails of *Livonia's* original suit, the first coming under the heading '*A schooner of 280 tons by M. Ratsey for J. Ashbury Esq. to be named the Livonia*'. The motives behind Ashbury's choice can only be speculated upon but certainly the early 1870's correspond with the period when Tom Ratsey was first beginning to successfully exert his influence on the development of the firm's output.

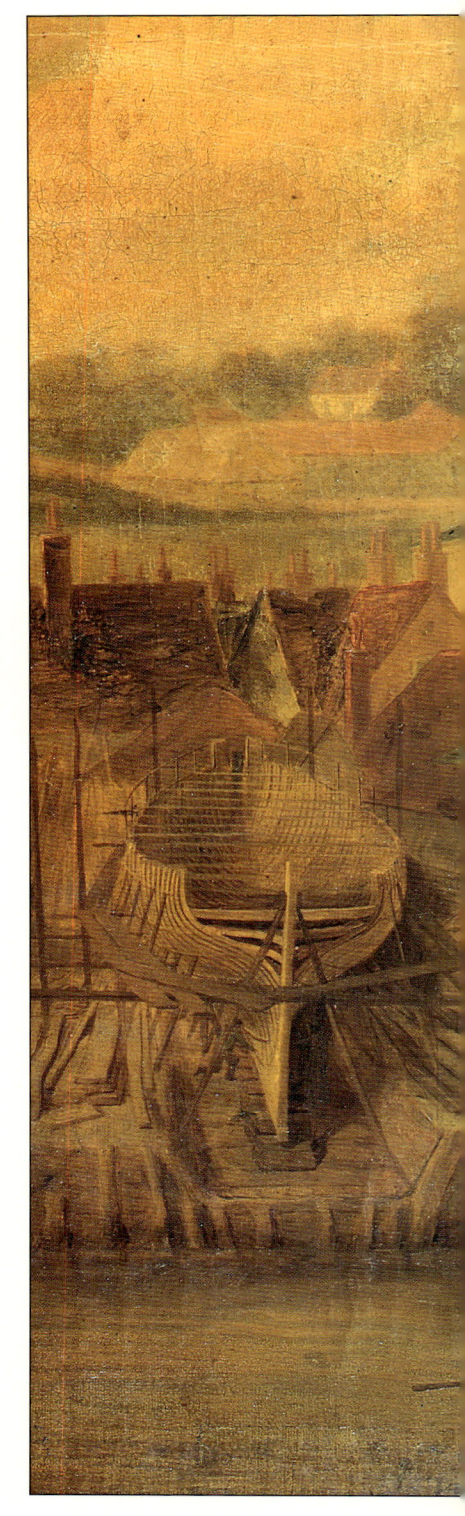

Left: The radical John Harvey-built yawl *Jullanar* of 1875 sailed through all the loopholes of the contemporary rating system and heralded a period of rapid design evolution. This last photograph of the celebrated yacht shows her being dismantled by Camper & Nicholsons in 1905. The Lapthorn loft is in the background. / *Photo by A. W. Nicholson, Author's Collection*

Above: The ship and yacht building Ratseys were distantly related to the sail making Ratseys. Their yard on the Cowes water front as painted by Charles Gregory in 1845 was adjacent to the sail loft and it was on these slips that M. E. Ratsey built *Cambria* and *Livonia*, the first two America's Cup challengers. / *Harold A. Ratsey*

Above: Michael E. Ratsey (1830-1915) the third and final of the yacht building Ratseys. Through his association with America's Cup challenger James Ashbury and many other prominent yachtsmen he became one of the most highly regarded British yacht designers and builders of the 1860s and 70s. / *Harold A. Ratsey*

Above: In 1870 the Ratsey-built *Cambria* became the first challenger for the America's Cup. The races for the cup were delayed so that owner, James Ashbury, could be present at the opening of the Suez Canal. Consequently *Cambria* was the first sailing yacht to pass through the canal. Flying Lapthorn sails *Cambria* was defeated in the America's Cup but won the transatlantic race that preceded it against the crack American schooner *Dauntless*. / *Harold A. Ratsey*

Over: James Ashbury's second challenge for the America's Cup in 1871 was with the new Ratsey-built schooner *Livonia*. For the sails he switched his allegiance from the Lapthorn to the Ratsey loft signalling its return to the forefront of yachting under Tom Ratsey's stewardship. / *Harold A. Ratsey*

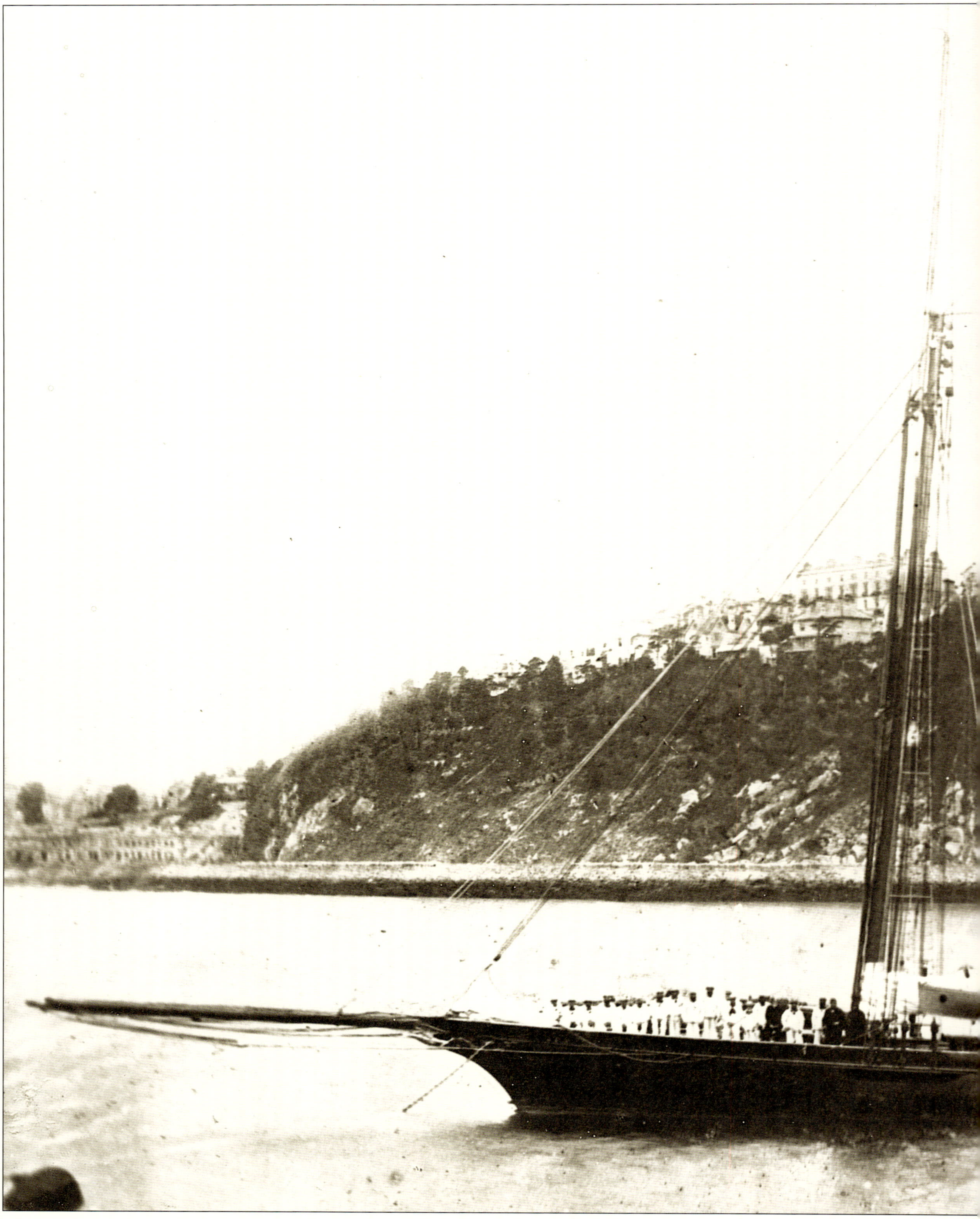

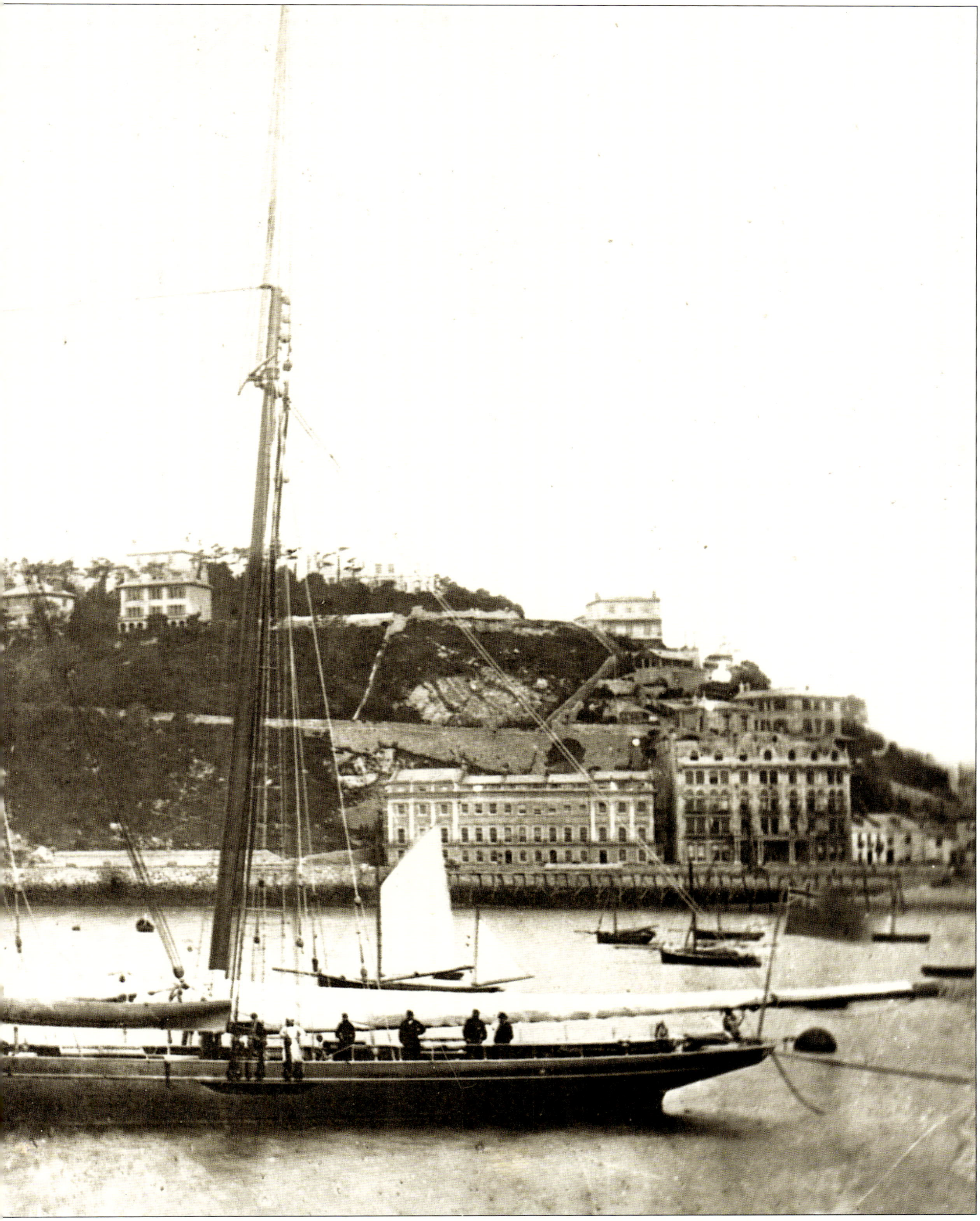

From *America's* 1851 victory on, most commentators have correctly listed her cotton sails high amongst the attributes that contributed to her advantages over the British yachts with their flax sails. Additionally *America's* fore and main sails were laced to the booms and could consequently be set flatter than the loose-footed English sails. Although the impact of *America's* victory was very widely felt throughout the British yachting fraternity and the yacht itself was bought by English yachtsmen, the lessons were slowly learnt. On first seeing *America*, veteran yachtsman the Marquis of Anglesey had remarked '*If she is right, we must all be wrong*', but ten years later the Lapthorns were making *America* a new suit of new loose footed flax sails. With specific regard to the evolution of sails William Cooper, a leading commentator of British yachting of the 1870's, wrote: '*We cannot reconcile any deviation from established custom with our notions of the way things should be. Very few yachtsmen are disposed to experimentalize with yachts or their equipment; it is rather an expensive hobby when indulged in to any extent.*'[11] Thomas W. Ratsey's great achievement was in overcoming the innate conservatism that dominated the debates in British sail-making throughout the latter half of the nineteenth century.

The tradition of flax sails was centuries old, and in a yachting culture that still predominantly viewed a sail as bag with which to catch and retain the wind, it seemed to be the ideal sail making material. It is a naturally baggy fabric and stretches every time it is set. Indeed, amongst relative sophisticates a technique of wetting sails for windward sailing existed since in this way the flax could be shrunk into a less baggy surface that would be more efficient when sailing on the wind. Additionally, flax is a soft material, easily handled and very durable. Cotton, on the other hand, becomes hard and extremely difficult to fold when wet, it is also prone to mildew. Beyond these simple parameters there were others which contributed to the widespread use of flax for yacht sails until around 1900. The cotton *America* had used was of excellent quality but with the rise of steam power, weaver's interest in maintaining the quality of cotton duck for ships sails declined, a point Tom Ratsey made forcibly in 1921:

Cotton and sailmaking so far as we know it has become a lost art due to competition and steam. The duck is not to be compared with what it was 50 years ago. I am not speaking without knowledge as I remember all about *Henrietta, Fleetwing, Vesta, Dauntless* and *Sappho's* sails and unless the cloth can be improved, there will never be decent fore and aft sails made again. The unfortunate part is, from all we hear, that these duck manufacturing companies keep on changing hands and the successive managers or directors, keep on succeeding each other and all they apparently think about is how much money they can make. Then again the weavers die out and I very much doubt if their successors profit by the experience and interest which their predecessors gained during their lifetimes.[12]

Opposite: The schooner *America* whose 1851 victory began the greatest of yachting competitions. After her victory she passed into British ownership and despite the clear advantage that her relatively flat cotton sails had given her, her British owners re-equipped her with loose footed flax sails. *America* is seen her in 1885 when again in American ownership she was outfitted with cotton sails which were laced to the booms. / *Beken of Cowes*

Above: Throughout his life Tom Ratsey was closely identified with his yacht *Dolly Varden*. Indeed, the yacht became almost as famous as the man. In the mid-1930s when *Dolly Varden* was over 60 years old, Uffa Fox still believed her to be the fastest cutter of her length in the world. Ratsey raced her avidly, used her for countless experiments and lived aboard her in the summer. / *Beken of Cowes*

Over: Yachts drying sails off Cowes. Although Ratsey & Lapthorn introduced their own anti-mildew composition the threat of rot and the consequent need to ensure that sails were dried remained one of the main drawbacks of cotton sails. / *Beken of Cowes*

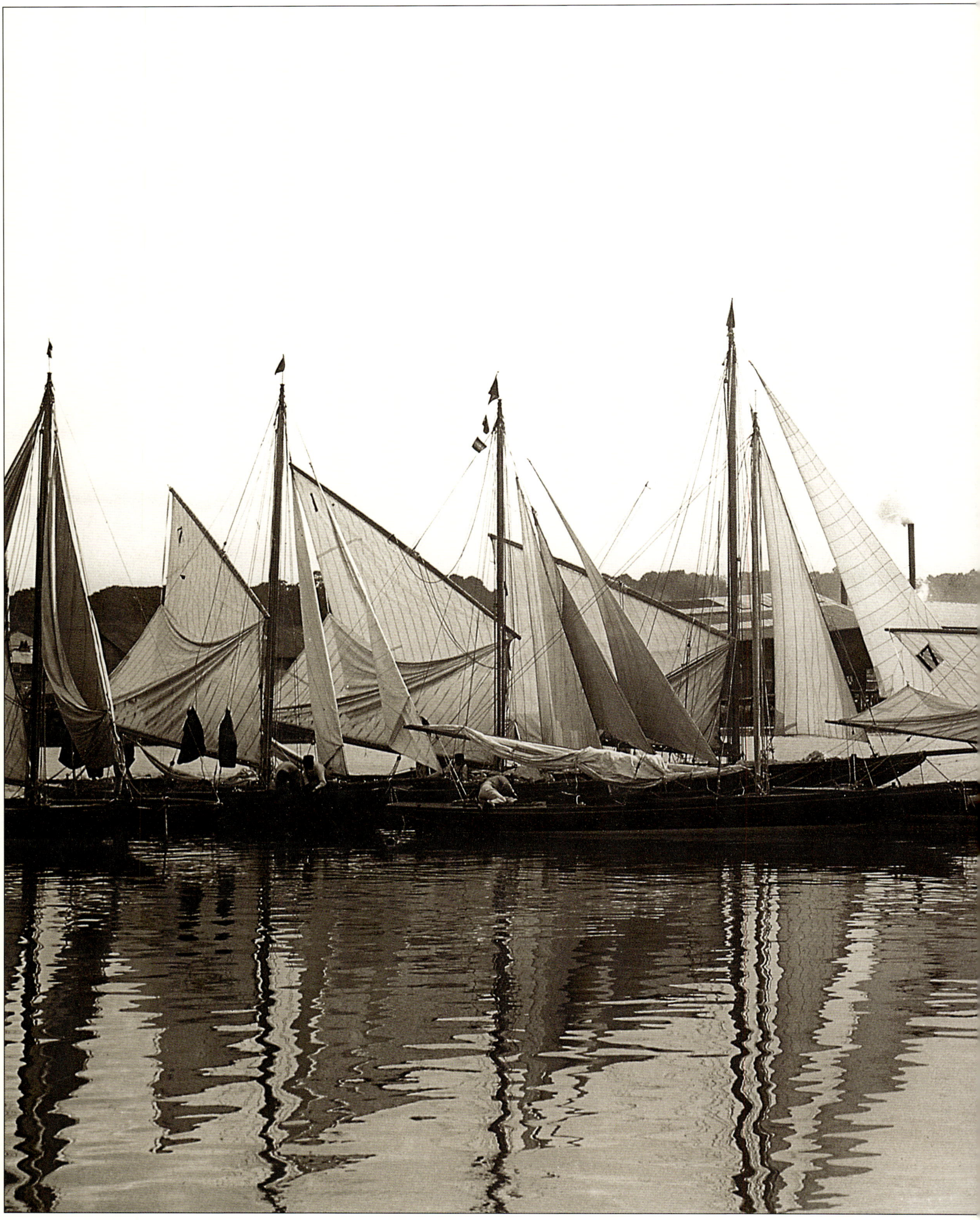

33

In general Ratsey was right and the lack of consistently good cotton duck greatly hampered the adoption of cotton sails in Britain. However, his statement above was disingenuous since it was his resolution of the supply problems influencing the use of cotton duck which was arguably the greatest factor in the later success of Ratsey & Lapthorn. When he made the sails for *Livonia*, Ratsey turned to a range of cloth suppliers most of which were American; however, unreliable quality and other problems forced him to look elsewhere. As early as 1869 the London-based George Rogers Ratsey II had been seeking information on the Lapthorn's suppliers of cotton cloth. This highlights the Ratseys awareness of the commercial importance of obtaining good cloth but the resolution of this problem was more complex than simply finding the best existing supplier. In the event the breakthrough for the Ratsey loft was two fold. In general terms, the American civil war, 1860-66, forced British weavers to look elsewhere for cotton and acted as a catalyst for the increasing use of Egyptian-grown cotton. When woven Egyptian cotton proved stronger that the best of the American cloths, Tom Ratsey was able to capitalise on this because of his firm's close relationship with the Crewkerne weavers Richard Hayward & Son.

Richard Hayward, who founded the firm in 1789 was a contemporary of the first George Rogers Ratsey and had supplied flax cloth to him from at least as early as 1806. With the accession of the third Richard Hayward in 1868, a number of internal problems in the firm were resolved and it was restructured as R. Hayward & Co. Seemingly, the third generations of both the Ratsey and Hayward families faced similar challenges. Over a relatively long period Tom Ratsey and Richard Hayward worked together to perfect the weaving of Egyptian cotton sail cloth and although little evidence of their collaboration survives, their cloth appears to have been reaching high quality levels in the 1870s. Additionally, by soaking the cotton duck in a solution of sugar, lead and alum, Ratsey succeeded both in pre-shrinking it and making it resistant to mildew. Having instigated the development process, Ratsey obtained sole rights to all the sail cloth woven by Hayward & Co. This monopoly on Hayward's output remained in place until World War II and was a key factor in the firm's competitive advantage and growth. In 1903, as the firm's new loft in New York sought to impose itself in America on the strength of the cloth it could use, the master sailmaker of the U. S. Navy yard in Brooklyn was so impressed by the quality of their canvas and so frustrated at the firm's monopoly on Hayward's output that he sought to challenge it via the U. S. naval attaché in London.

In parallel with his work in developing and obtaining quality cotton sail cloth, Tom Ratsey was a pioneer in his approach to the issue of sail shape. *America* had introduced flat sails and with few exceptions all sought to emulate these. Even those who persevered with loose footed main sails did so since they considered this the best way of keeping a sail flat. A laced sail, it was argued, would be more prone to spilling wind as a yacht moved through any seaway since the motion of the hull would be more easily transmitted to the sail through the boom. In 1856, James Lapthorn expressed the view thus:

We quite agree with you that all sails should be made to stand as flat as possible, this is what we aim at. We do not hold with sails being laced to the boom for vessels of any size, and unless a vessel has very fine lines, it is a great injury, it does not give sufficient life, which a vessel at all full lined requires.[13]

To the dogma of flat sails, Tom Ratsey brought his childhood observations of birds in flight. He studied the ratios of length, breadth and width in wings and applied this to sailmaking. As a result, he was one of the first to realise that a considerable part of the driving force of a sail is provided by its lee side and that a sailing boat is to some extent pulled along by the wind as well as pushed. Prior to this sailmakers had graduated the panel widths of the sail cloths by increasing the seam overlap in the middle of the sails order to achieve a uniform flat surface, indeed this method was patented in 1852, but none prior to Tom Ratsey had considered the sail as an aerofoil.[14] Although late in his life he condemned the excess of shape that some sought to give sails, he first introduced the modern concept sail shape wherein relatively fuller luffs and tighter leeches reproduced the principles he had observed in bird's wings.

In 1881 G. L. Watson commented that *'In no department of yacht building has greater perfection been reached than with the sails, and whatever point we may have got to with hulls of yachts, some of the mainsails turned out by Messrs Lapthorn or by Mr Charles Ratsey are simply perfection.'*[15] However, just as Tom Ratsey was turning his father's business round and laying the foundations of his future success, the Lapthorn loft was undergoing changes which would culminate in threatening its dominant market position. Indeed, within a year of Watson's statement the two firms had merged. In 1867, for all the British yachts for which the sailmaker can be identified, the Lapthorns had made sails for 75 per cent, the Ratseys accounted for a mere 5 per cent. The following year, James Lapthorn, the founder of the Gosport business, died leaving the loft to his sons James II and Edwin and precipitating a relatively rapid period of change. James II died young in 1869 leaving his own son James III under the guardianship of his brother, Edwin Lapthorn, who assumed sole control of the loft. Through the 1870's, the firm continued to prosper, indeed it could hardly fail to given its links with the Camper & Nicholson yard. Nevertheless it was loosing market share to the more dynamic Ratseys and an increasing number of competitors. Towards the end of the 1870's a change in Ben Nicholson's business strategy and local factors affecting the usage of Portsmouth harbour by yachtsmen had a serious impact on Edwin Lapthorn's perception of his business.

The impact of young, scientifically-trained designers such as G. L. Watson was beginning to have serious implications for Camper & Nicholson's order book. Additionally, large sailing yachts were being eclipsed by their steam powered counterparts and Nicholson had not invested in the required infrastructure to build these. Aware that the period in which he would remain a leading designer would invariably be limited, Nicholson had developed a large yacht maintenance business in parallel with his original yacht building yard and from 1880 onwards he increasingly began to rely on this as the source of his revenue. Camper & Nicholsons only re-emerged as substantial yacht builders in the late 1890's once Ben Nicholson's son Charles E. Nicholson had established himself as one of the premier designers. With his close connections to the Nicholsons, Edwin Lapthorn must inevitably have been aware of this threat to his core business.

Explanations of the method Edwin Lapthorn adopted to resolve the looming difficulties only become credible when considered in the context of the entrepreneurial exhaustion that he appears to have succumbed to. Of his two sons, only Edwin W. had followed him into the business; Thomas H. F., his twin, was training to become a solicitor. This movement away from the traditional business towards the professions combined with the business changes introduced by Edwin Lapthorn and his subsequent behaviour betray his desire to gradually remove himself from the manufacturing process and increasingly become a rentier. In 1882 such motivations led Edwin Lapthorn, who was still responsible for 50 per cent of all sails in usage on British yachts to initiate a merger with the Ratseys whose market share had only risen to 8 per cent.

Above: In 1873 G. L. Watson (1851-1904) established the first independent yacht design office in Britain; twenty years later he designed the peerless *Britannia*. Watson brought scientific principles to yacht design and fully realising the importance of good sails recruited Tom Ratsey to work with him on *Thistle*, his 1887 America's Cup challenger. / *Author's Collection*

Over: The amicable rivalry between the two Ratsey half brothers certainly extended on to the water. Like Tom Ratsey's *Dolly Varden*, George Rogers Ratsey II's *Marionette* was another typical example of the Itchen Ferry type cutter. She is seen here flying a complete suit of patent sails including the short lived patent mainsail. / *Beken of Cowes*

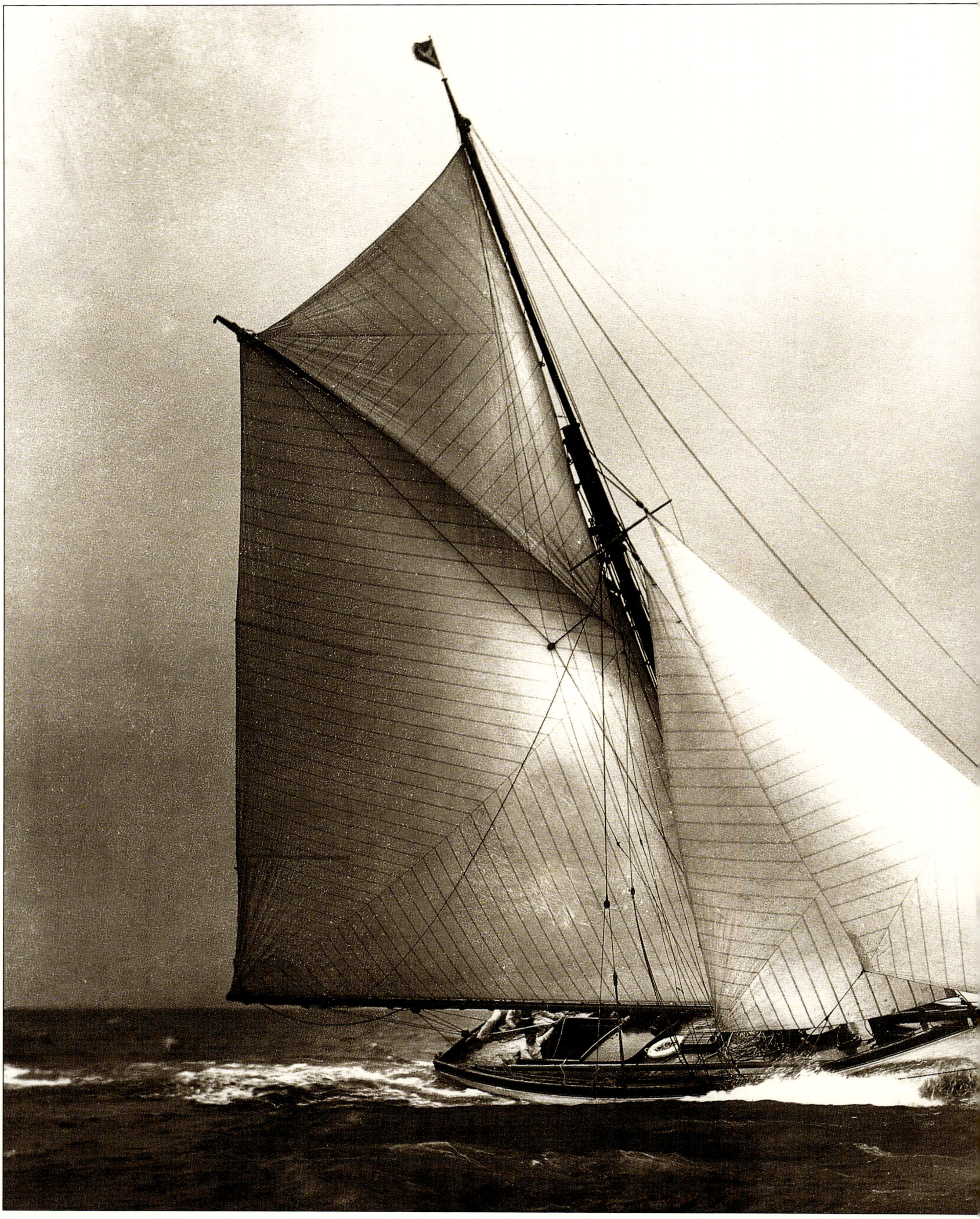

Charles Ratsey left the matter entirely in his sons' hands; Tom Ratsey was clearly the leading light but his brother George Rogers Ratsey II, still working London, had a significant interest in the firm. Rather naturally the two young men were flattered by the proposal. Since the closure of M. E. Ratsey's yard four years earlier they had been aware of the decline in yacht building in Cowes and the consequent need to find new markets but they failed to realise that they were already beginning to cut into the Gosport loft's trade. Furthermore, they had no insight into the specific situation affecting yachting and yacht building in Gosport. When the two parties met in neutral Ryde, the two young Ratseys were undoubtedly over eager and agreed to the partnership on Edwin Lapthorn's terms. As a consequence they contributed their entire profits for many years towards buying into the Gosport sail loft. Although now a partnership, neither party was willing to forego their name's first place; thus the Cowes loft became Ratseys & Lapthorn whilst that in Gosport became Lapthorn & Ratseys.

Despite the punitive terms of the merger, both the Ratsey brothers made some gains. In Cowes the volume of business increased immediately with Thomas W. Ratsey being responsible for 25 per cent of the new firm's output in the first year. More significantly, George Rogers Ratsey II at last found a place in the expanded firm. He moved to Gosport and was able to represent Ratsey family interests in the uneasy partnership. Edwin Lapthorn had brokered a partnership that effectively reduced work load whilst increasing profits. Additionally, it decreased his personal duties by allocating a share of these to George Rogers Ratsey II. With time on his hands Edwin Lapthorn set about consolidating his and his son's positions. His sole control of the firm had originated in his elder brother's early death and he now sought to deal with his nephew, James Lapthorn III who might exercise his considerable claim over the firm. James Stanley Lapthorn later recorded the incident:

> When my father was about 28 years old, his uncle asked if he knew the business and thinking that he was going to get a rise or be made a partner, said '*Yes*'. He was then informed that the terms of the will (to be taught the business) had been carried out and that his services would not any longer be required as he had taken the Ratsey's and his own son Edwin Walter Lapthorn into partnership.

The Ratseys when they heard my father had been discharged, took great exception to this, for it reduced the value of the business, for my father might have started up on his own, or been taken into partnership with some other sailmaker.[16]

The situation was eventually resolved by opening a new Lapthorn & Ratseys sail loft on the Clyde in April 1884. Initially this was located with the Scott & Co. ship and yacht building yard in Greenock but it soon relocated downstream to James Adams' Cove yard in Gourock where in remained operational until James Lapthorn III's death in 1928.[17]

These difficulties and the sense of having been taken advantage of in the initial agreement set the tone for what remained an awkward partnership. There are clear indications that communication between the various lofts was little better than if the firms had still been operating independently. At Gosport in particular George Rogers Ratsey II and the Lapthorns always had a strained relationship. This was compounded by the contrast between the Ratsey's relative poverty and entrepreneurial hunger and the Lapthorn's wealth and disinterest. But the differences ran deeper, the Ratseys were staunch Church of England Conservatives; the Lapthorns non-conformist Liberals, indeed there was little common ground between them. Eventually in 1909 both Edwin and his son Edwin Walter Lapthorn decided to sell out and retire. They then became victims of their own partnership agreement. Typically this stipulated that the parties could only sell shares to other share holders and the Ratseys united to take advantage of the situation. The low value the Lapthorns were forced to accept reflected the undue profits they had originally made from the partnership. In Scotland the news was well received. Not only did the Ratseys give the Scottish Lapthorns a chance to buy back into the firm but James 'Stanley' Lapthorn IV moved to Gosport finally inheriting what his branch of the Lapthorn family always considered to be their birth right. He also recorded his father's *'delight that his uncle with all his cleverness and sharp practise, had been stung.'*

Opposite: Internal rivalries led to James Lapthorn III to leave Gosport and establish a new loft on the Clyde in 1884. After a brief period in Greenock he moved to Gourock where he remained until his death in 1928 when the loft was closed. This is the only known photograph of the Gourock loft. / *Mystic Seaport Museum*

Above: In 1909 the Edwin Lapthorns, father and son, sold out of the business. This facilitated a return to Gosport of the Scottish branch of the family in the form of James Lapthorn III's son, James Stanley Lapthorn IV who commissioned this painting. Renewing his historic links with Gosport he specifically instructed local artist Martin Snape show Portsmouth harbour, complete with convict ships, as it had appeared in the mid-nineteenth century before his family was split by feud. / *James F. Lapthorn*

Over: The 1899 William Fife-designed and built cutter *Yvette* at the 1996 Imperia Regatta. / *Franco Pace*

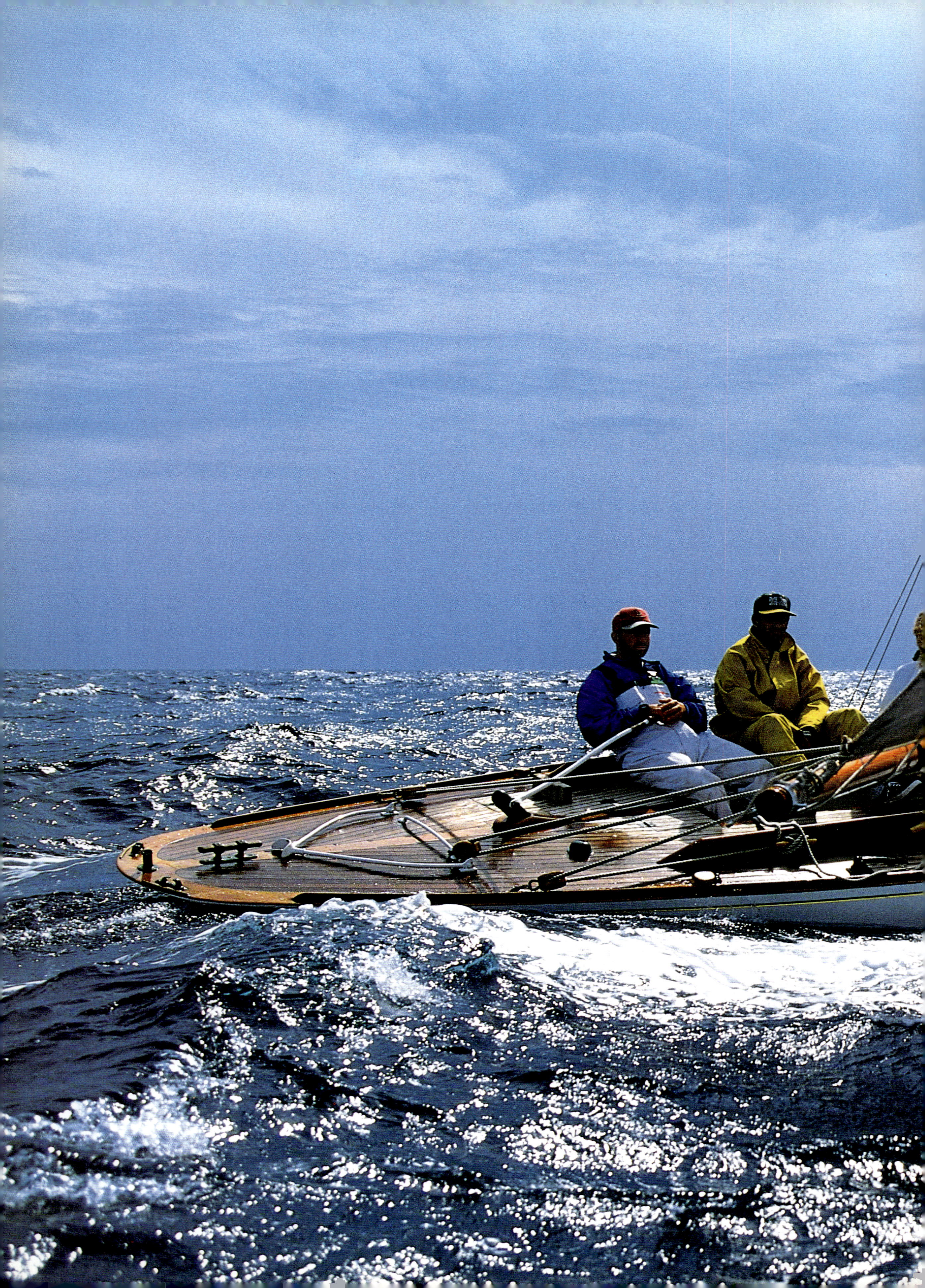

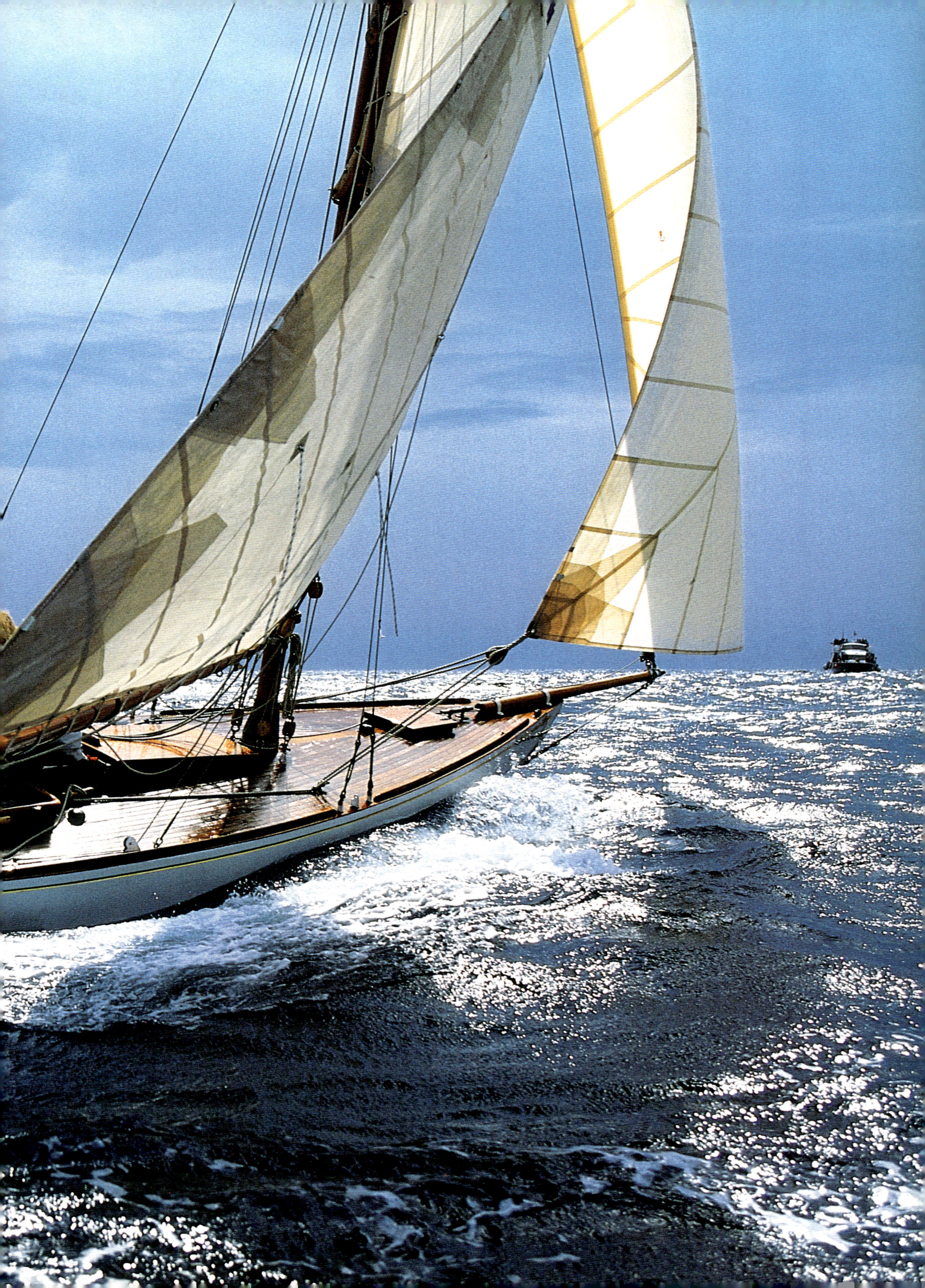

Despite the thirty years of internal difficulties that the merger of the two firms engendered, these years also saw the firm triumph in the explosion of yachting that spanned the final years of the nineteenth century and the pre-World War I period. Eight America's Cup challenges were fought and lost; the Prince of Wales' *Britannia* was launched initiating active Big Class racing; and a succession of rating rules finally gave way to the International Rule and the first of the metre classes. No other period has seen international yacht racing on this scale and Tom Ratsey rose through it to become one of the key arbiters in yacht racing development.

In 1885 and 1886 when *Genesta* and *Galatea* made their futile bids for the America's Cup, they sailed under Lapthorn canvas. There was no particular criticism of their sails and Edwin Lapthorn even travelled to New York to oversee *Genesta's* wardrobe. This said, the sails of both yachts were consistent with the rather gentlemanly and amateurish standards of these challenges. In 1887 the Scottish syndicate that challenged with the G. L. Watson-designed *Thistle* involved Tom Ratsey in their plans from the outset. Ratsey and Watson were good friends. Watson took a close interest in the design of *Thistle's* sails and together they accompanied the challenger to America to assist in the racing. Watson was the first British yacht designer to fully realise the fundamental importance of good sails and Ratsey took full advantage of the opportunity to enhance his reputation and that of his trade. Whilst in New York, Tom Ratsey met many of the leading characters in American yachting. He had already formed firm friendships with many of the American yachtsmen who had visited Cowes, including such figures as the outstanding schooner designer and skipper Bob Fish, but in 1887 he laid the foundations of a strong network of personal relationships that would last for the rest of his life. Indeed, this went hand-in-hand with a genuine enthusiasm for America and all things American. In return, American esteem for Ratsey was achieved by dint of the developments he brought to sailmaking in the 1890s.

Right: In 1885 the James Beavor Webb-designed *Genesta* was the first cutter to challenge for the America's Cup. The narrow beam and deep draft was typical of British cutters of the period. Edwin Lapthorn made her sails and travelled to New York to make alterations to these before the unsuccessful Cup races against *Puritan*. / *Beken of Cowes*
Over Left: *Galatea*, the second of the Beavor Webb-designed America's Cup challengers was defeated by *Mayflower* in 1886. Again Edwin Lapthorn was responsible for her sails. / *Beken of Cowes* **Over Right:** Tom Ratsey's long association with the America's Cup began in 1887 with the G. L. Watson-designed challenger *Thistle*. / *Beken of Cowes*

43

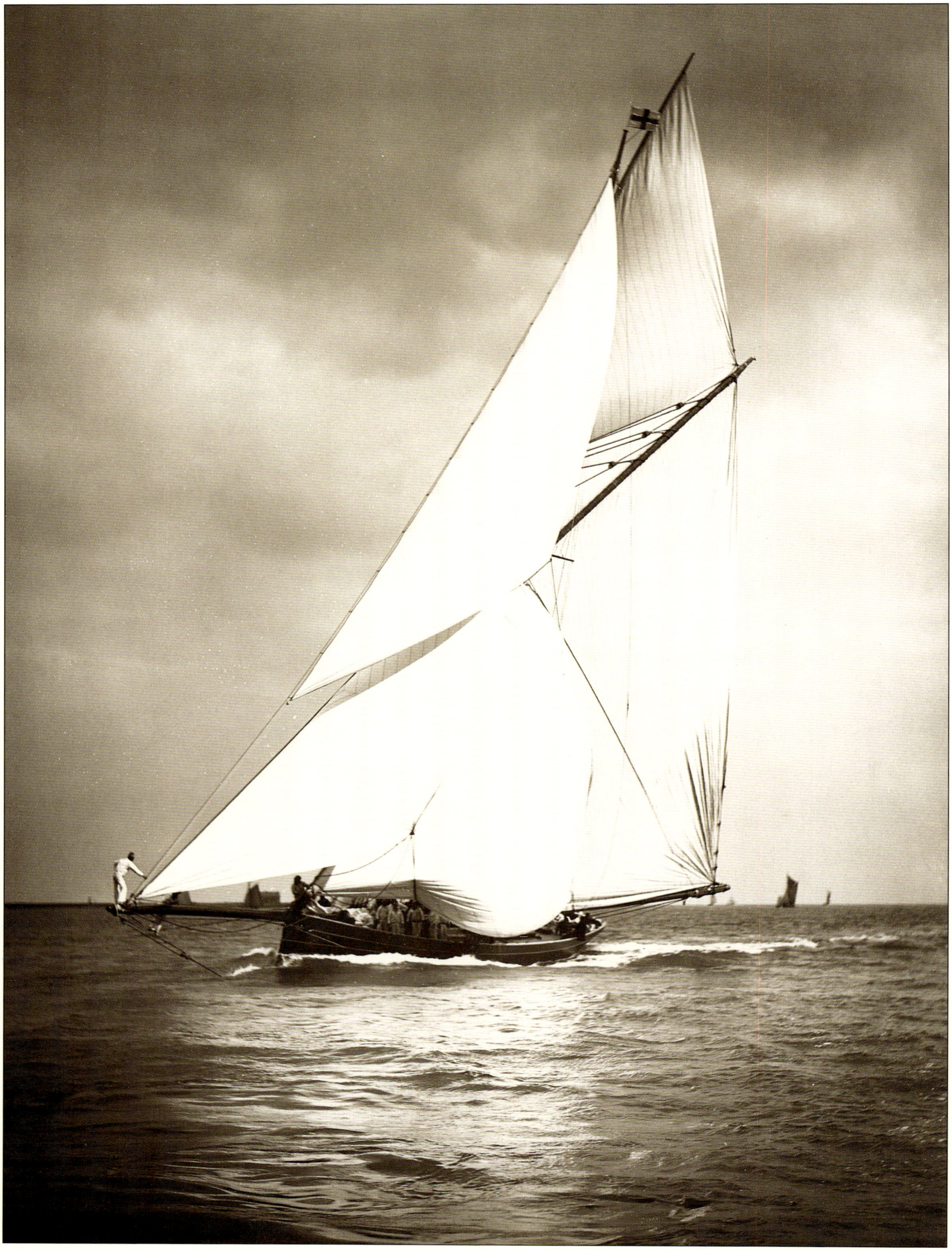

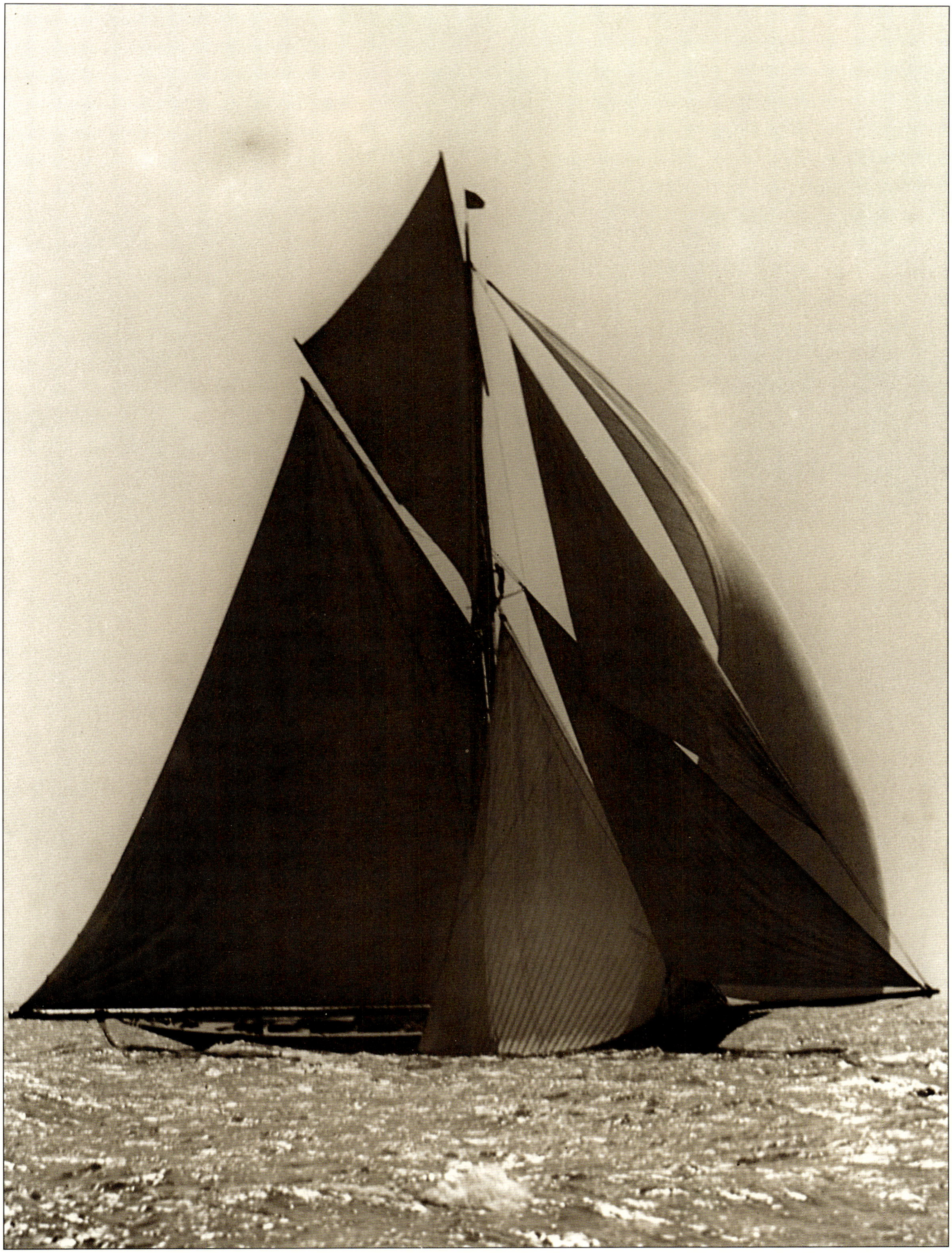

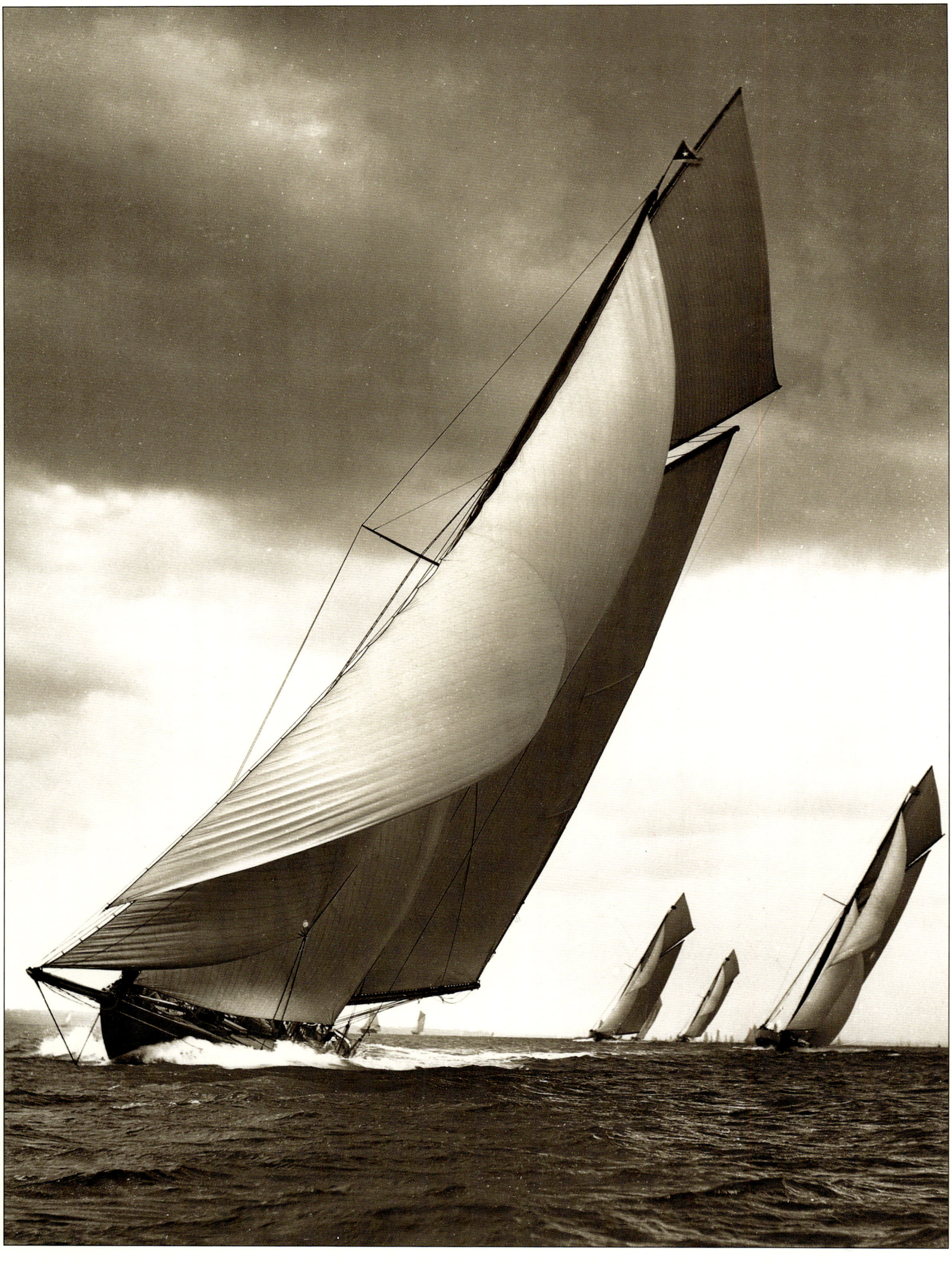

Sail cloth was generally woven in 18 or 24 inch widths. As early as the 1830's when flax was still the only fibre they used, the Ratseys had been false seaming their cloths in the middle to increase its strength and reduce stretch. These individual cloths were then assembled as sails with vertical or horizontal seams. In the latter part of the nineteenth century vertical seams, parallel to the leech (the aft vertical edge of the sail), were preferred for mainsails since these allowed the leech to stand better. A good mainsail cut in this manner could avoid the need for battens which Tom Ratsey regarded as *'an everlasting nuisance and abomination.'* [18] Despite increasing refinements in the weaving of cotton duck, simple logic dictates that this will stretch more in length (along the warp) than in width (along the weft). Consequently, mainsails with vertical panels were the more prone to stretch and when poor quality weaving lead to differing amounts of stretch in the sail's constituent panels all shape was lost. This problem was addressed on both sides of the Atlantic.

In Bristol, Rhode Island, the great American yacht designer Nat Herreshoff had become so frustrated at the poor quality of sails supplied to his yachts that he had established a small loft to re-cut and alter these. In 1894 he enlarged this facility and began sailmaking proper. The motivation of this sprang from his introduction of cross cut sails wherein the panels are arranged perpendicular to the leech. This arrangement allowed the more even distribution of strain along the weft of the cloth and additionally facilitated the mak-

Below: Tom Ratsey patented a new system of cutting sails in England in 1892 and in America two years later. This arrangement of the panels minimised stretch and although the patent mainsail was soon superseded by the Herreshoff-designed cross cut sail, Ratsey's patent introduced the definitive approach to head sail cutting. / *Author's Collection*

Left: The American Herreshoff-designed cutter *Navahoe* raced in British waters in 1893. She is seen here leading *Calluna*, *Iverna* and *Satanita* but was no match for *Britannia* and experienced the same frustrations as had characterised British yachting ventures in US waters. / *Beken of Cowes*

Over: Although *Valkyrie II* failed in her bid for the America's Cup, 1893 was a vintage year in British yachting. *Valkyrie II* (left) and *Britannia* (right) were just two of four new first class cutters launched that year. Despite the universal admiration *Valkyrie II*'s sails had received in America, the Prince of Wales stipulated an outdated vertically cut flax main sail for *Britannia*. / *Beken of Cowes*

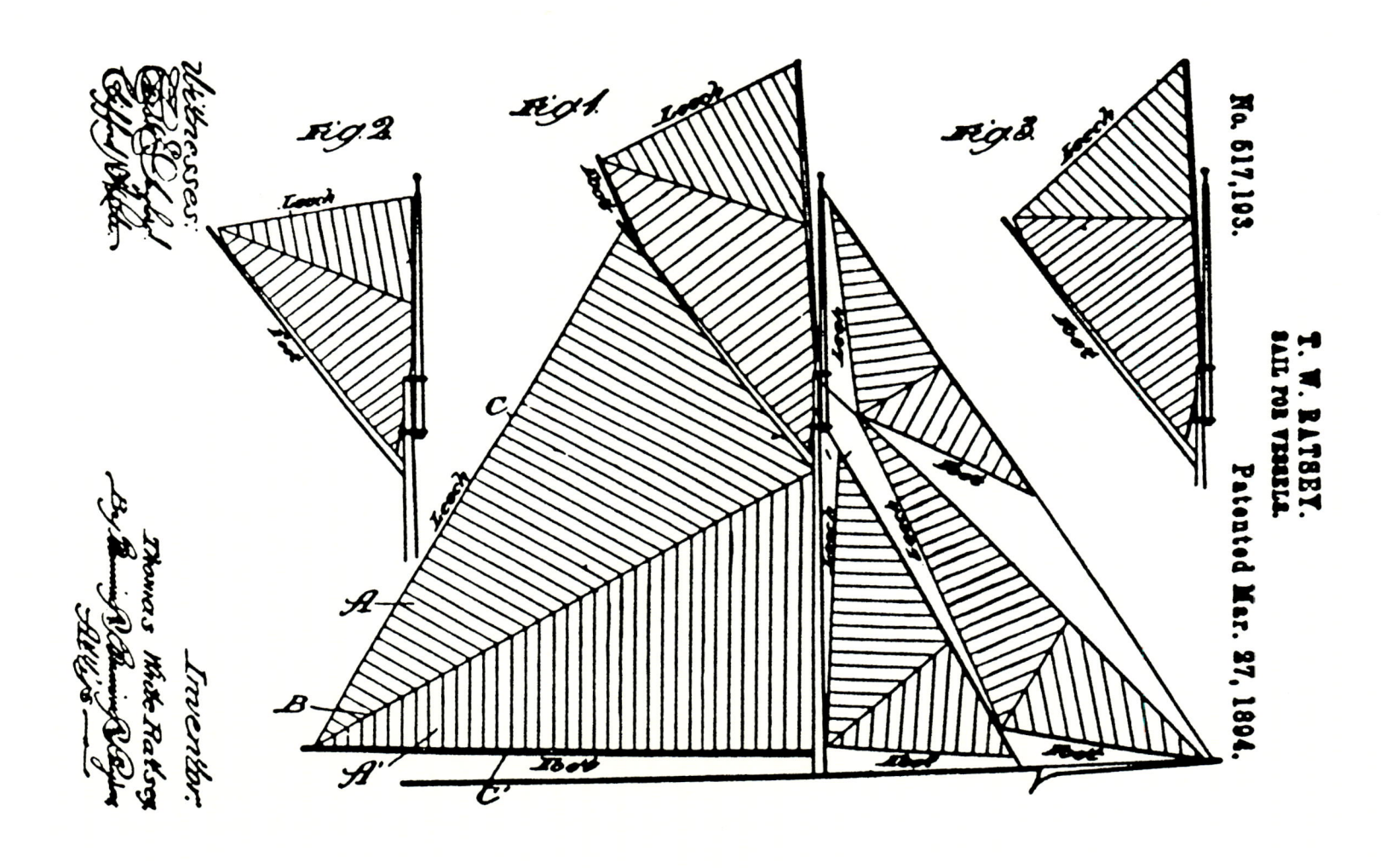

ing of sails that would stand better. It also introduced the possibility of cutting a sail with roach. In vertically cut sails, the leech, or after edge of the sail, was straight since it was formed by the edge of panel that ran the full height of the sail. With cross cut sails, the panels could be extended so that the leech was no longer straight but convex, adding to the sail's driving power in a way that sail measurement for rating purposes did not penalise.

Prior to Herreshoff's development of cross cut sails, Thomas Ratsey had already introduced a more sophisticated solution to the problem which he patented in England in 1892 and in America two years later. The innovation of Ratsey's diagonal seamed sails was in having two panel directions. By combining the vertical and cross cut principles he minimised sail stretch along the foot and leech. Thus Ratsey's patent sails were made in two halves, the lower half had panels arranged perpendicular to the foot and the higher half had panels perpendicular to the leech. The two sections were then stitched together along a diagonal seam. Having largely eliminated the cause of stretching, Ratsey predicted that *'these sails will be made to the full size of the spars and will stand as well at first as after the first month, or in other words they will not require to be stretched to bring them into shape.'*[19] In practise the patent main sails were short-lived since they could not be given roach or shape as easily as the simpler cross cut variety. However, for head sails, Ratsey had introduced the definitive approach to sail cutting which was practised as long as natural fibres were used in sail making. More importantly he made the sailmaker responsible for the shape of the sail when it left his loft rather than relying on flawed methods of stretching in situ to give a sail shape.

The practical assertion of superiority of Tom Ratsey's development in sail cutting was given in the America's Cup races of 1893, the first of the Earl of Dunraven's challenges. Again Ratsey travelled with the challenger and although *Valkyrie II* lost, her sails won only praise. In America, the Cup's Herreshoff era had begun, the Bristol-based designer and builder being chosen to design the defender in the wake of Edward Burgess who had been responsible for the three previous defenders. Whilst Herreshoff was clearly aware of the importance of good sails, *Valkyrie's* raised the standard beyond anything previously seen. General Paine who had been the principal force behind the financing of the three previous defences commented that her suit *'fitted like a glove;*

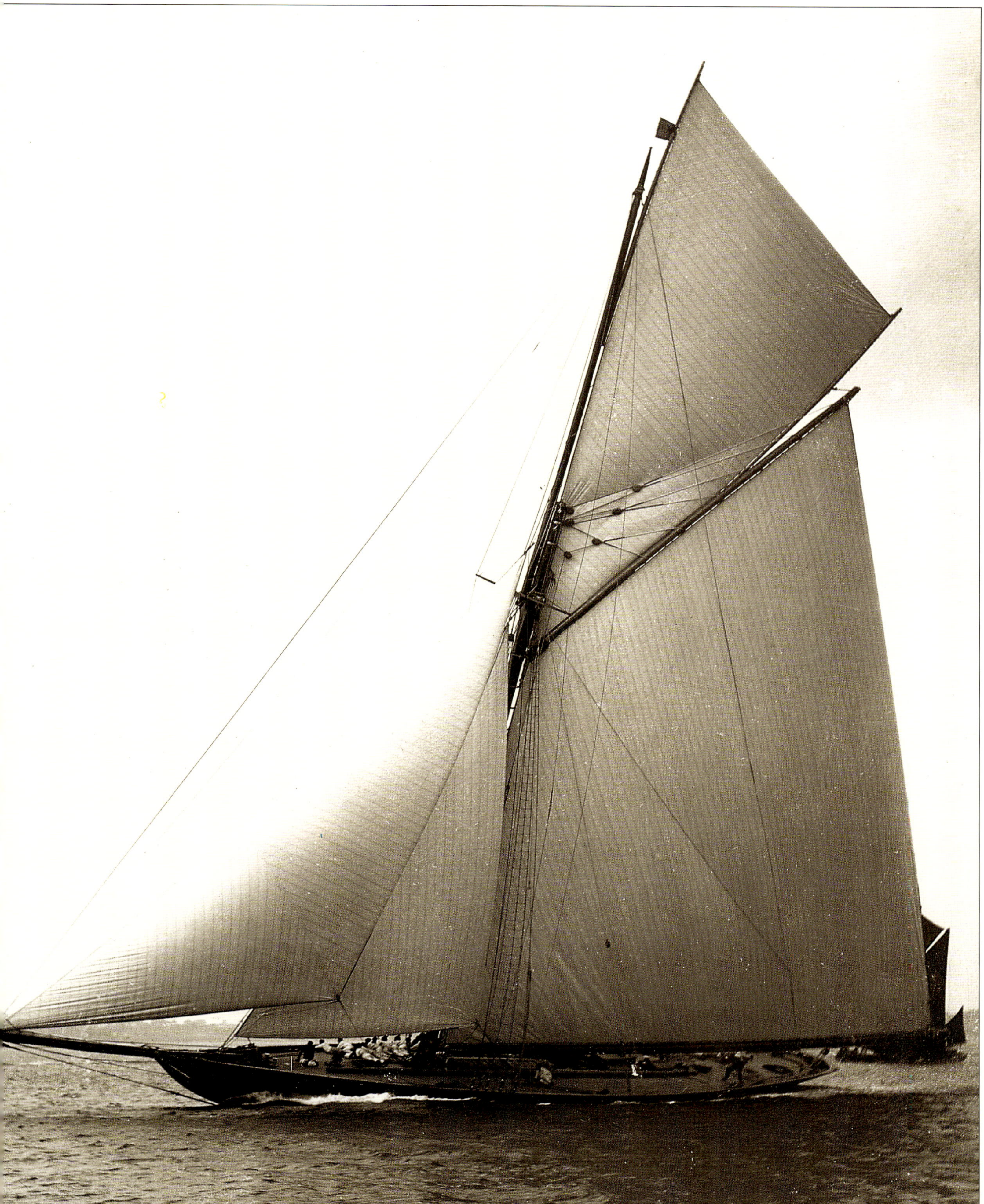

the most perfect canvas he had ever seen in America.'[20]

The America's Cup aside, 1893 was a vintage season; the Prince of Wales' *Britannia* was launched and was joined in a vibrant Big Class by the other newly-built cutters *Calluna* and *Satanita* and the American visitor *Nahavoe*. In addition to *Valkyrie II*, Ratsey & Lapthorn made the sails for all the new British cutters. The tables were turning and the firm's Cowes loft was dominant as racing yachtsmen clamoured for Tom Ratsey's sails. The impact of Ratsey's success heralded something of a revival in Cowes' yacht-related businesses. Although no longer a centre of yacht building, its craftsmen were nevertheless indispensable in other fields. A contemporary yachting magazine commented:

> There is no place in the world like Cowes for sails, blocks and boats [i.e. tenders] and the number of sub-contacts this winter is something enormous. Messrs Hansen & Sons and then White & Sons with boats, Ratseys & Lapthorn for sails and Mr Arthur Rowe for blocks. These being destined for yachts in all parts of the habitable globe.[21]

The firm's Cowes loft was not prospering alone; at the same time as it was preoccupied with the sails for the four new Big Class cutters, James Lapthorn III in Gourock was cutting sails for 33 yachts.

Above: Ratsey & Lapthorn's original loft in Cowes remained in use through till the 1930s and was again in service during World War II when its replacement was bombed. This building was demolished in the 1960s although another of the firm's eighteenth century lofts remains as the Sir Max Aitken Museum. / *Beken of Cowes*

From a British point of view, the 1894 season had all the ingredients required to improve on the vintage year which it succeeded. *Vigilant*, the 1893 America's Cup defender was in UK waters for the season, as was *Valkyrie II*, now returned from her American exertions. In all five big cutters were to be racing in a re-run of the America's Cup and on one of them was the Prince of Wales. The sport's popularity had never been greater and despite the unsuccessful America's Cup attempt British confidence was running high: '*We had been taught to believe that we had lessons to learn from the Americans as to the shape and set of our sails. Messrs Ratseys & Lapthorn upset all that last year.*'[22] In the event, there was no America's Cup re-run because *Valkyrie II* was sunk in a collision with *Satanita* but, such misfortunes not withstanding, it was a good year for the British. *Britannia* which had been widely considered slower than *Valkyrie II* proved superior to *Vigilant*, beating her in 11 of 16 races. By mid-season *Vigilant's* owner was so alarmed that he sought to order a new suit of sails from Ratseys & Lapthorn. Tom Ratsey, however, declined the order saying: '*No, let this be America against Britain, in ships, sails and seamen.*'[23]

The projected image of the firm, endlessly able to supply top quality sails and generally willing to do so is too simple. In addition to the clear discrimination the firm exercised in significant Anglo-American races, it also reserved favours for particularly significant clients and consequently graduated the benefits accrued by yachtsmen who bought their sails. Having developed a technique of sail cutting and an experienced work force, the main in-house differential remained the sail cloth used. The firm was always willing to use cheaper cloth if a client so desired but equally it developed some premium cloths. Naturally as orders grew and incremental adjustments were made to the weaving process Haywards, the weavers, acquired new looms. For consistency, cloth from only one loom was used in each sail and some looms achieved such a state of perfection that they were named after the yacht that flew their cloth. The '*Valkyrie* loom' of 1893 is the first documented case but others followed. In the course of *Britannia's* long racing career several '*Britannia* looms' succeeded each other. Equally, some yachts acquired a number of looms, indeed the 1893 *Valkyrie II* certainly had named looms for her mainsail as well as her Belfast linen and silk spinnakers. Access to the cloth from these looms was always purely discretionary.

Above: The Ratsey's house on City Island, New York. / *Franklin Ratsey-Woodroffe*
Over 1: Edward, Prince of Wales boarding his yacht *Britannia* whilst the crew hoist the jack yard top sail by riding down on the halyard. / *Beken of Cowes*
Over 2: *Avel* was built to C. E. Nicholson's design at the Camper & Nicholson yard in 1896. Decommissioned in 1928, she was used as a houseboat until 1991 when her restoration was undertaken by Maurizio Gucci. She was relaunched in 1994. / *Franco Pace*

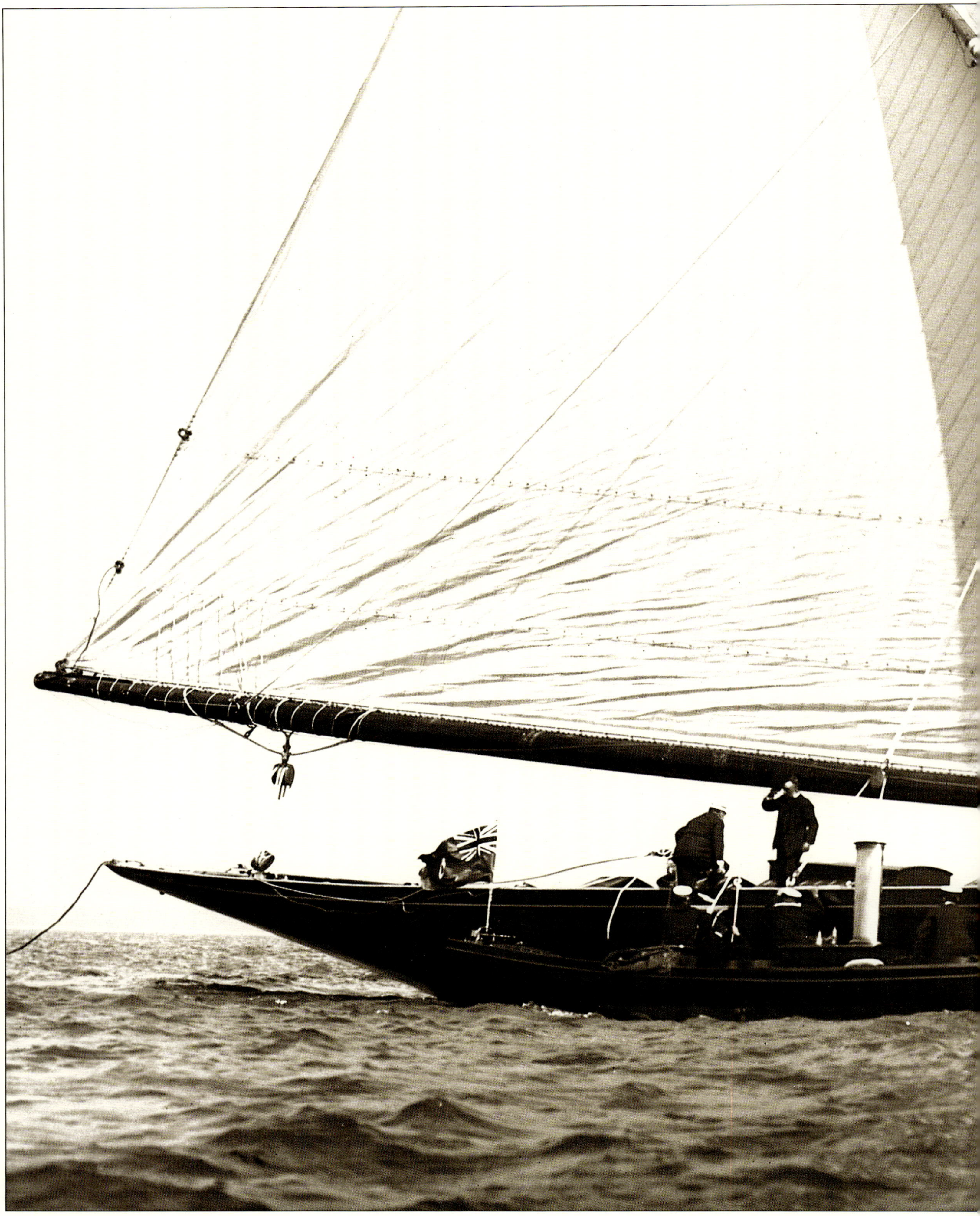

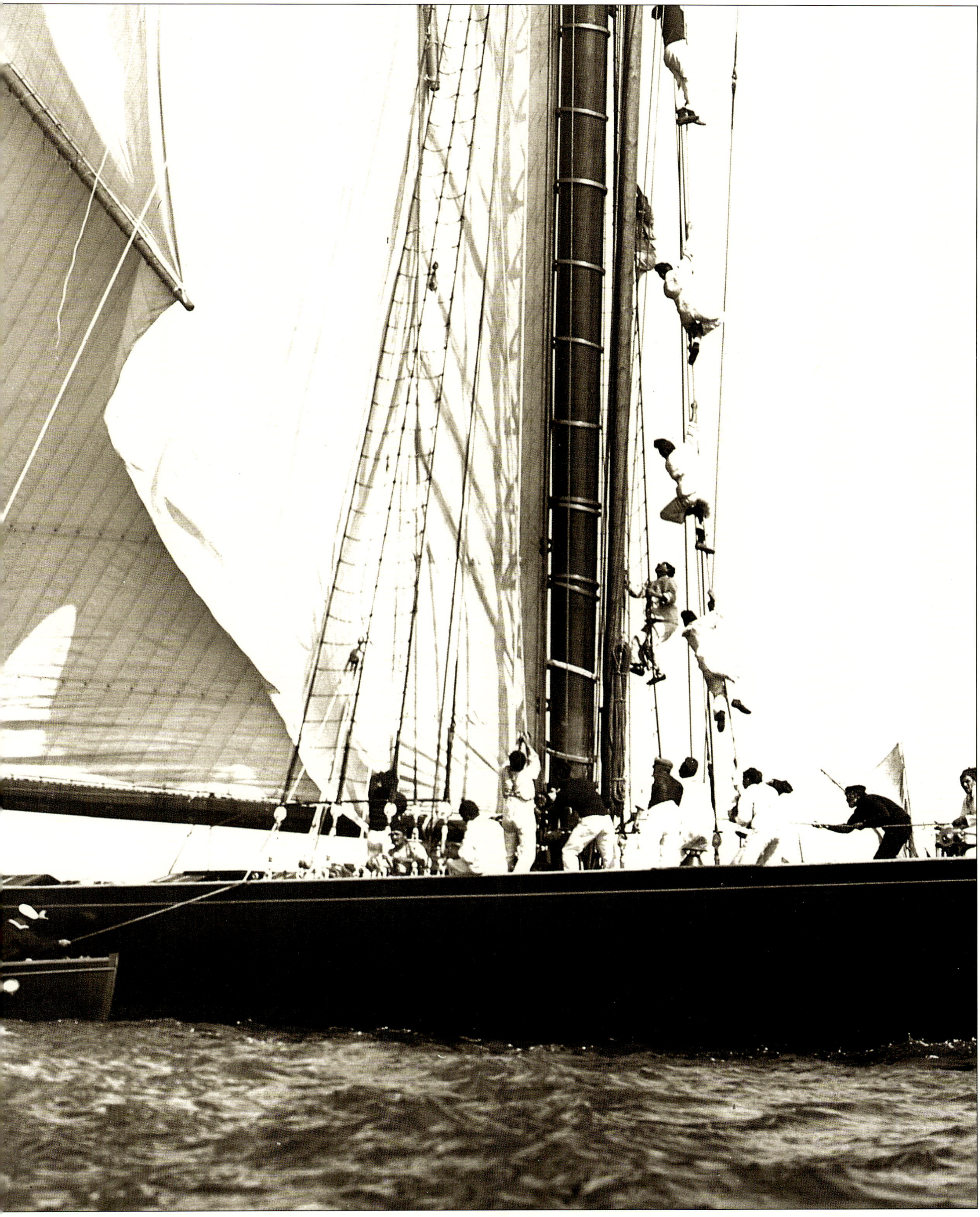

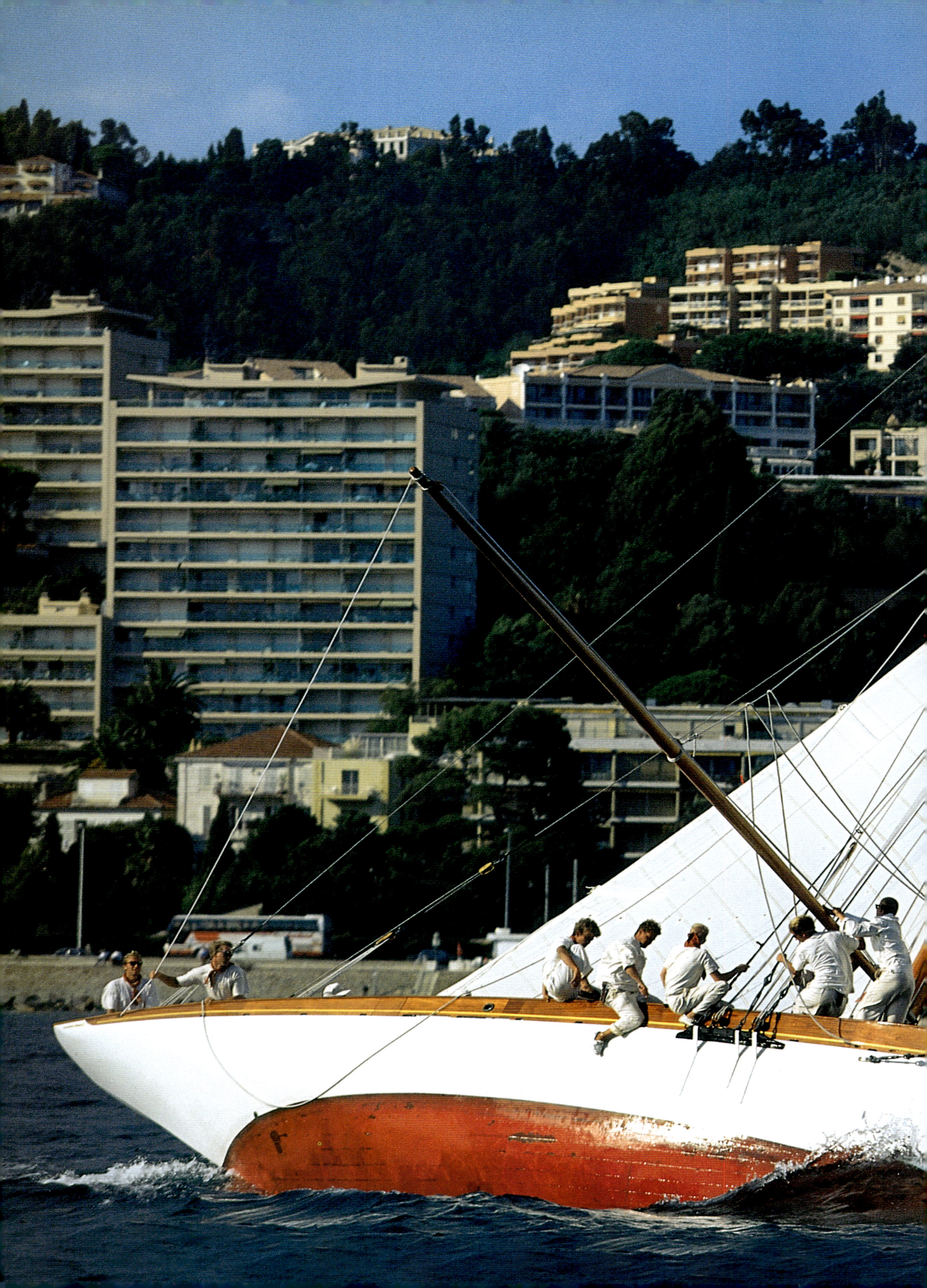

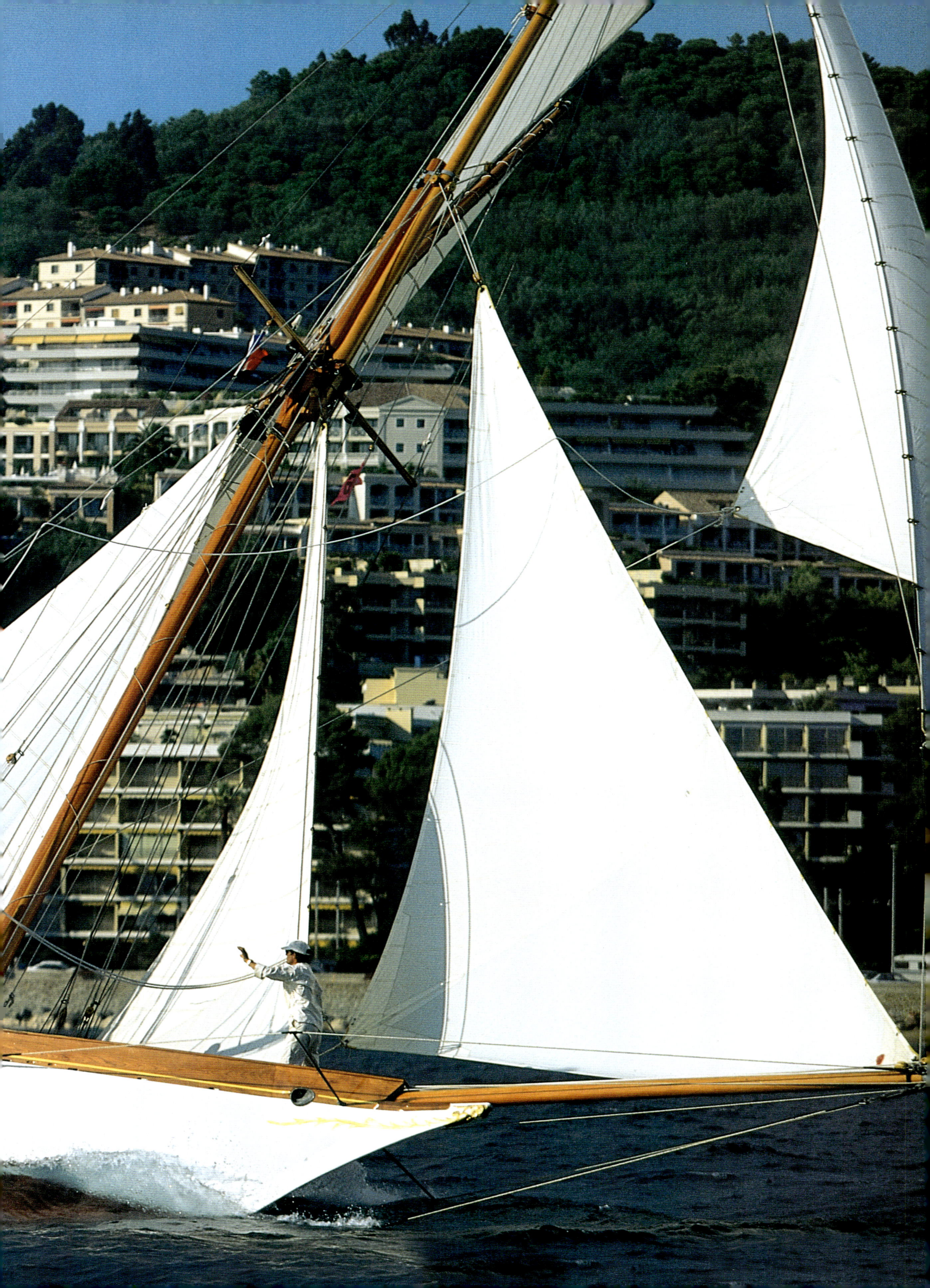

Having stitched up the UK, and to a large extent, the continental sailmaking market and become recognised as the world's leading brand, the only theatre for the company's expansion was America. Thomas W. Ratsey was in New York with *Valkyrie III* for the Earl of Dunraven's last America's Cup attempt in 1895 and returned with Sir Thomas Lipton's first challengers, *Shamrock I & II* in 1899 and 1901. An increasingly familiar figure in American yachting circles he secured a number of sail orders for the Cowes and Gosport lofts. But, such long distance business with little first hand engagement by the sailmaker and no possibility of any after sale service was far from satisfactory. During the 1901 Cup contest Ratsey was approached by a group of leading New York yachtsmen who, eager that he should establish an American loft, promised him their business. Additionally Robert Jacob, the owner of a large yacht maintenance yard on City Island, offered to build him a sail loft since he saw the benefits of an alliance between his and Ratsey's business. A long term admirer of things American, Ratsey rose to the opportunity with enthusiasm. In a rare surviving letter of 1902 to W. G. Jameson, the amateur manager of *Shamrock II*, Ratsey reported:

> I have been very busy since our voyage to America. I returned here in November and arranged for building the sail loft. I brought my

Left: The 1893 America's Cup defender Vigilant raced in British waters during the 1894 season. The accidental sinking of *Valkyrie II* prevented a re-run of the previous year's America's Cup but *Britannia* (right) with her Ratsey & Lapthorn sails proved superior leading the visitors to seek a new suit of sails but Tom Ratsey declined their order. / *Beken of Cowes*

Below: *Valkyrie III* setting a cloud of Tom Ratsey's canvas during trials prior to the 1895 America's Cup contest. / *Beken of Cowes*
Over: *Avel* at the 1995 Regattes Royales in Cannes with all sails pulling in the evening breeze. / *Franco Pace*

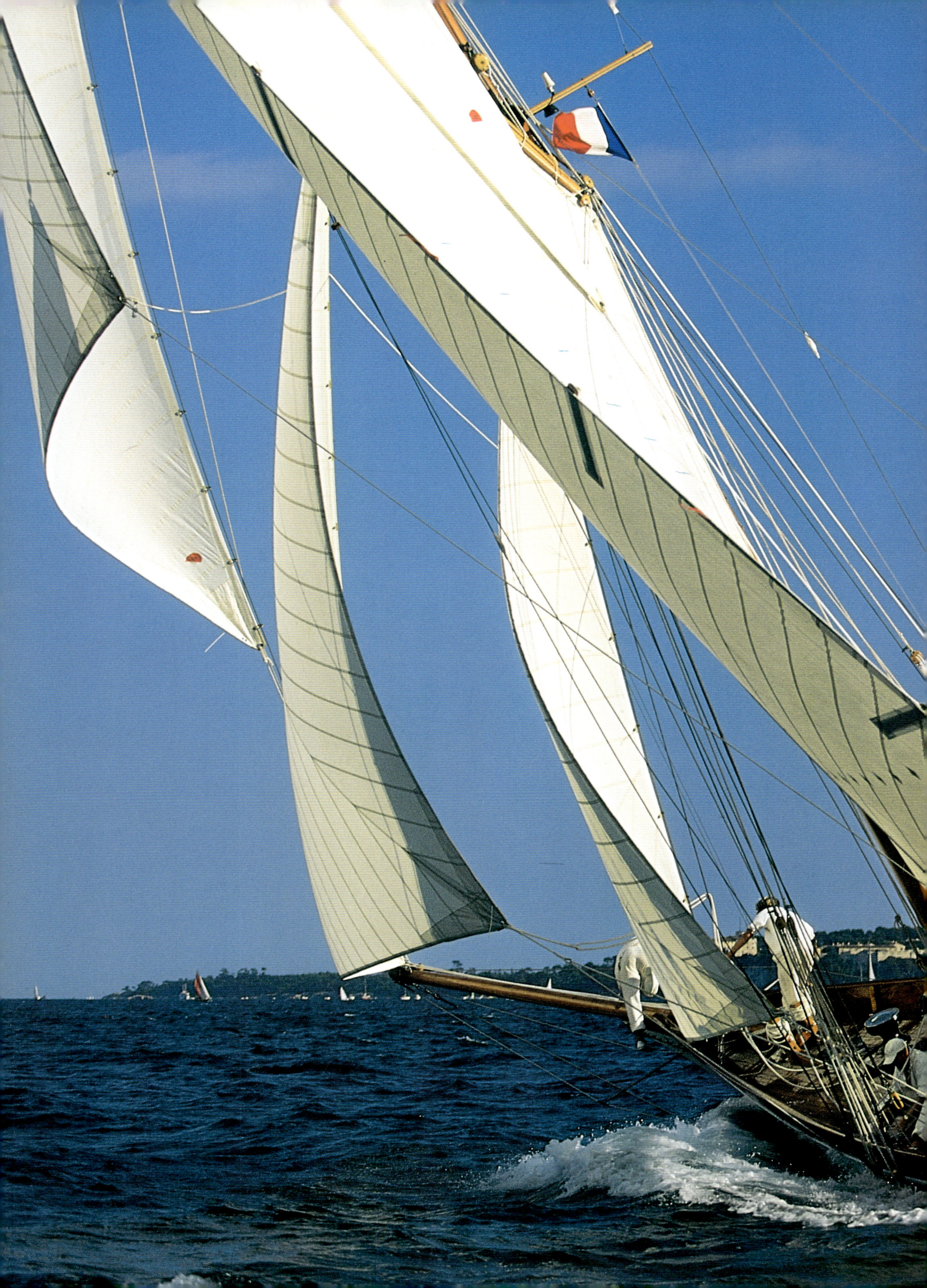

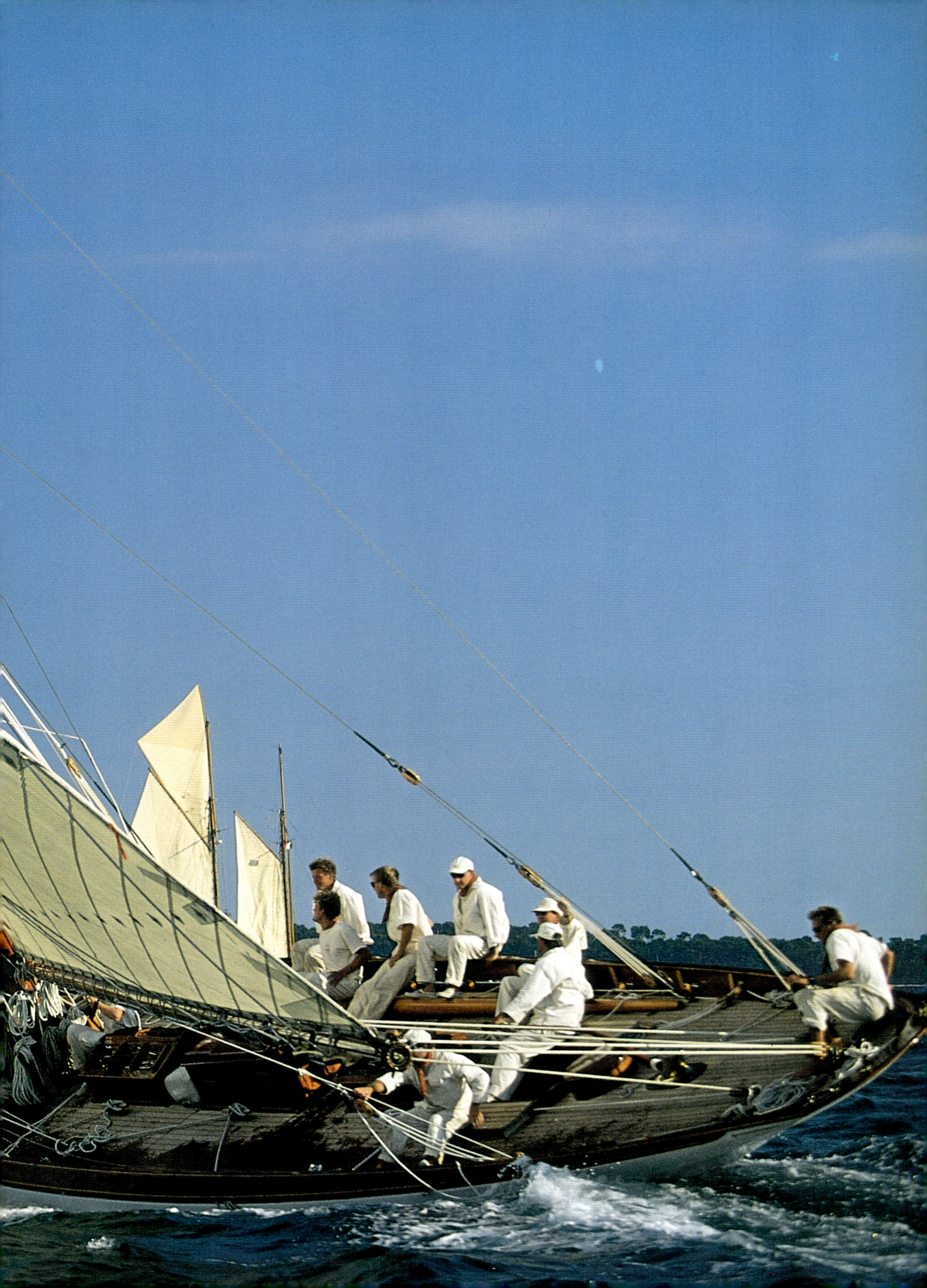

```
#0.  Thos. Ratsey
#1.  Wm. Wavell
#2.  Harry Read
#3.  Fred Denjafield
#4.  Geo. Abrook
#5.  Wm. Hunt
```

wife, daughter and Edwin Lapthorn Jnr with me just to show them the country where they will probably live a portion of their lives.

We returned just before Christmas. After that I had two and a half months of hard work at home getting the work well forward for this season at home and sailed for here on the 15th of March. Since then as you can imagine I have been very busy. I found the new sail loft which is a magnificent structure, the largest private loft by far in the world.[24]

By 14 April 1902 the loft was open for business and Ratsey reported back to Cowes: *'This is our first day of opening. As you can imagine I have been exceptionally busy since my arrival. Everyone is so nice and willing to do all they can to help us especially Mr Jacob, it makes things go very easily.'*[25] Having been part of the group that originally invited Tom Ratsey to

Above: For the 1895 America's Cup, Tom Ratsey travelled to New York with a team of sailmakers who looked after *Valkyrie III's* wardrobe. / *Mystic Seaport Museum*

Opposite Above: The first of Sir Thomas Lipton's *Shamrocks* challenged for the America's Cup in 1899. After the failures of three G. L. Watson-designed challengers William Fife was chosen to design *Shamrock* but despite the immaculate Ratsey sails, including cross cut main, victory remained elusive. / *Beken of Cowes*

Opposite Below: *Shamrock II's* sails were the principle victims of a serious rigging failure in 1901. Such incidents were not uncommon and certainly contributed to Ratsey & Lapthorn's business. / *Beken of Cowes*

Over: *Avel* (right) and *Thendara* under spinnakers at the 1995 Regattes Royales in Cannes. / *Franco Pace*

61

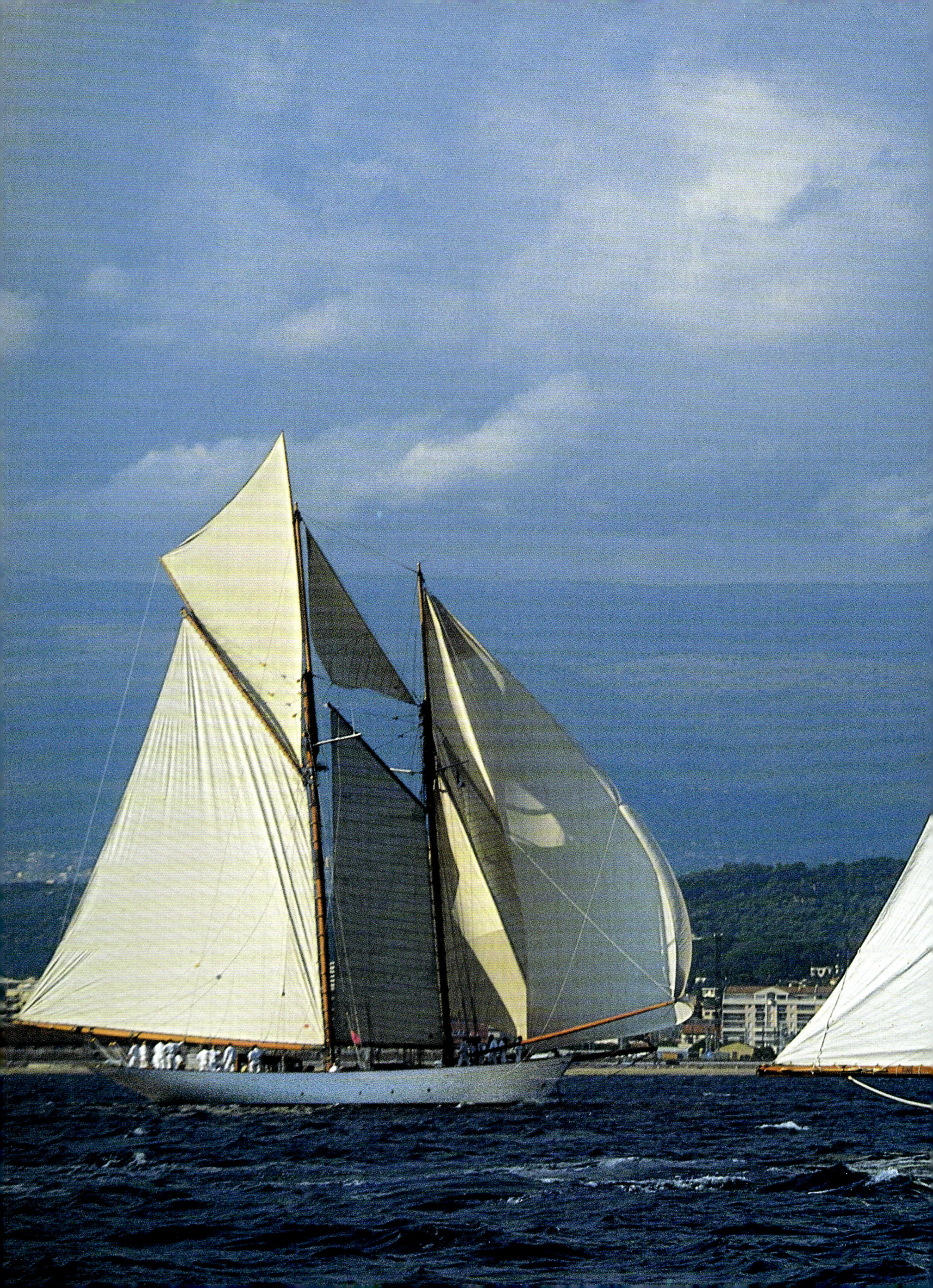

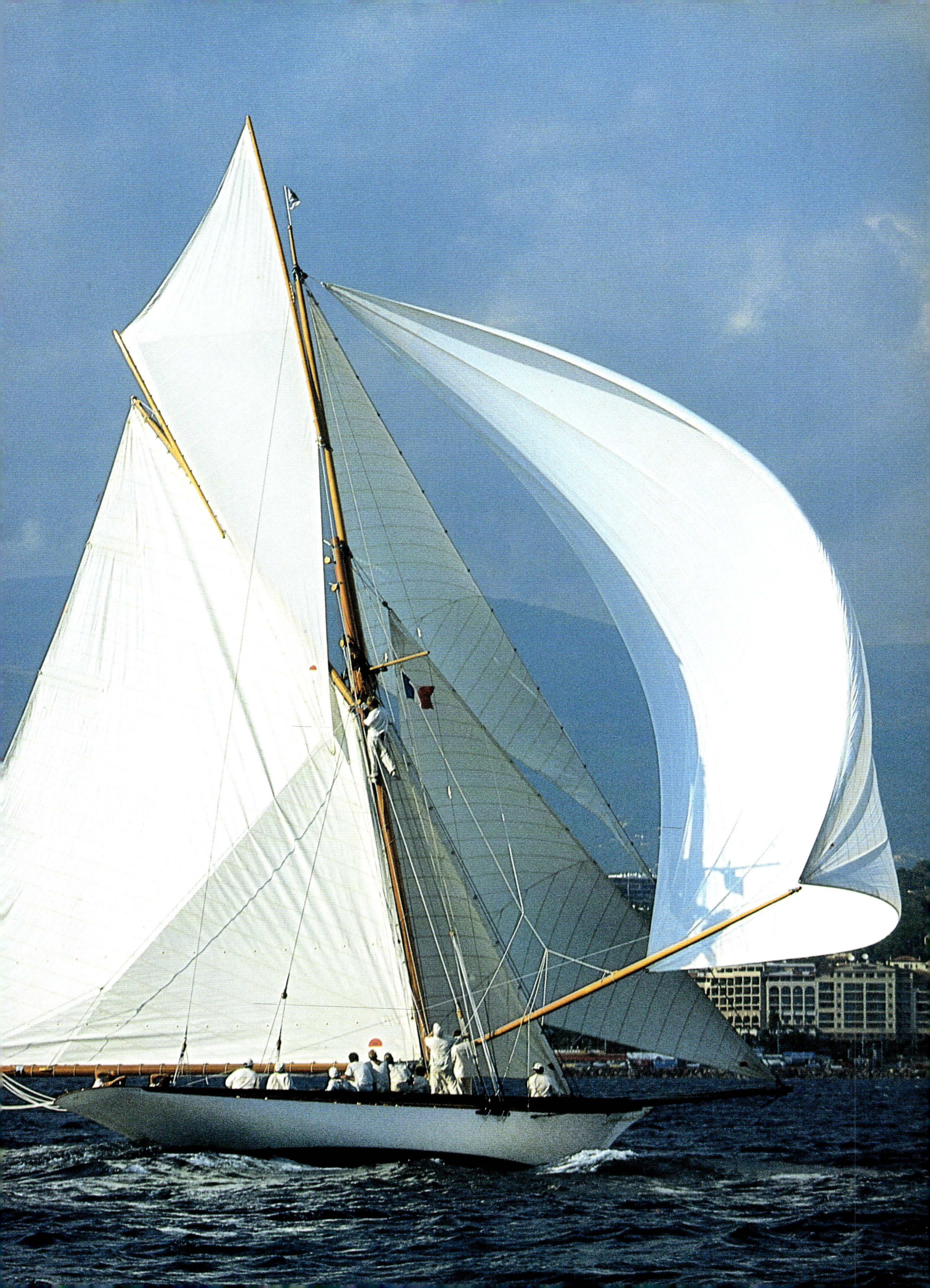

Above: Cornelius Vanderbilt was the first American yachtsman to order racing sails from Ratsey & Lapthorn's New York loft. The sheer perfection of the mainsail the firm made for his New York 70 *Rainbow* created a stir in yachting circles and established the new loft's reputation. / *Photo by James Burton, Rosenfeld Collection, Mystic Seaport Museum*

Right: J. P. Morgan was instrumental in persuading Tom Ratsey to establish a loft in New York and his order for new awnings and sails for his 300' *Corsair* helped establish the new venture. / *Photo by Charles Edwin Bolles, Rosenfeld Collection, Mystic Seaport Museum*

establish in New York, J. P. Morgan was true to his word and immediately ordered new suits of sails and awnings for his 300' steam yacht *Corsair* (third of the name). Such business was undoubtedly helpful in getting the new loft off the ground but it was a far cry from the type of work Ratsey had had in mind; he had set his sights on the New York 70 class. These were the New York Yacht Club's premier class and at 70' on the water line, the largest one design class ever built. Amongst their owners, Cornelius Vanderbilt was the first to succumb to the allure of improved sails and in July 1902 Ratsey was able to report back to Cowes that Vanderbilt's *Rainbow* had '*won with the new suit of sails we supplied. Everyone is talking about the mainsail. It is certainly a very beautiful sail.*' He continued '*The Rainbow's mainsail is admired by everyone. No such sail has ever been seen on a 70 footer before.*'[26] The New York loft's reputation had been secured.

Tom Ratsey had immersed himself in the establishment of the new loft but it was never his intention to stay in America. Rather, he saw this as an opportunity for the younger generation. He had instigated Edwin W. Lapthorn's early involvement but even in New York the collaboration between the Ratseys and Lapthorns proved difficult and although Edwin W. Lapthorn initially succeeded Thomas W. Ratsey, the arrangement did not last and he returned to Gosport in January 1903. Thomas W. Ratsey then instituted a rather far-fetched rota scheme whereby his eldest sons, Donald, Clayton and Stephen and George Ernest Ratsey, the son of his half brother George Rogers Ratsey II, would spend six months in turn in New York. Stephen Ratsey never joined in the arrangement but until World War I the remaining three spent six months in turn in New York before returning to England for a year.

The apparently seamless manner in which the Ratseys & Lapthorn expertise was transferred to New York was greatly facilitated by the company's monopoly over Hayward's cloth. To actually make the sails Tom Ratsey brought three of his leading hands from Cowes and recruited all the others locally. A week after opening the loft Tom Ratsey reported that they had '*15 sailmakers at work, 3 lady machinists, 3 boys, 3 labourers and 3 Britishers besides the office staff*.' He had himself taken on the cutting and seaming of new sails.[27] Within a month he had hired another 30 hands although such rapid growth did lead to one or two '*ghastly mistakes*'. The threat of competition for both clients and workers from Ratsey & Lapthorn became so great that its principal competitors in New York, led by Wilsons & Silsby, banded together to stop any further erosion of their work force.[28] Herreshoff was the only competitor outside New York and his vested interest in sailmaking led to his being one of the few American designers who did not actively welcome the British invasion. A. Cary Smith remained faithful to the established New York lofts but other American designers such as W. Starling Burgess, B. B. Crowninshield, Gardner & King and yards such as Townsend & Downey were all happy to endorse Ratseys & Lapthorn sails for their yachts. In return, some were able to extract very confidential information on the work of the rivals. James Beavor-Webb, for example, managed to get the New York loft to obtain the rig dimensions of the German Kaiser's Cary Smith-designed schooner *Meteor III* from their Gosport counterparts and pass these on to him. Others settled for the standard five per cent commission.

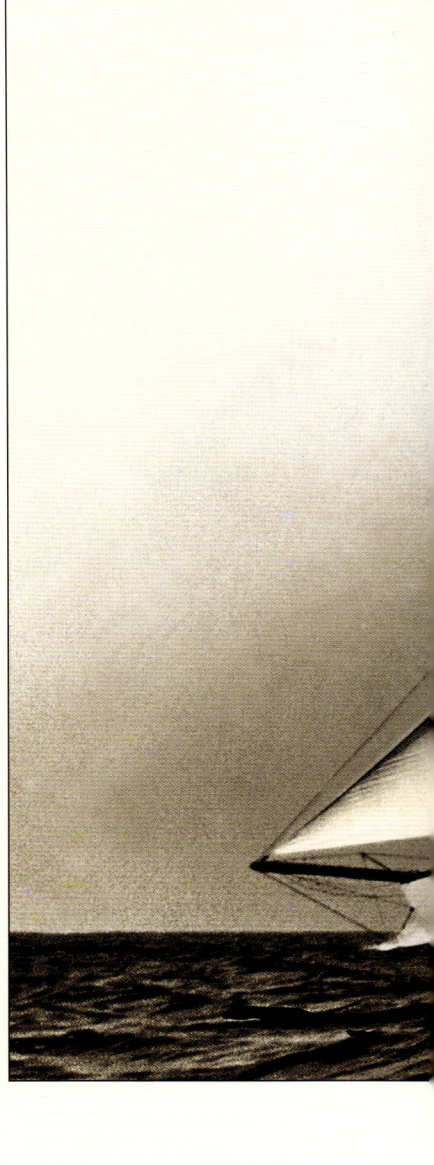

Left: Sailmakers at Ratsey & Lapthorn's Cowes loft with an enormous mainsail thought to be that of the 1903 America's Cup challenger *Shamrock III*. / *Mystic Seaport Museum*

Above: The William Fife-designed *Shamrock III* was defeated in the 1903 America's Cup races by Nat Herreshoff's *Reliance*. These were the largest gaff rigged cutters that ever raced. / *Beken of Cowes*

Over: The Nat Herreshoff-designed schooner *Mariette* was launched in 1915. In 1995 she was restored to her original rig and she is seen here in the gusty conditions that typify Porto Cervo during her first post-restoration regatta. / *Franco Pace*

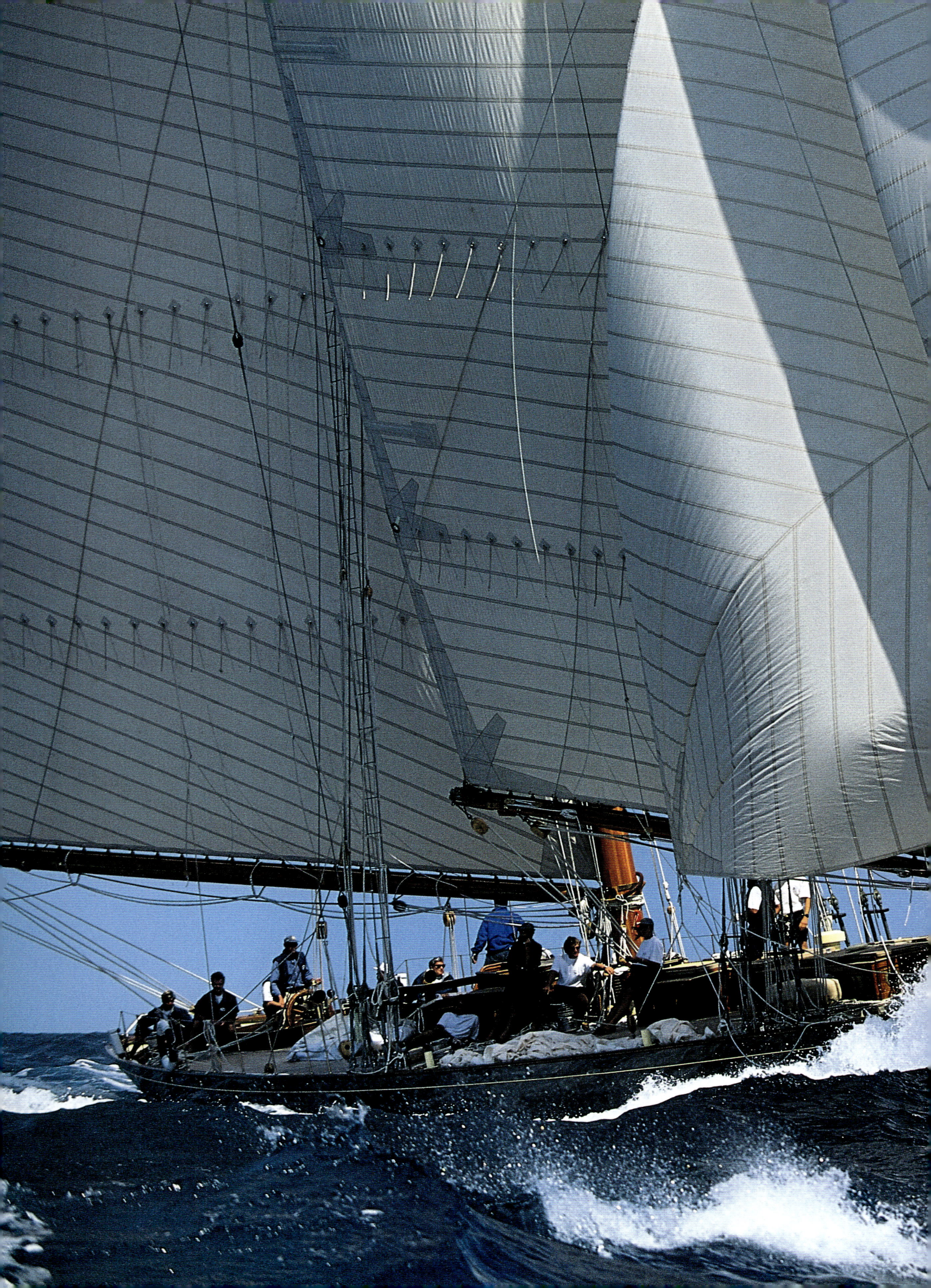

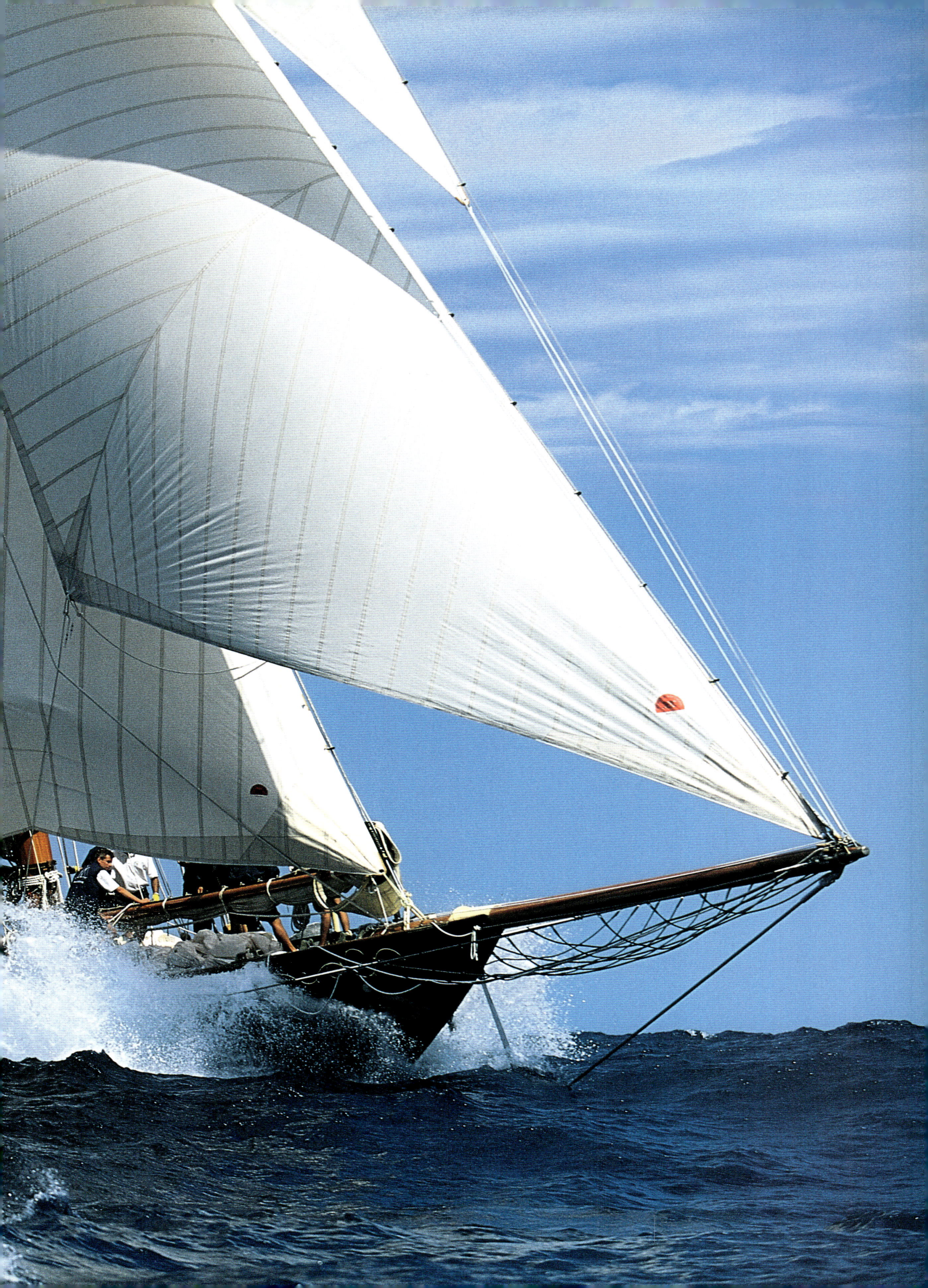

Such breaches of etiquette were minor compared to the dilemma that American yachtsmen anticipated the company facing when Sir Thomas Lipton challenged again for America's Cup in 1903. Initially the New York loft was only involved in providing sails for the trial horses, the 1899 defender *Columbia* and *Constitution*, an unsuccessful candidate for the 1901 defence. Nat Herreshoff, suspecting that information on his design for *Reliance*, the eventual defender, would be leaked back to England refused to allow the firm any contact with his new creation. When supplying the trial yachts, Edwin W. Lapthorn was cautious, but only on business grounds. He checked his quotes against those given in England for *Shamrock III* since '*it would never do for us to let them off better than Sir Thomas. There is the Challenge.*'[29] Consequently E. D. Morgan was forced to point out to the firm that their quote for *Columbia* was considerably higher than Herreshoff's but they still secured the order.[30] Although eager to secure business, it is clear that Ratseys & Lapthorn's were relatively expensive and that the firm was happy to maintain this clear indication of quality differential even if it lost a few orders. In the loft's second year Edwin W. Lapthorn reported back to Cowes that '*We find our prices tend to stick in the throats of one or two of them and we have lost one or two orders in consequence.*'[31]

Despite relatively poor sails *Reliance* was chosen over the two older yachts and the particular reasons for Herreshoff's secrecy gradually became apparent. In hull dimensions *Reliance* and *Shamrock III* were very close but the American yacht carried more than 12 per cent extra sail area. C. Oliver Iselin, manager of *Reliance*, sought to upgrade her canvas and cautiously approached Ratsey & Lapthorn fully expecting the same rebuttal that *Vigilant*'s owner had received 10 years earlier. The firm had, however, worked out its policy regarding such matters; their New York loft was American. Consequently Edwin W. Lapthorn received Iselin's invitation to quote '*with great pleasure*' adding that '*it is what we came here for.*' For his part Iselin '*thanked us and said he should not have been surprised if the reverse had been the case and that he should have understood our position.*'[32] This, however was only the beginning of difficulties; Herreshoff refused to give Iselin a copy of the sail plan and obstructed the British sailmakers throughout.[33] Eventually they had to measure *Reliance* on board before being able to cut and make her sails. When these were supplied the firm achieved a monopoly on the America's Cup sails on both sides of the Atlantic that lasted until the 1950s.

Left: In 1903 Ratsey & Lapthorn's New York loft built its first America's Cup sails, these were for the 1899 defender *Columbia* which acted as trial horse against the newly built *Reliance*. / *Photo by James Burton, Rosenfeld Collection, Mystic Seaport Museum*

Right: The Herreshoff-designed and built *Reliance* was originally equipped with his sails but these did not compare well to those Ratsey & Lapthorn had supplied for *Columbia*. Although Herreshoff refused to allow the firm to have a copy of the sail plan, they eventually built the sails that were used in the 1903 Cup races. / *Photo by James Burton, Rosenfeld Collection, Mystic Seaport Museum*

Over Left: *Mariette* on passage from Falmouth to Cowes after competing in the 1997 transatlantic race. / *Franco Pace*

Over Right: *Mariette* in her restored glory off Porto Cervo in 1995. / *Franco Pace*

Over 2: The New York 30 class *Linnet* is a survivor of the New York Yacht Club's many pre-First World War Herreshoff-designed one design classes. She is seen here in 1997 on the first sail trial following her restoration in Santo Stefano. / *Franco Pace*

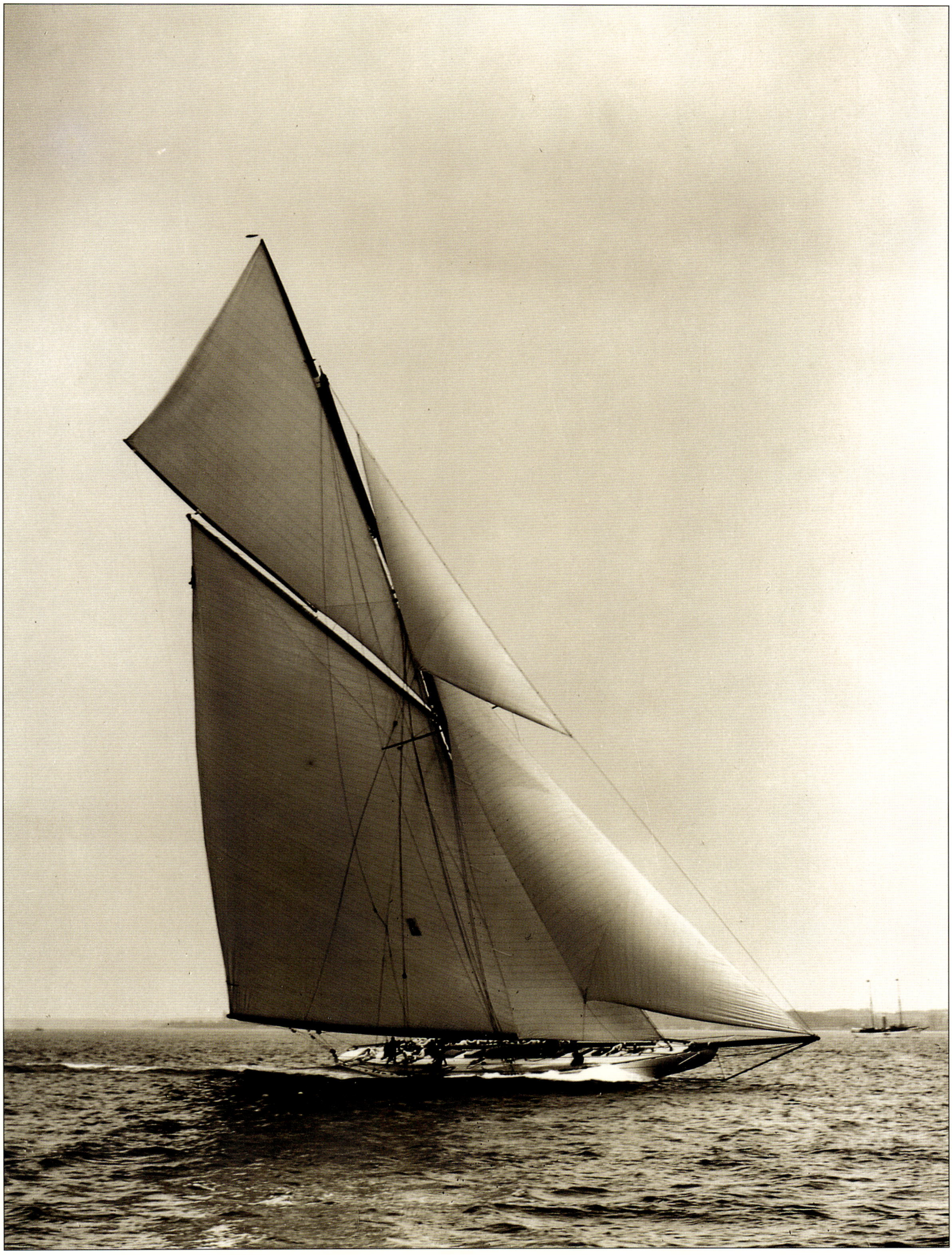

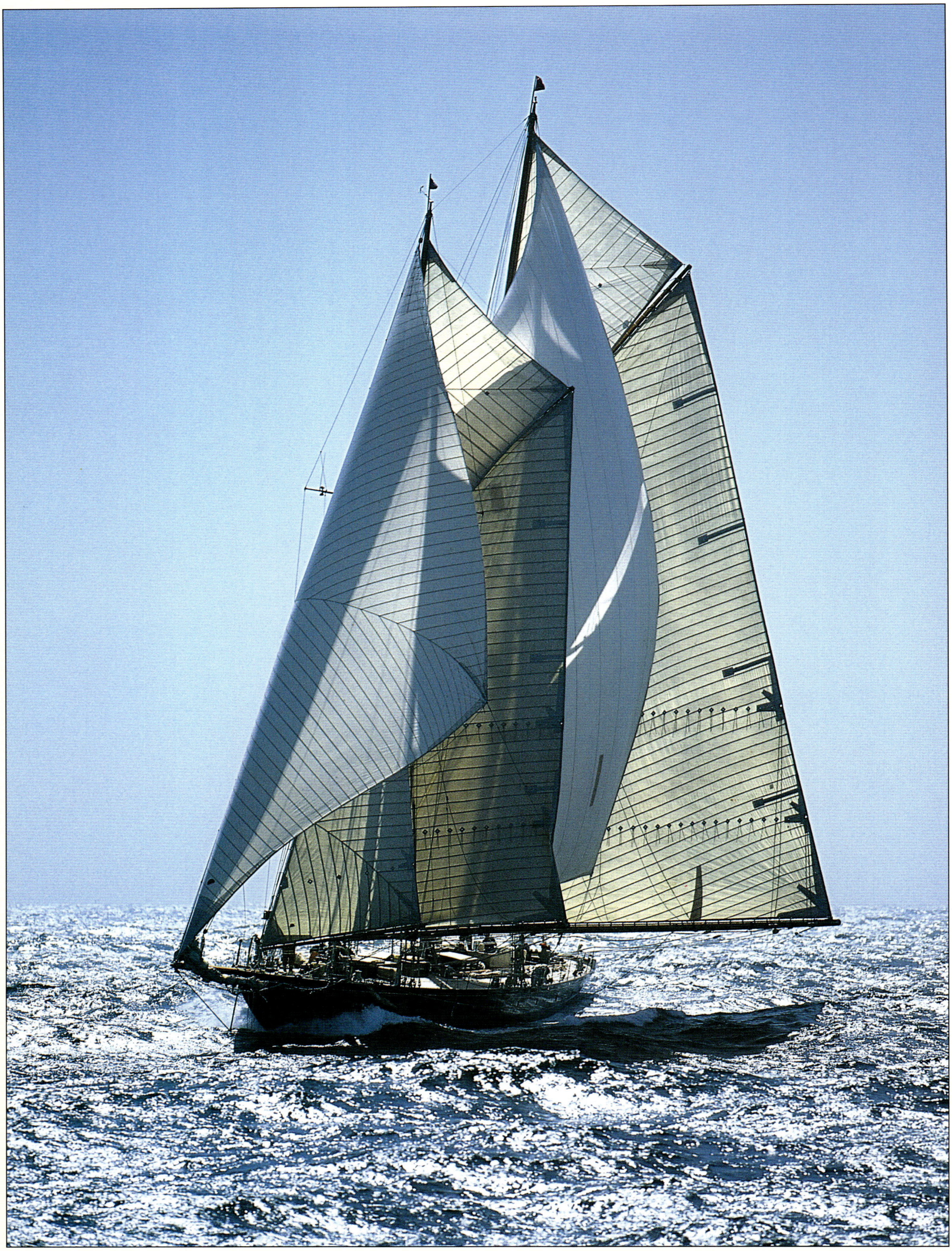

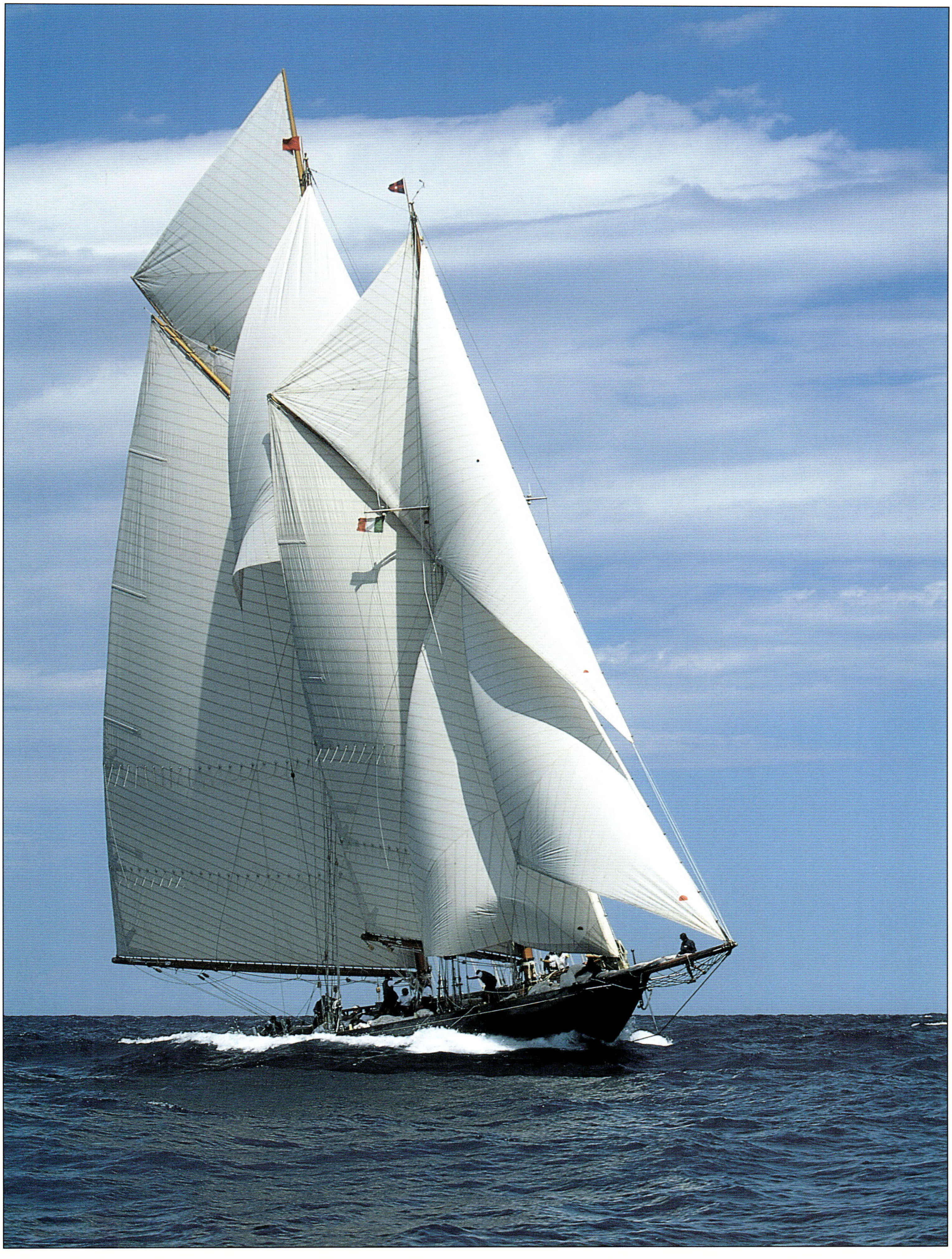

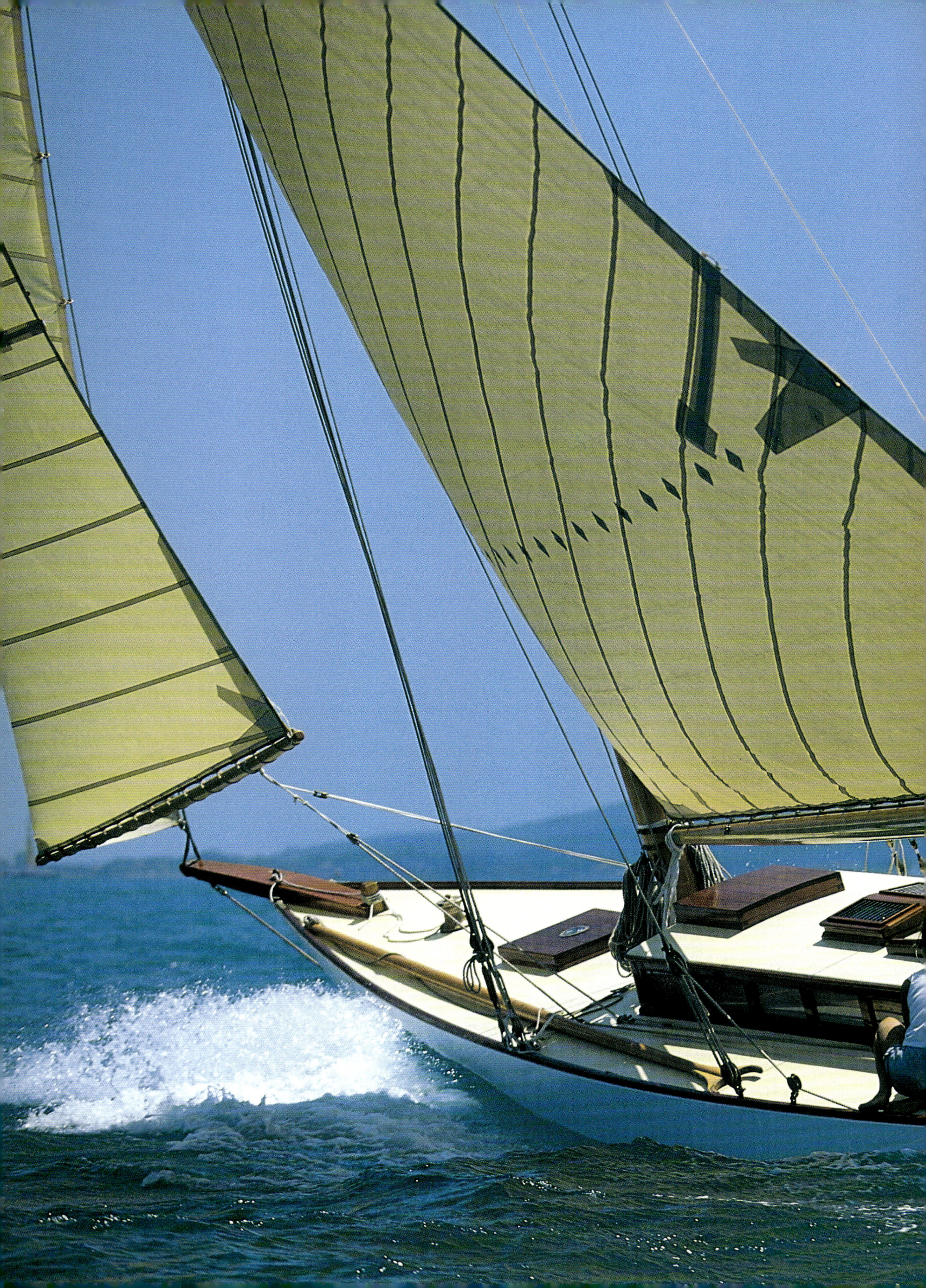

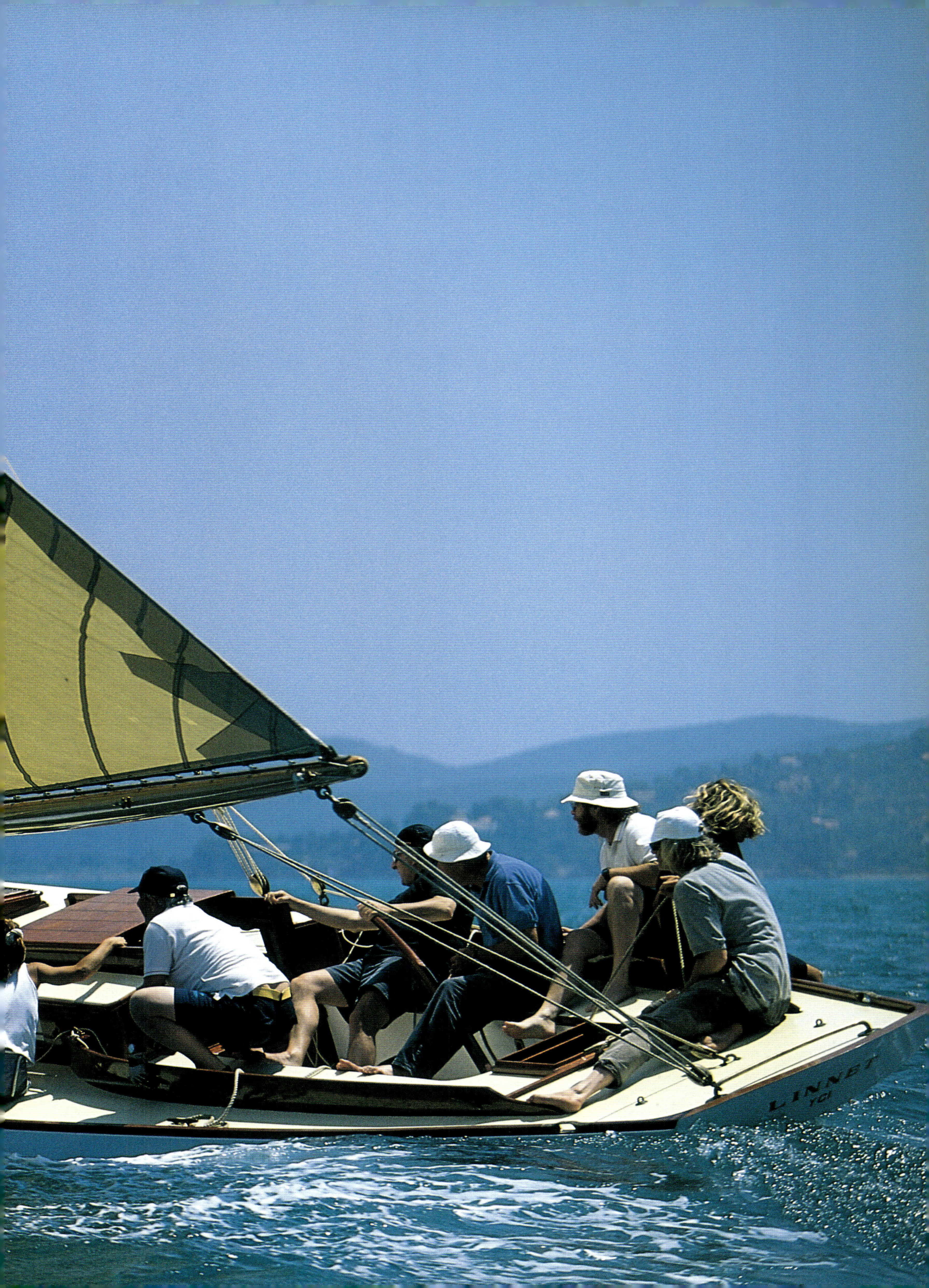
LINNET
YCI

In 1903 the firm finally settled the issue of its name when it assumed limited liability status. The overwhelming contribution of the Ratseys in the firm's three major lofts and James Lapthorn III's subordinate status within his own family left the Gosport Lapthorns little bargaining power. By way of compensation the Ratseys dropped the 's' but from then on they came first, and the firm became Ratsey & Lapthorn Ltd. Despite this, Edwin Lapthorn secured the position of chairman with his son Edwin W. and the Ratsey half brothers Thomas W. and George Rogers II all being appointed joint managing directors. This situation persisted until the Gosport Lapthorns withdrew from the firm in 1909 and were replaced by James Stanley Lapthorn (IV) who had trained under his father James III at the Gourock loft.

The arrival of James Lapthorn IV in Gosport coincided with the emergence of C. E. Nicholson as Britain's senior yacht designer. G. L. Watson had died in 1904 leaving William Fife Jnr and C. E. Nicholson as the principal rivals. In 1906 Nicholson designed *Nyria*, his first Big Class cutter and the first racing yacht to be built to Lloyd's Register classification. The success of this yacht not only increased Nicholson's prominence but paved the way for the 1907 introduction of the First International Rating Rule inclusive of Lloyd's Register scantling regulations. Initially Nicholson secured few orders for the new metre class yachts but in 1912

Above: A 1910 water colour sketch of the Gosport loft by Frank Mason. / *James F. Lapthorn*
Below: Charles E. Nicholson (1868-1954) whose yacht design talents were responsible for the revival and expansion of Camper & Nicholsons yard from the mid-1890s through to World War II. He is seen here in a yard launch with his brother Arthur W. Nicholson (left). / *Author's Collection*
Opposite: In 1912 C. E. Nicholson pioneered the Marconi gaff rig on his 15 Metre class yacht *Istria*. It was the greatest refinement in gaff rig and propelled him to the forefront of British yacht design. / *Beken of Cowes*

Over: The 1909 Fife-designed First International Rule 15 Metre class *Tuiga* approaching hull speed during the 1995 Cannes to St Tropez race. / *Franco Pace*
Over 2 Left: After being discovered in Cyprus in 1989, *Tuiga* was restored by Fairlie Restorations. In 1993 she won her first Nioulargue. / *Franco Pace*
Over 2 Right: Restored to her original rig, *Tuiga's* boom is 56 feet long and with an equally authentic deck layout there are no winches to ease sail handling. / *Franco Pace*
Over 3: *Tuiga* punching through the waves in a strong breeze off St Tropez at the 1993 Nioulargue. / *Franco Pace*

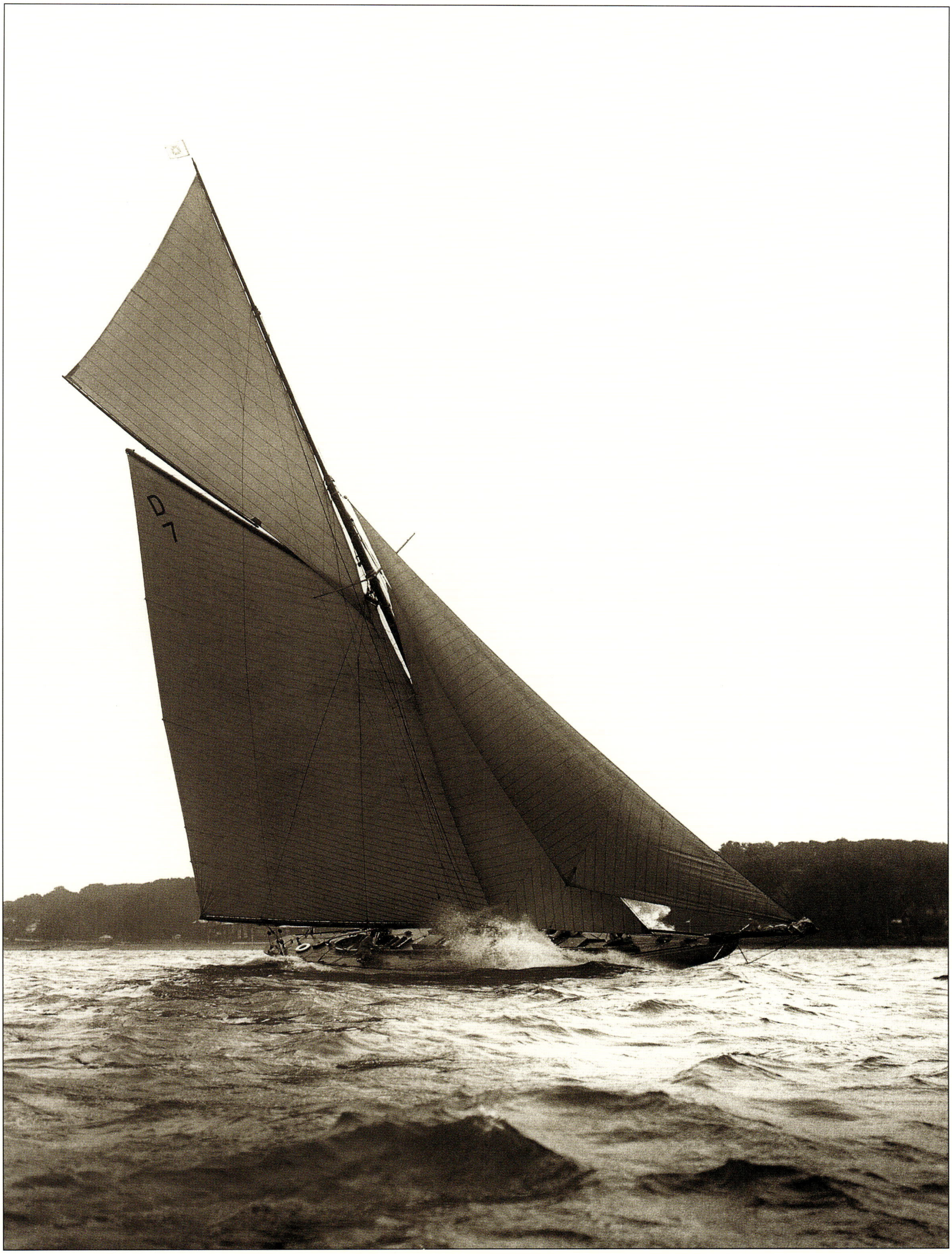
D 7

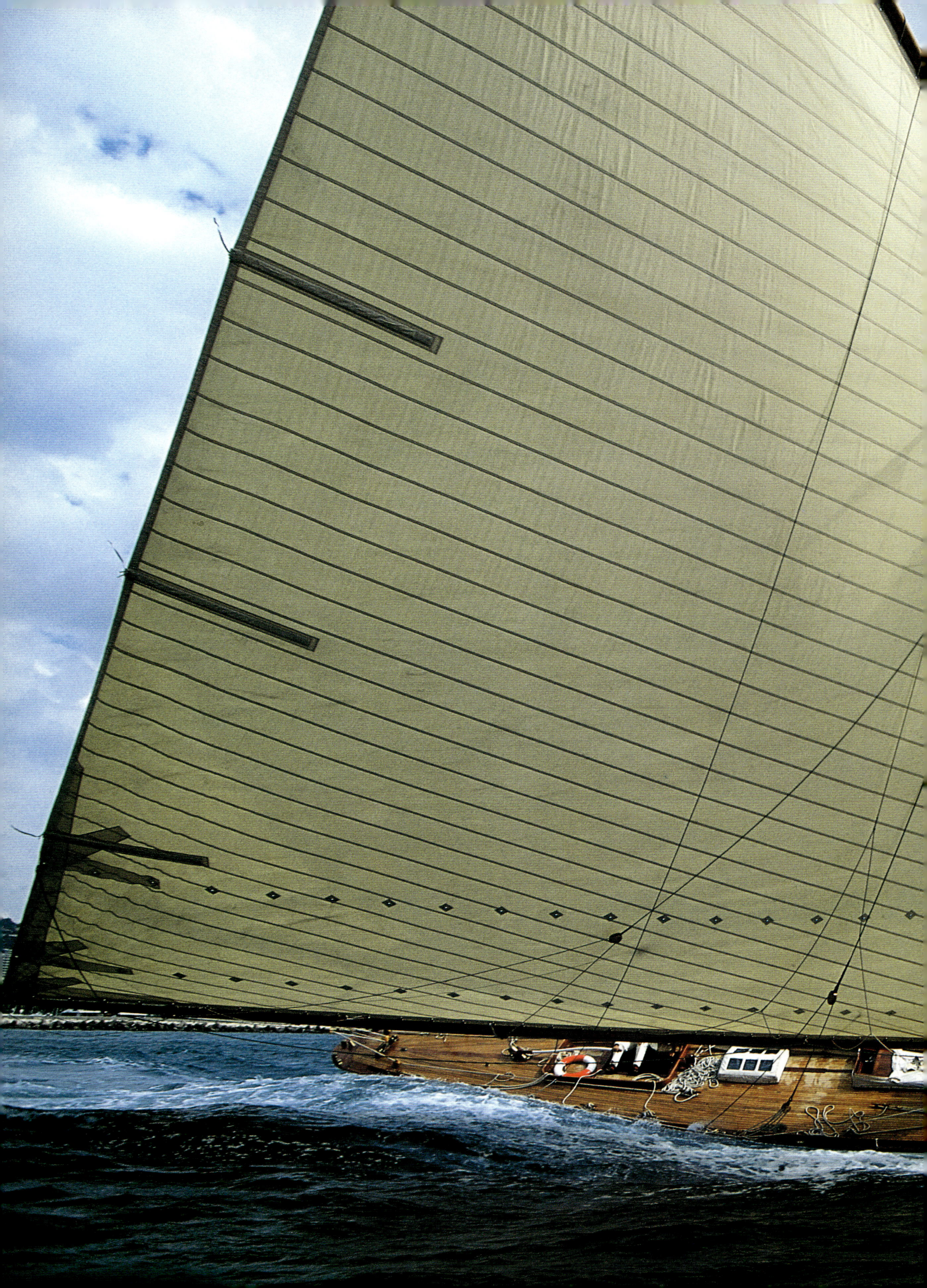

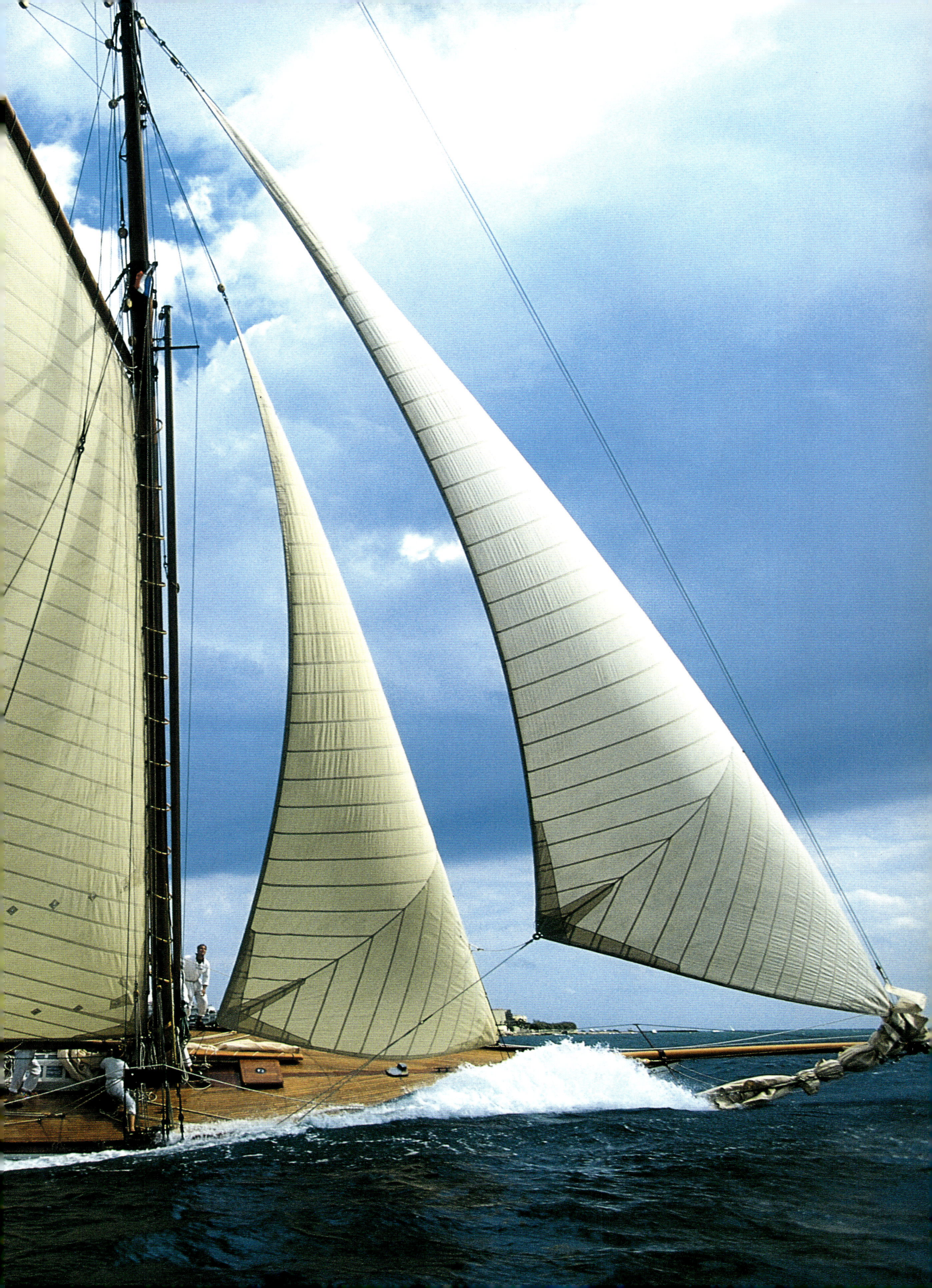

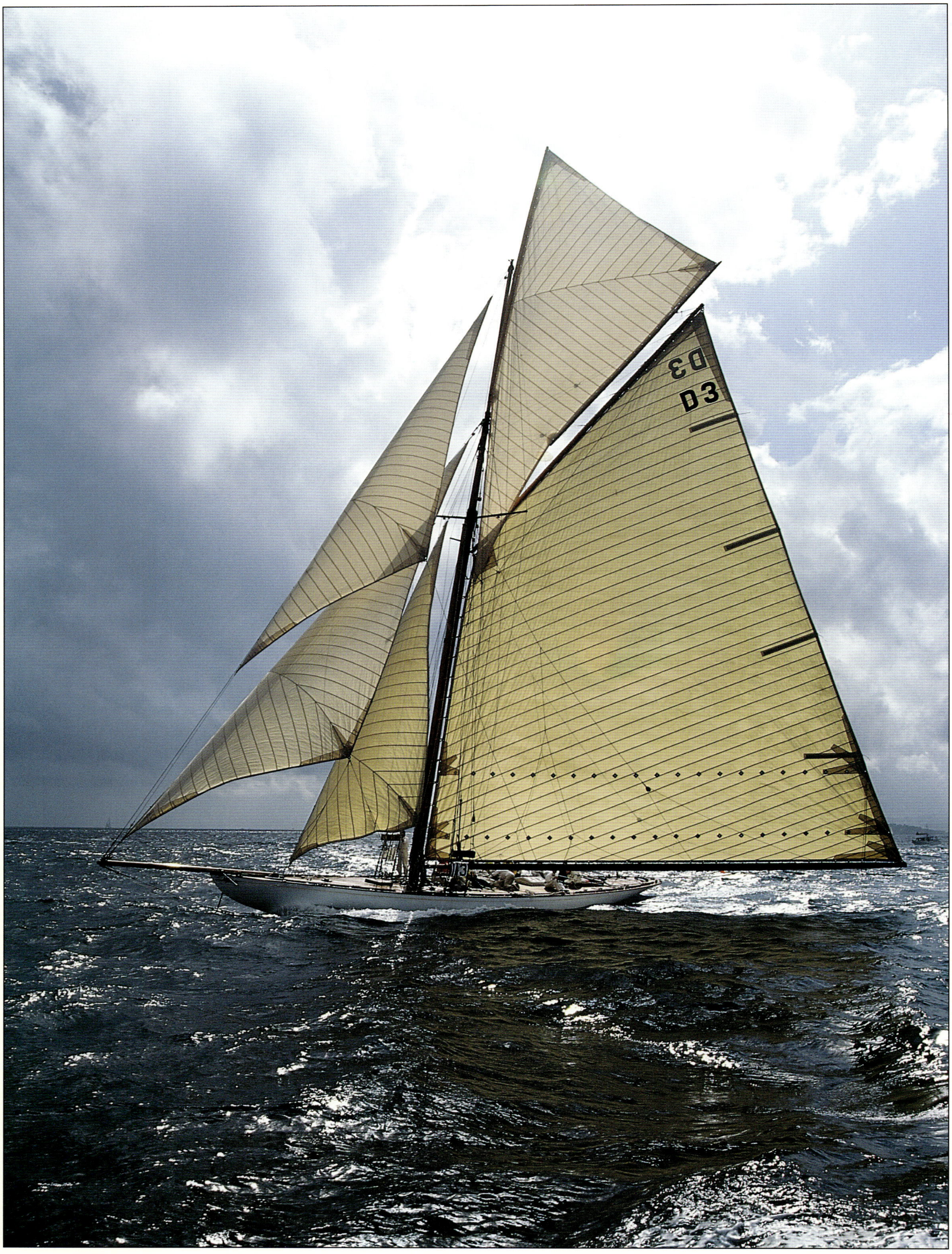
D3
D3

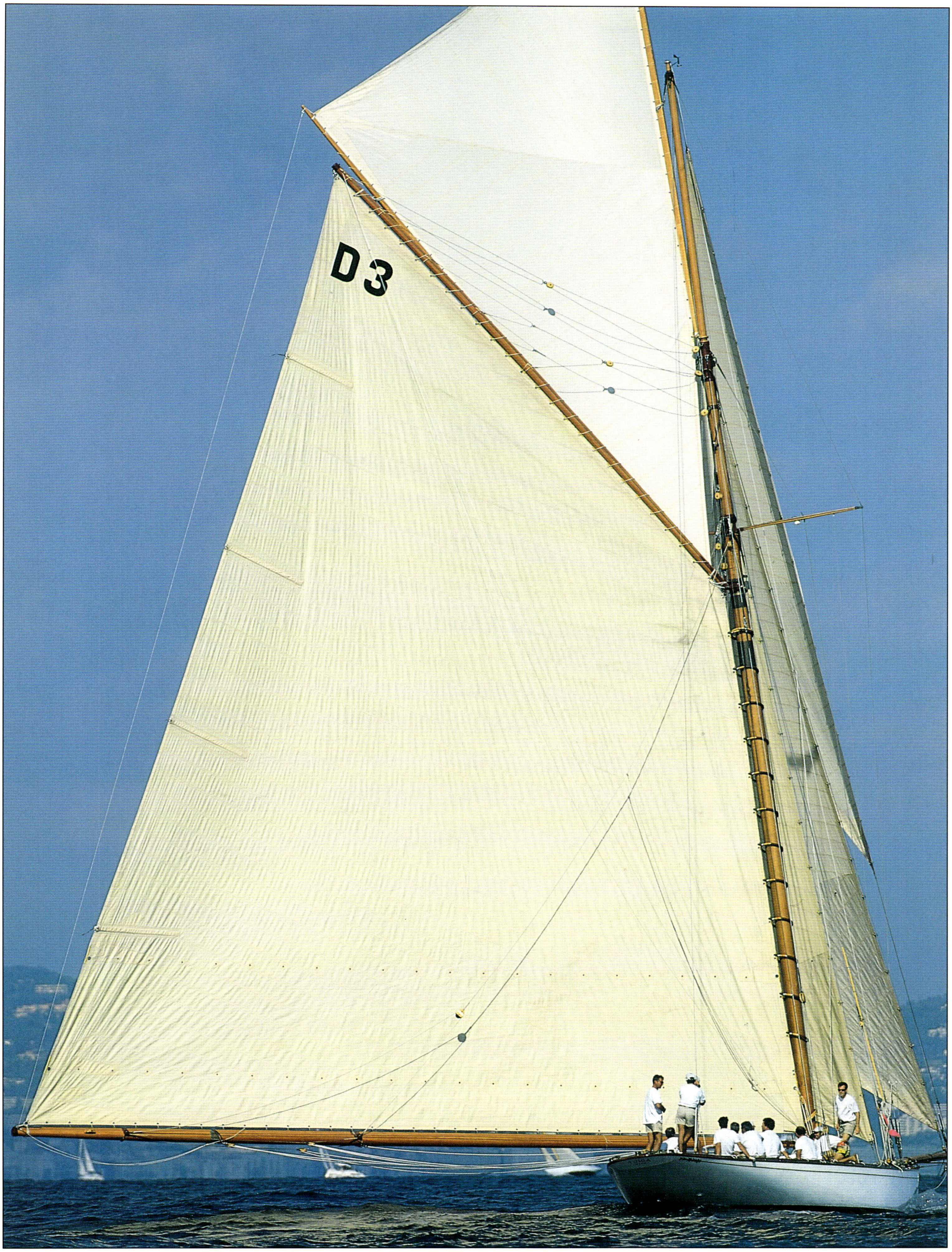
D3

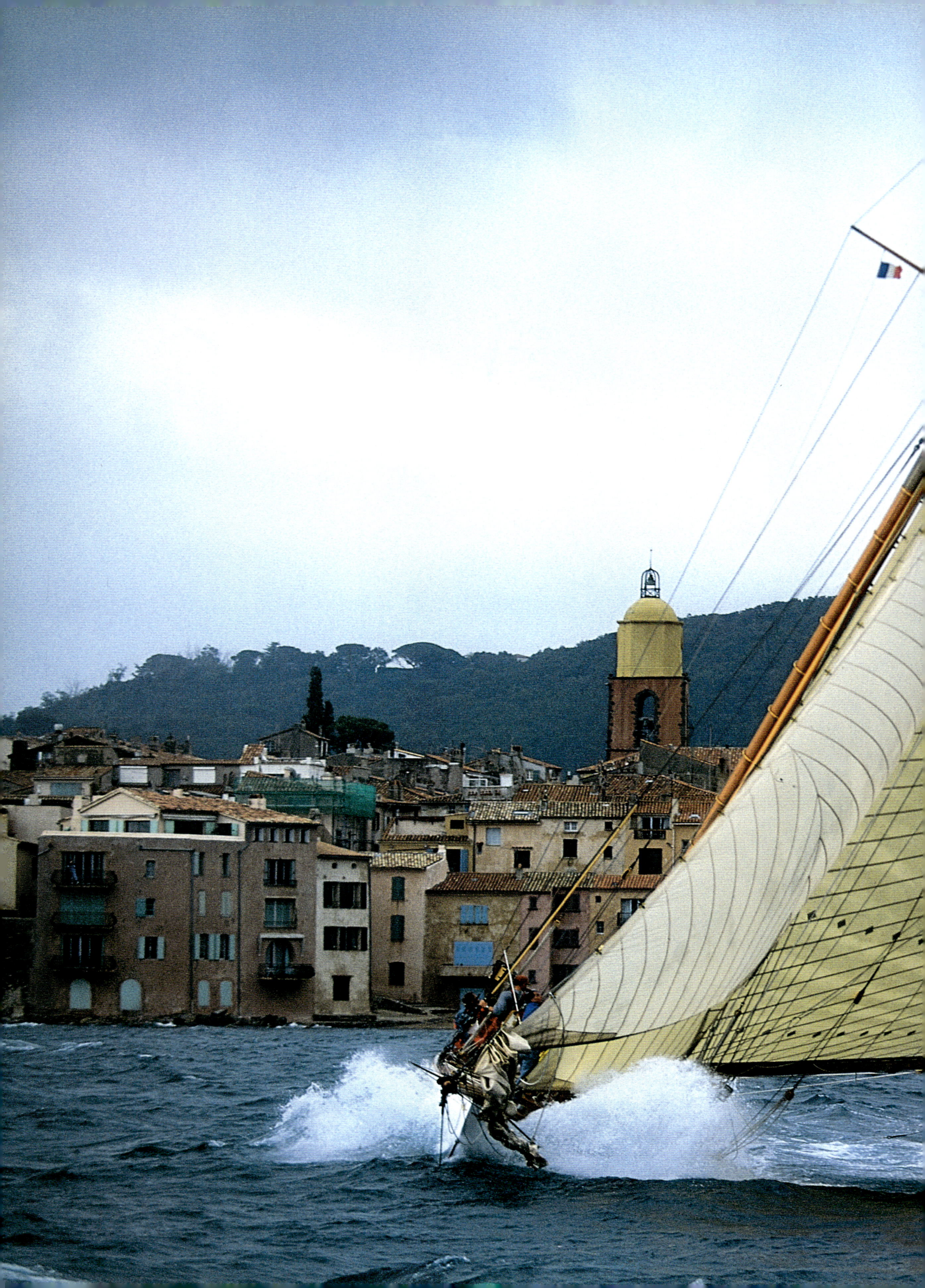

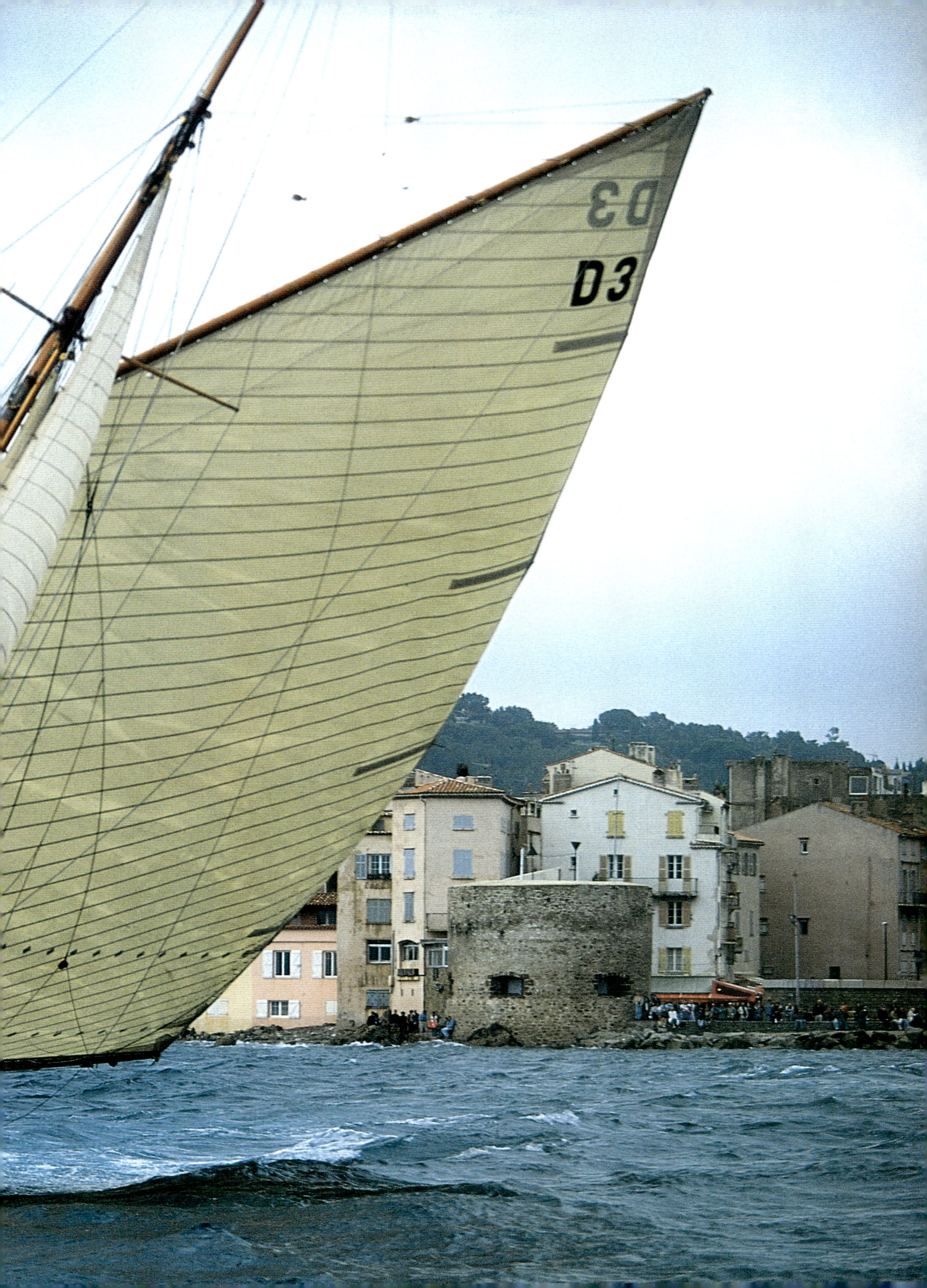
D3

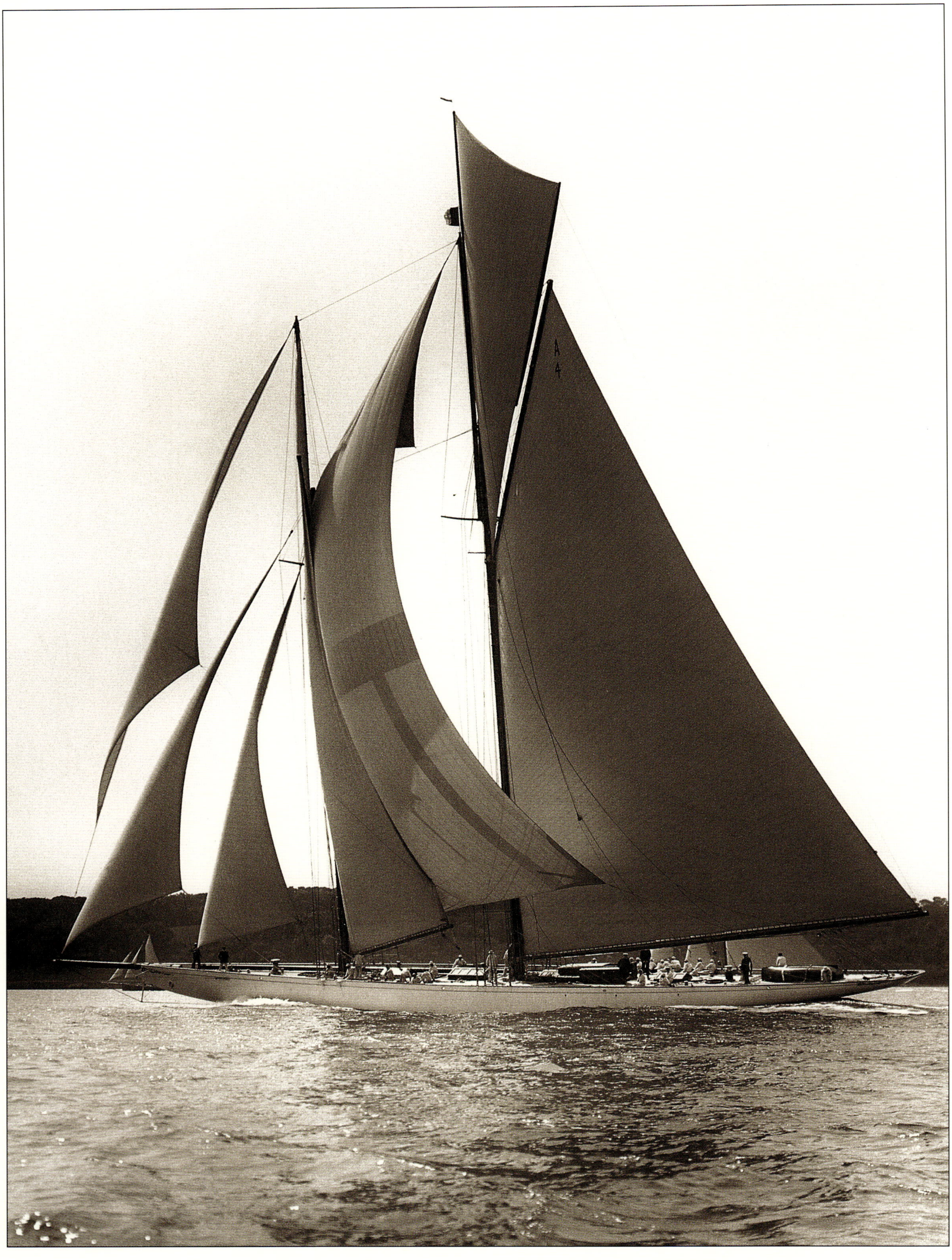
A4

his first 15 Metre design *Istria* set a precedent that revolutionised the rigging of racing yachts. His introduction of the Marconi rig was a refinement of the gaff rig. It dispensed with the upper yard of the traditional jack-yard topsail and thus considerably reduced weight aloft and increased the efficiency of gaff rig. Among the many orders Nicholson secured after *Istria's* great success were the commissions for *Margherita,* the replacement for Fife's failed A class racing schooner *Waterwitch*, and Sir Thomas Lipton's fourth America's Cup challenger *Shamrock IV.*

The sudden increase in racing yacht orders secured by Camper & Nicholsons in the immediate wake of the departure of the Edwin Lapthorns, father and son, gave James Lapthorn IV considerable opportunity to display his skills. Certainly George Rogers Ratsey II was his senior, but now in his late sixties, he was no longer active on the loft floor. It fell to James Lapthorn IV to design and cut the sails for Charles E. Nicholson's designs and the sails he produced were so good that he gradually took over the ageing Tom Ratsey's mantle. Charles E. Nicholson's son John summarised his firm's attitude towards the Ratseys and Lapthorns:

> Although there was a great deal of friendly rivalry between the Cowes and Gosport branches of the famous old sail making firm, we always considered Mr James Stanley Lapthorn [IV] as their best cutter, in tailoring parlance, and he cut and clothed these gracious ladies with a high degree of skill. His senior and I suppose the doyen of sailmakers, Mr Tom Ratsey, did not give Lapthorn too easy a time but he mellowed with age and we all loved him.[34]

Indeed, Thomas W. Ratsey's attitude to the newcomer may well have been coloured by the effect he had on the Cowes loft's order book. That Camper & Nicholsons trade should go to the Gosport loft was traditional but some yachtsmen became so impressed with the Gosport mainsails that they shifted their allegiance from Cowes to Gosport. Others maintained that the Cowes fore sails remained unrivalled and amongst the most dedicated racing men were several who split their orders between the two lofts; Gosport for

Opposite: The 1913 Nicholson-designed schooner *Margherita* is believed to have been the fastest racing schooner of all time. After winning all the major trophies in her first season, *Margherita* never raced again. / *Beken of Cowes*

Above: Tom Ratsey remained the head of the firm but with so may race winning yachts being built and outfitted in Gosport the supremacy of the Cowes loft was gradually eroded. / *Photo by W. Kirk, Franklin Ratsey-Woodroffe*

Over 1: *Tirrenia II*, a Fred Shepherd-designed ketch, was launched in 1914 and restored in 1992. She is seen here encountering the conditions that usually prevail off Bonifacio at the southern end of Corsica. / *Franco Pace*

Over 2: The First International Rule 10 Metre class *Tonino* was built in Bilbao to the designs of William Fife in 1911. Originally owned by King Alphonso XIII she was restored in Italy in 1993. / *Franco Pace*

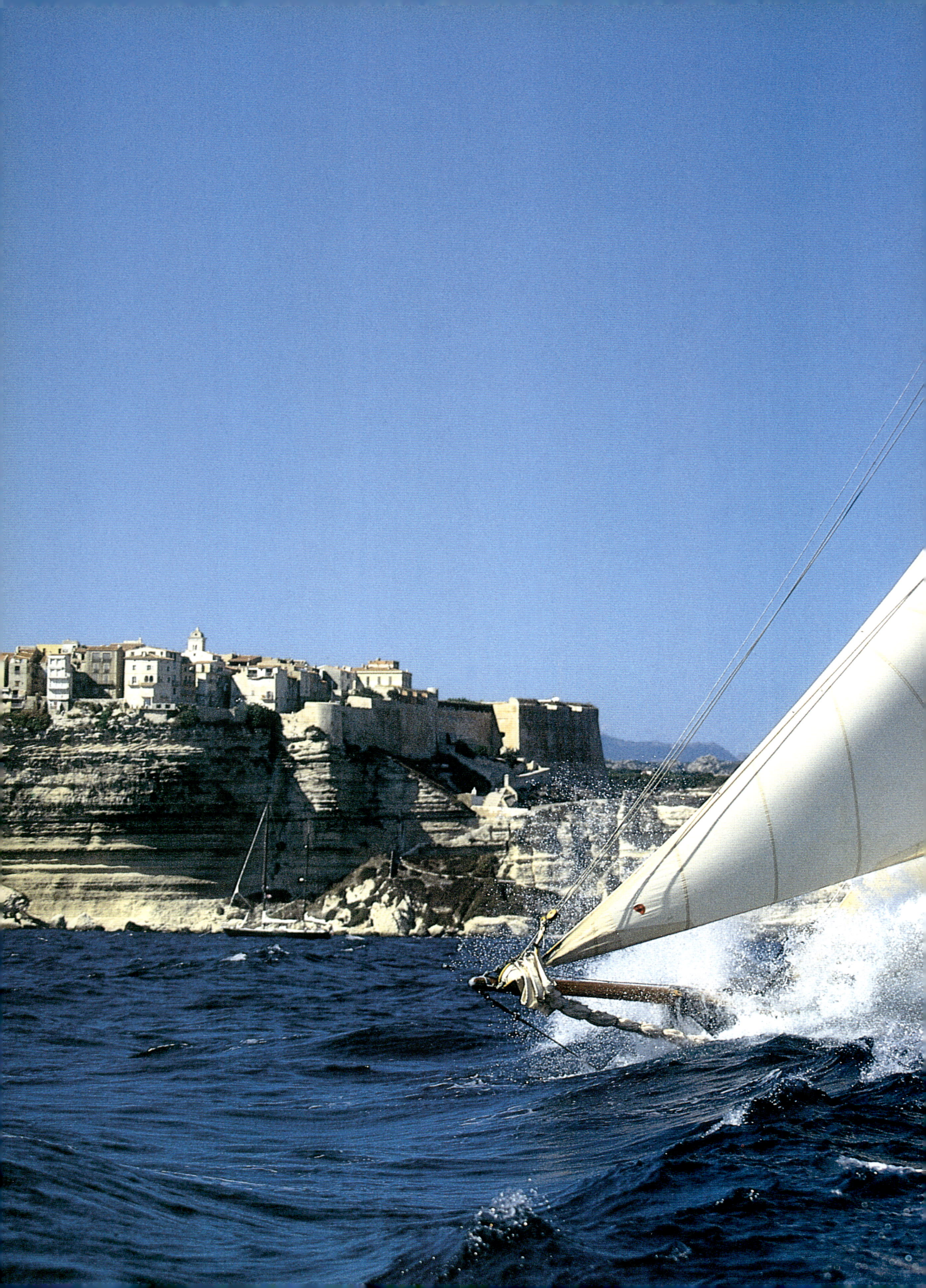

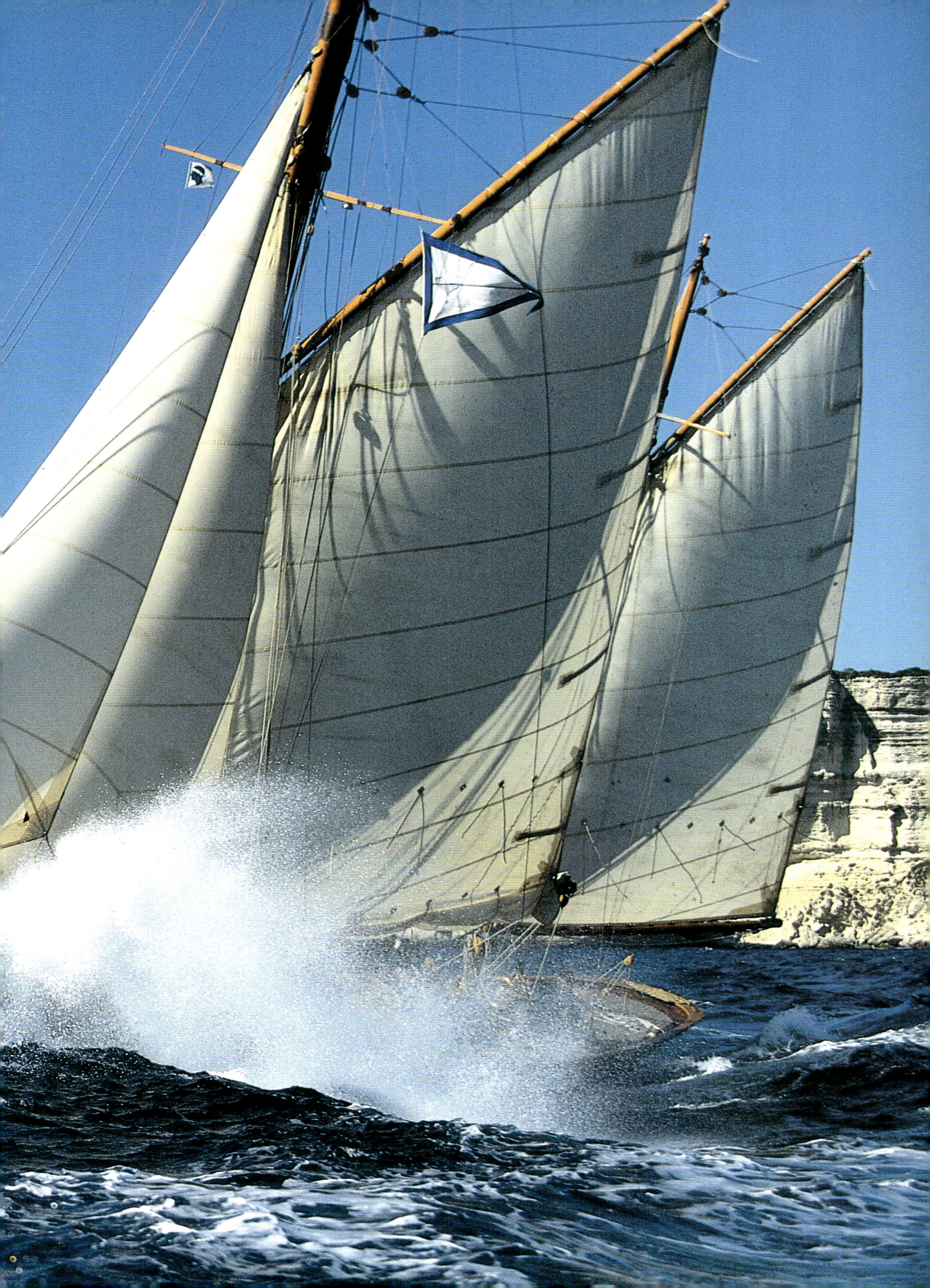

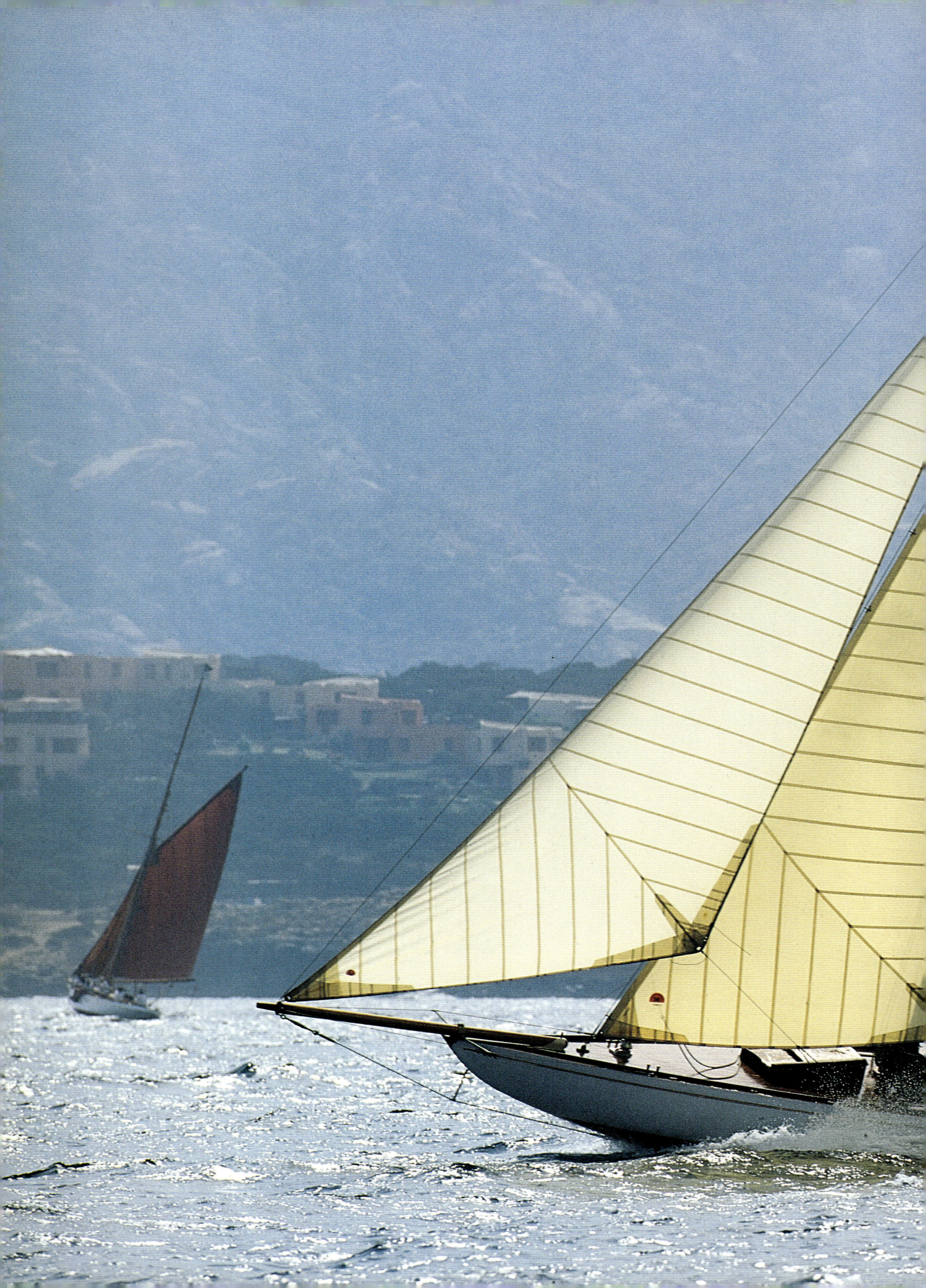

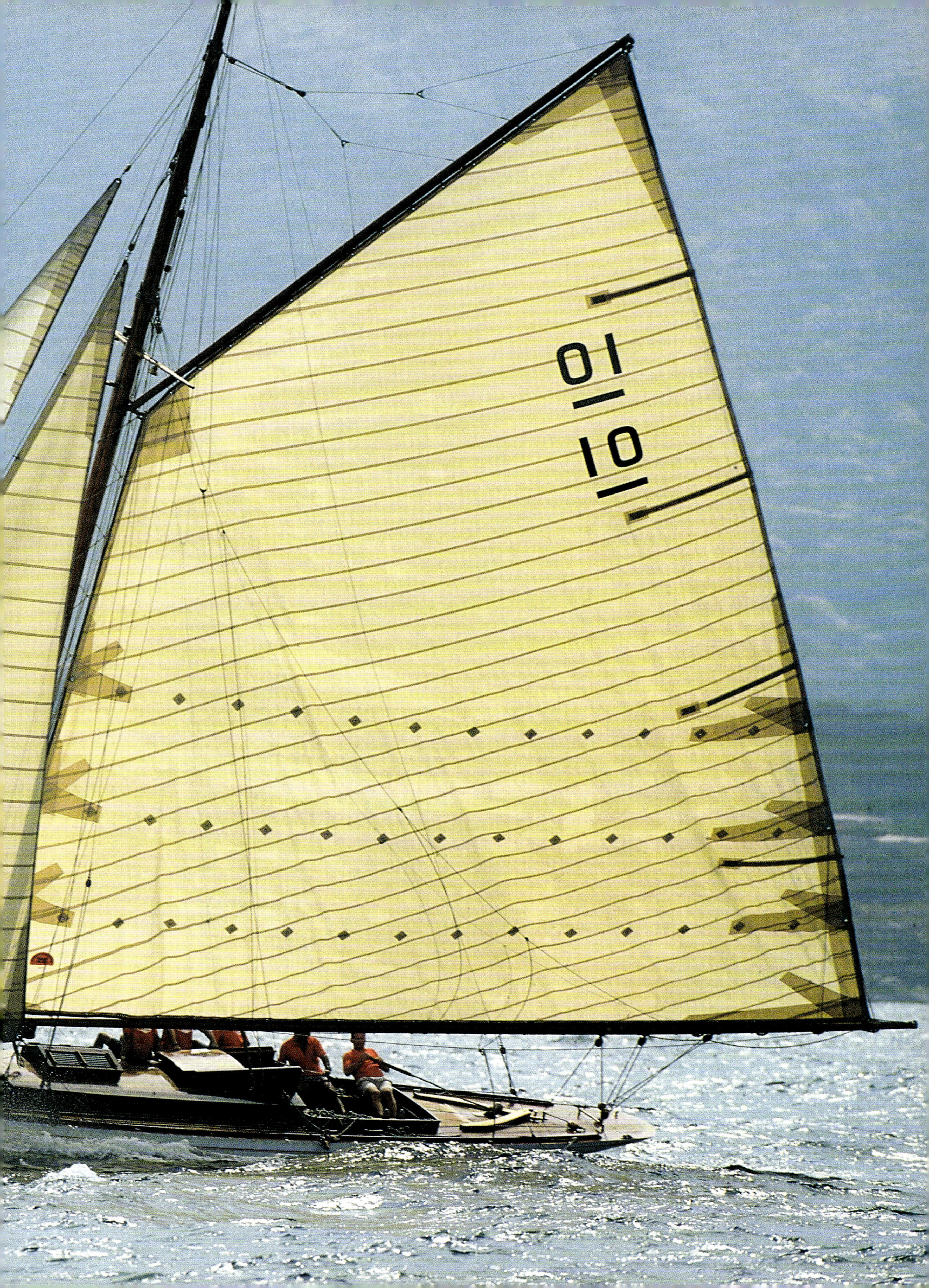
01
10

mainsails and Cowes for foresails.

The most important of James Lapthorn IV's early commissions was the sails for *Shamrock IV*. All these were made in Gosport; the first America's Cup sails since *Livonia* in 1870. Although tempted, Nicholson did not dare attempt a Marconi rig on such a large yacht. Instead he briefly toyed with a single fore sail replacing the standard jib and staysail but when this proved unmanageable he reverted to the standard cutter rig. The diversion was evidently good business for Lapthorn who was eventually to make a complete new suit of sails for *Shamrock IV* when all her gear burnt whilst in store; but before then the outbreak of World War I put an end to yachting. In C. E. Nicholson's words: '*The terrible reality of war seems to have at once obliterated Shamrock, the unimportance of such matters at a time like this having wiped out any regrets one would have keenly felt at a postponement under any other circumstance.*'[35] For Tom Ratsey World War I proved devastating. He had sailed regularly with both Edward VII and George V and made all the sails for *Britannia*. Equally he had raced with the Kaiser and made sails for his *Meteors*. Now in another competition he lost his three eldest sons.

When war broke out all Tom Ratsey's sons were at

home, it being George E. Ratsey's tour of duty in New York. Franklin, the fourth son, was already serving in the navy and came through the war unscathed. The eldest three Donald, Clayton and Stephen all joined the Isle of Wight Rifles. T. Christopher (Chris), the youngest, joined the navy as an able bodied seaman but had a miserable time and transferred to the army to be with his brothers. As a result all the Ratsey brothers, bar Franklin, were reunited, at Gallipoli. On 8 August 1916 they disembarked amongst the second wave of the stalled allied landing; Chris contracted dysentery and was immediately out of action. On the morning of the 12th the Isle of Wight Rifles were briefed before action. On hearing the

Left: The Nicholson-designed *Shamrock IV* tuning up with the Fife-designed 23 Metre class *Shamrock*. Nicholson's willingness to compromise all in the quest for speed is clearly shown in the contrast of his 'ugly duckling' with the elegant Fife. Note the experimental sloop rig on *Shamrock IV*. / *Beken of Cowes*

Above: The launch of the America's Cup challenger *Shamrock IV* from Camper & Nicholsons yard in 1914. With the Stars and Stripes flying from their loft, the Lapthorn's were displaying sporting if controversial loyalties. / *Author's Collection*

Below: Martin Snape's 1907 water colour of the Gosport waterfront showing Camper & Nicholsons' building sheds and Ratsey & Lapthorn's loft in the distance./ *James F. Lapthorn*

plan Capt. Clayton Ratsey responded '*My God we'll all be killed.*' He and his brother Donald died that day. Stephen escaped with injuries and after a stint in hospital in Alexandria was repatriated with his brother Christopher. By coincidence they travelled back to England with their brother-in-law Troop Officer Stanley Woodroffe, who had married their sister Muriel. After convalescence at Osborne House, Lt Stephen Ratsey rejoined his battalion at Gaza where it was dug in. Soon after he told his men that he was going to avenge his two brothers and went over the top alone. He was never seen again.[36]

Left: Four of Tom Ratsey's sons fought at Gallipoli, only two returned. By coincidence 2nd Lieutenants Christopher (left) and Stephen Ratsey were re-united with their brother-in-law, Troop Officer Stanley Woodroffe on the voyage home. / *Franklin Ratsey-Woodroffe*

Below: Christopher Ratsey at the memorial to the 29th Division which fell at Gallipolli. His brothers Donald and Clayton were killed on the same day and was Stephen injured. After recovering from his injuries Stephen rejoined his regiment at Gaza where he ran from his trench towards Turkish lines saying he was going to avenge his brothers, he was never seen again. / *Franklin Ratsey-Woodroffe*

Right: *Shamrock IV* in her final racing trim, the sloop rig was abandoned in favour of the proven cutter rig. The outbreak of war delayed the 1914 America's Cup until 1920 by which time Nicholson sought to introduce a range of further rig improvements. / *Beken of Cowes*

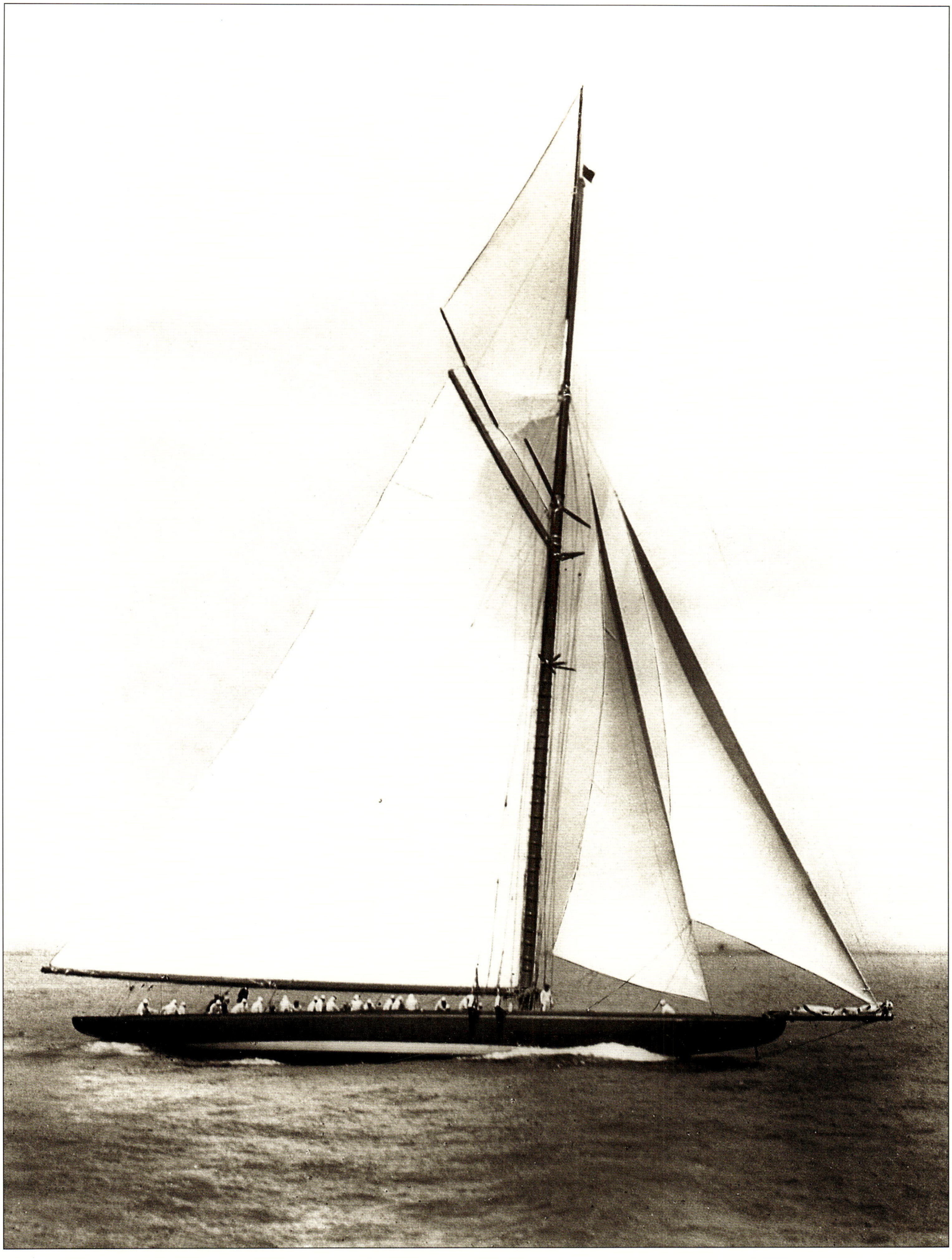

War devastated both Tom Ratsey's family and his business, recovery was a slow process. In Gosport the Lapthorn's had survived intact as had George E. Ratsey in New York. Sensing a faster recovery in America G. E. Ratsey thought the firm should have its own loft and shrewdly bought some land adjacent to the Henry B. Nevins yard where the greatest number of American racing yachts were built during the inter-war period. In 1919 he sought backing for his construction plans from Tom Ratsey but such was the latter's disinterest that he only replied '*Do as you think fit.*'[37] G. E. Ratsey did and built a loft with three 150' long floors which he extended ten years later to be able to lay out whole J class mainsails. But such sails, like many of the inter-war developments, were not welcomed by Thomas W. Ratsey. He never adjusted to Bermudan rigs saying publicly '*I have no use for them, and I consider any such rig positively dangerous outside the Solent, perhaps inside too.*'[38] Gradually he began to display some of the same deep-rooted opposition to all things new that he had faced 40 years earlier. In 1929 he summarised his position:

> The secret of my success is that we attend to our business and follow in the footsteps of our fore-fathers, make such changes from time to time as we think will be improvements. My dear boy Donald, who was killed in the War, was rather fond of making changes and I used to say to him, '*All right Donald, by all means make changes when it is an improvement, but do not make changes for the sake of changing, otherwise we shall go astern.*' Then I always believe in letting the young ones take the lead, even to steering the course, we luff to a free puff and we always go about directly the wind heads us. Whenever we make a change it is always with the approval of the Senior.'[39]

With Tom Ratsey firmly in place as 'the Senior' the loss of three of his sons presented the firm with an immediate succession problem. To solve this he withdrew his immediate family from involvement in the New York loft; this became the preserve of George E. Ratsey who was joined in 1919 by his eldest son Ernest A. Ratsey and from 1924, for six months a year, by his second son G. Colin Ratsey.

Above: Ratsey & Lapthorn's new loft on City Island was built next door to the Henry B. Nevins yard where the greatest number of American racing yachts were built during the inter-war years. / *Rosenfeld Collection, Mystic Seaport Museum*

Gosport was jointly run by James Lapthorn IV and George Rogers Ratsey II until the latter died in 1923 and it reverted wholly to Lapthorn control. This arrangement left no heir to the Gourock loft and it closed with James Lapthorn III's death in 1929. In Cowes the changes were greater; Chris' medical studies and ambitions to become a surgeon were aborted and he was co-opted into the family firm. Franklin Ratsey had ongoing commitments in the Navy, and only retired in 1939; just in time to join up again; nevertheless he served on the firm's board from 1932. In was in this context that Tom Ratsey invited his only daughter, Muriel, on to the firm's board in 1920 and although there is little tangible evidence of her activities, her influence on the firm appears to have been strong. She was married to Stanley Woodroffe, the naval officer Chris and Stephen Ratsey had met up with on their return from Gallipoli. Since Stanley was normally away at sea she lived with her father, kept house for him and played a role in the company's administration.

Above: 1921 saw the first appearance of the Bermudan rig in the British Big Class. Designed by C. E. Nicholson for the Big class cutter *Nyria*, it was a resounding success. *Nyria's* mainsail was cut by James Stanley Lapthorn IV and built in Gosport. Note the mast hoops to the spreaders and track above; a short lived transitional arrangement. / *Photo by Mary Nicholson, Author's Collection*

Left: Tom Ratsey standing in *Lulworth's* companionway in August 1929. *Lulworth* was the last gaff Big Class cutter to be built and for all Tom Ratsey's disapproval of the Bermudan rig, her failure to convert to it ended her racing career. / *Franklin Ratsey-Woodroffe*

Over 1: *Creole* remains one of C. E. Nicholson's great masterpieces. When originally launched from Camper & Nicholsons Gosport yard in 1927 her three masted staysail rig was a major breakthrough in rig design, she is seen here at the 1993 Nioulargue. / *Franco Pace*

Over 2: William Fife's choice of the Bermudan rig for his 1926 offshore cruiser *Hallowe'en* caused consternation at a time when gaff rig still prevailed. A record breaking performance in the Fastnet race silenced the critics. *Hallowe'en* is seen here at start of the race from Porto Rotondo to Porto Cervo in Sardinia in 1993. / *Franco Pace*

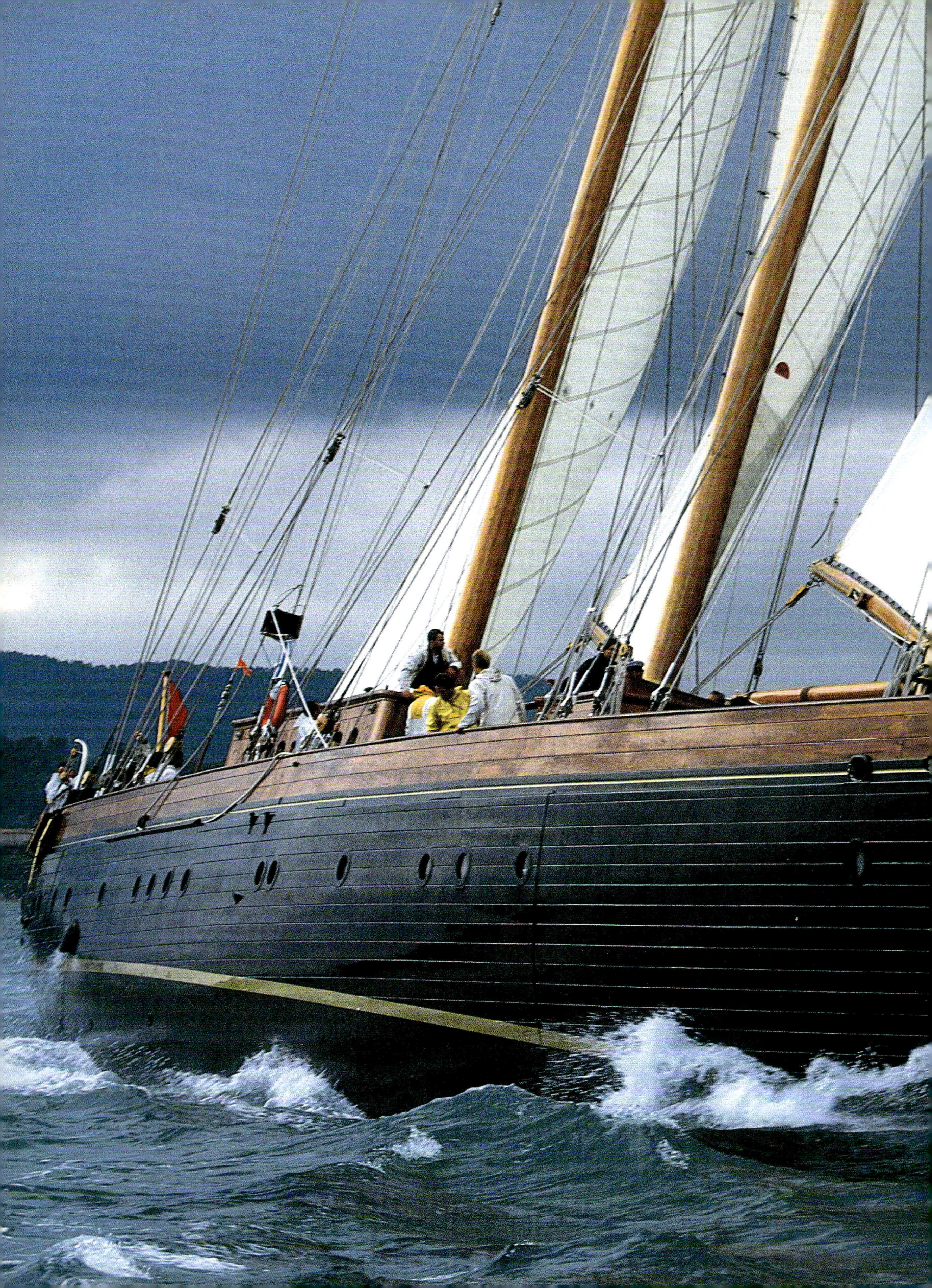

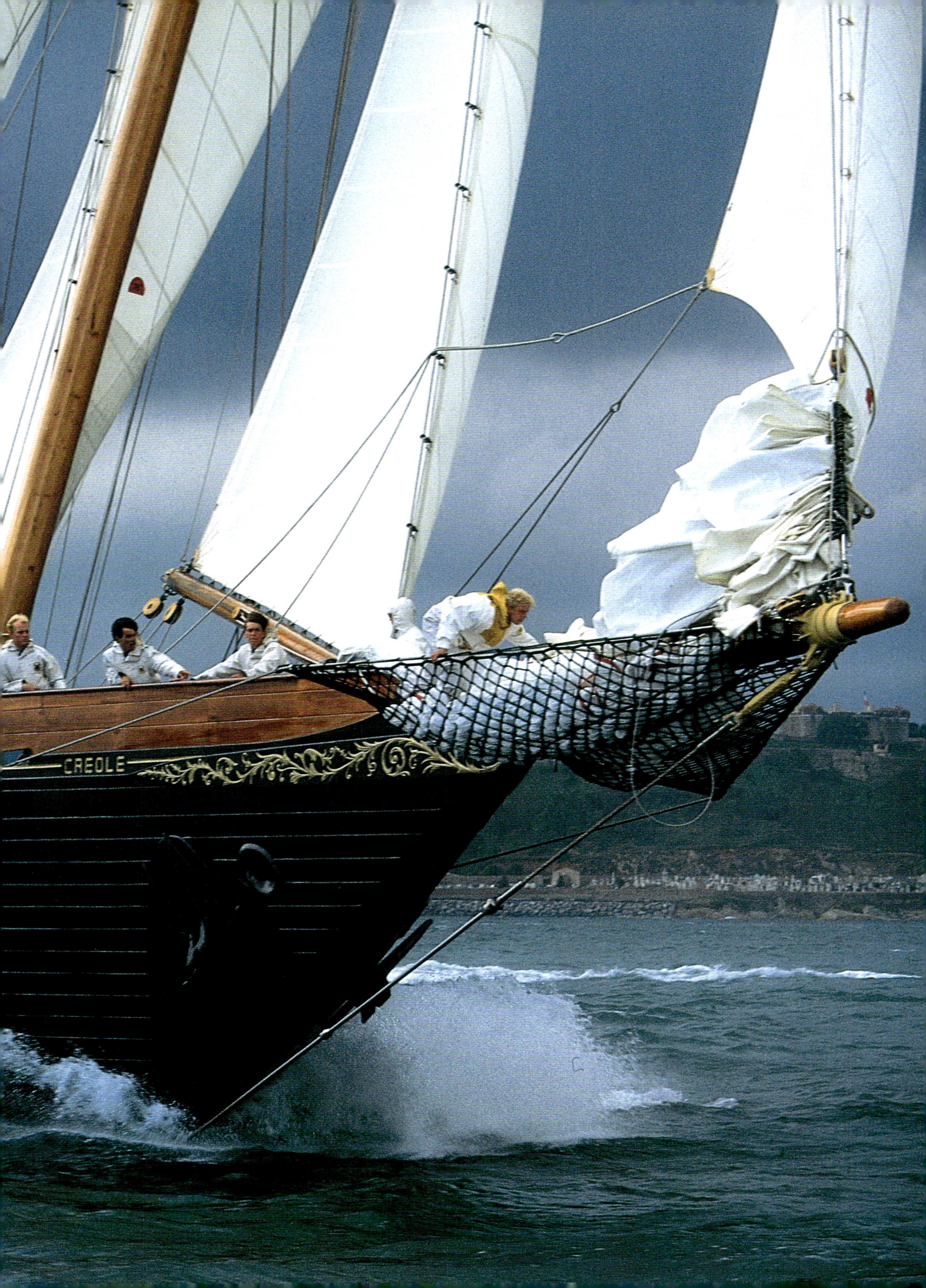
CREOLE

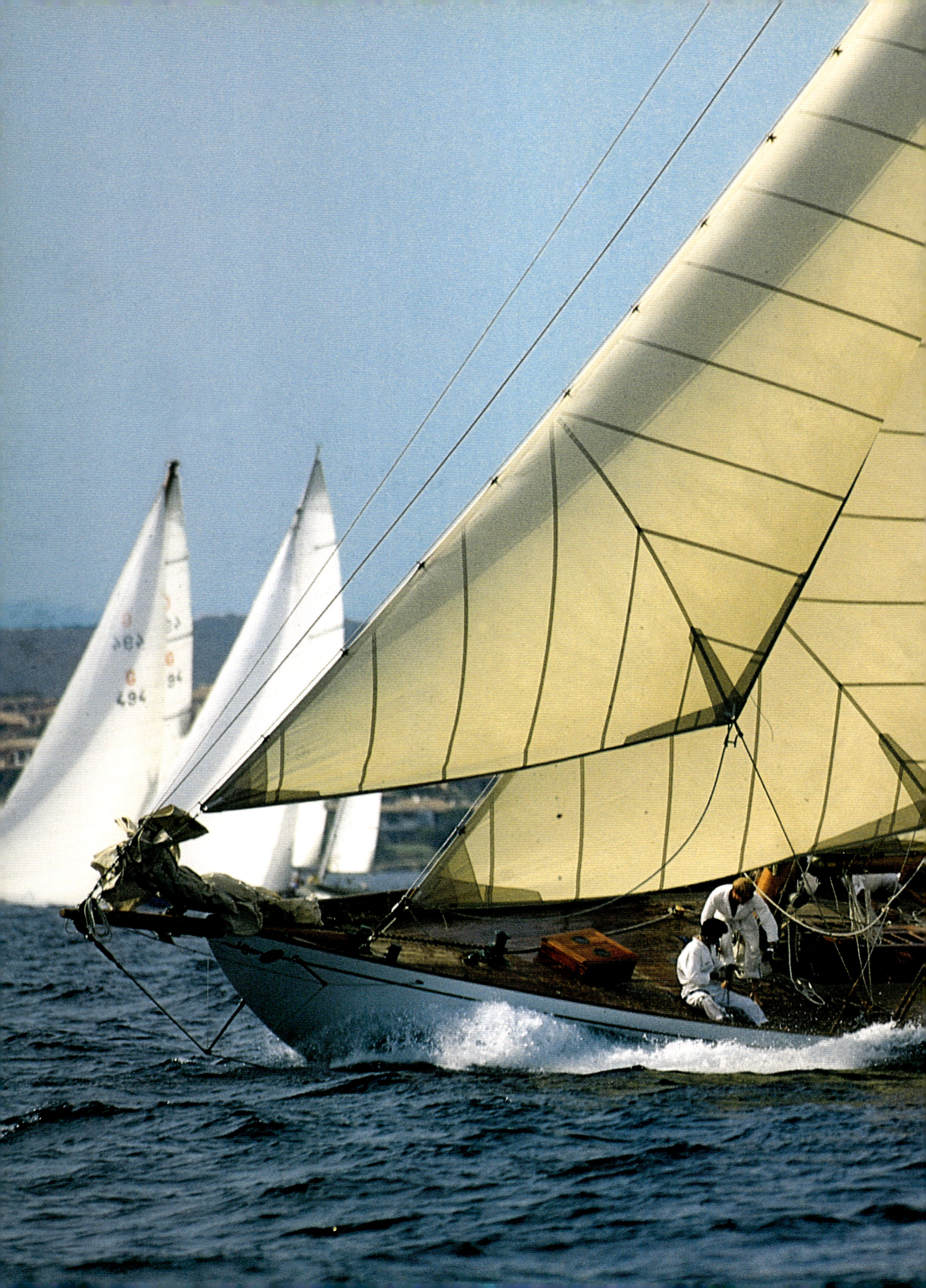
494

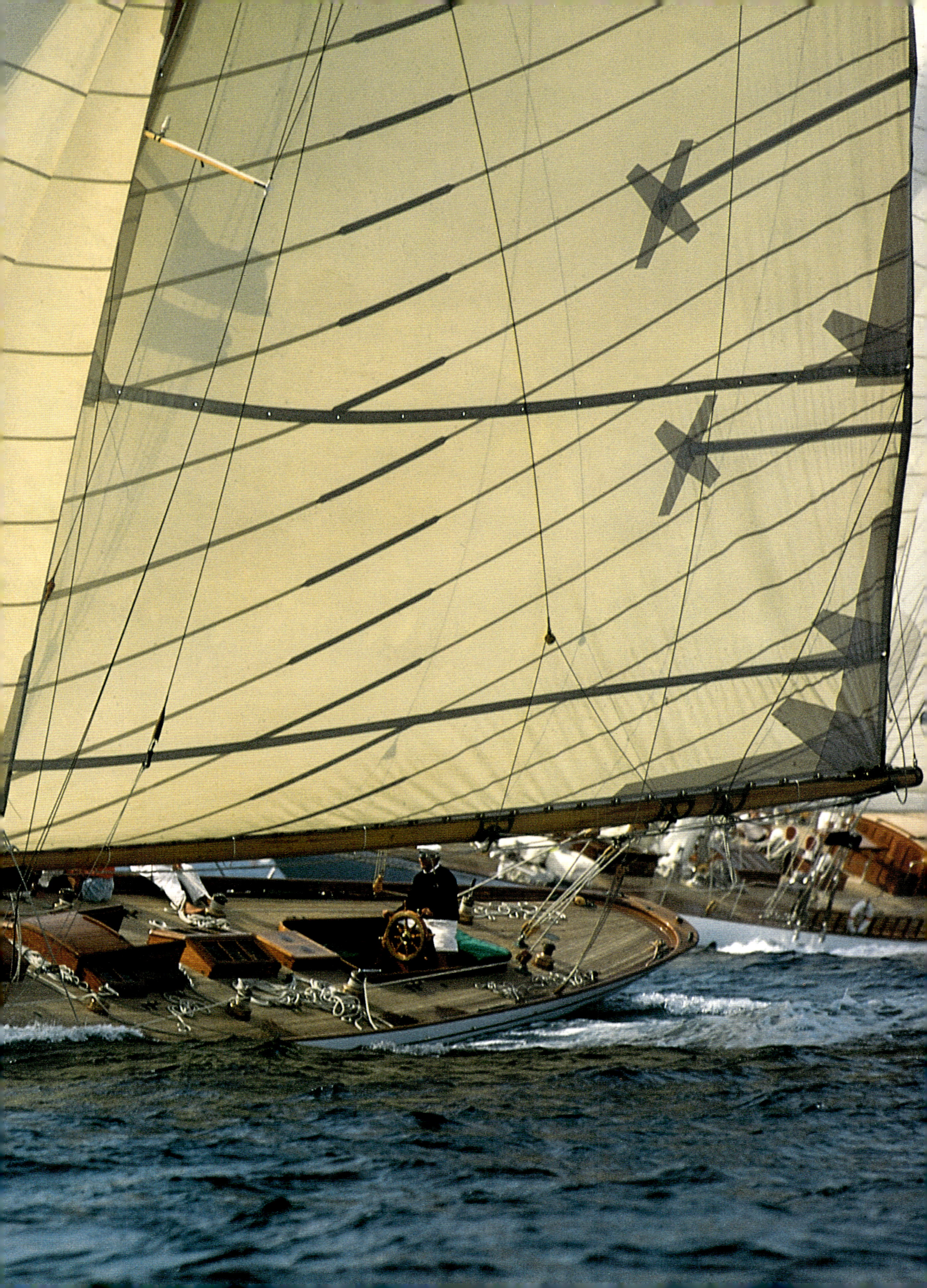

Above: In 1928 Fife and Nicholson designed the first new Bermudan rigged Big Class cutters. In this 1930 photograph, the Fife-designed *Cambria* is leading Nicholson's *Astra* and the gaff rigged, Herreshoff-designed schooner, *Westward*. / *Beken of Cowes*

Above Right: *Britannia* flying her new Bermudan sails, her escort ship is standing by. / *Beken of Cowes*

Over 1: Restored in 1995, the 1923 Fife-designed and built ketch *Kentra* made the pilgrimage to her place of birth on the Clyde for the 1998 Fife Regatta. / *Franco Pace*

Over 2 Left: The Second International Rule 8 Metre class Osborne was built to Fife's designs for the Queen of Spain in 1929. Restored to her original appearance in 1997, she is seen here at the 1998 8 Metre World Championships on Lake Geneva. / *Franco Pace*

Over 2 Right: A grey day at the Cannes' Regattes Royales in 1994. The 1930 Fife-designed and built 8 Metre *Fulmar* ghosts along with her genoa set. / *Franco Pace*

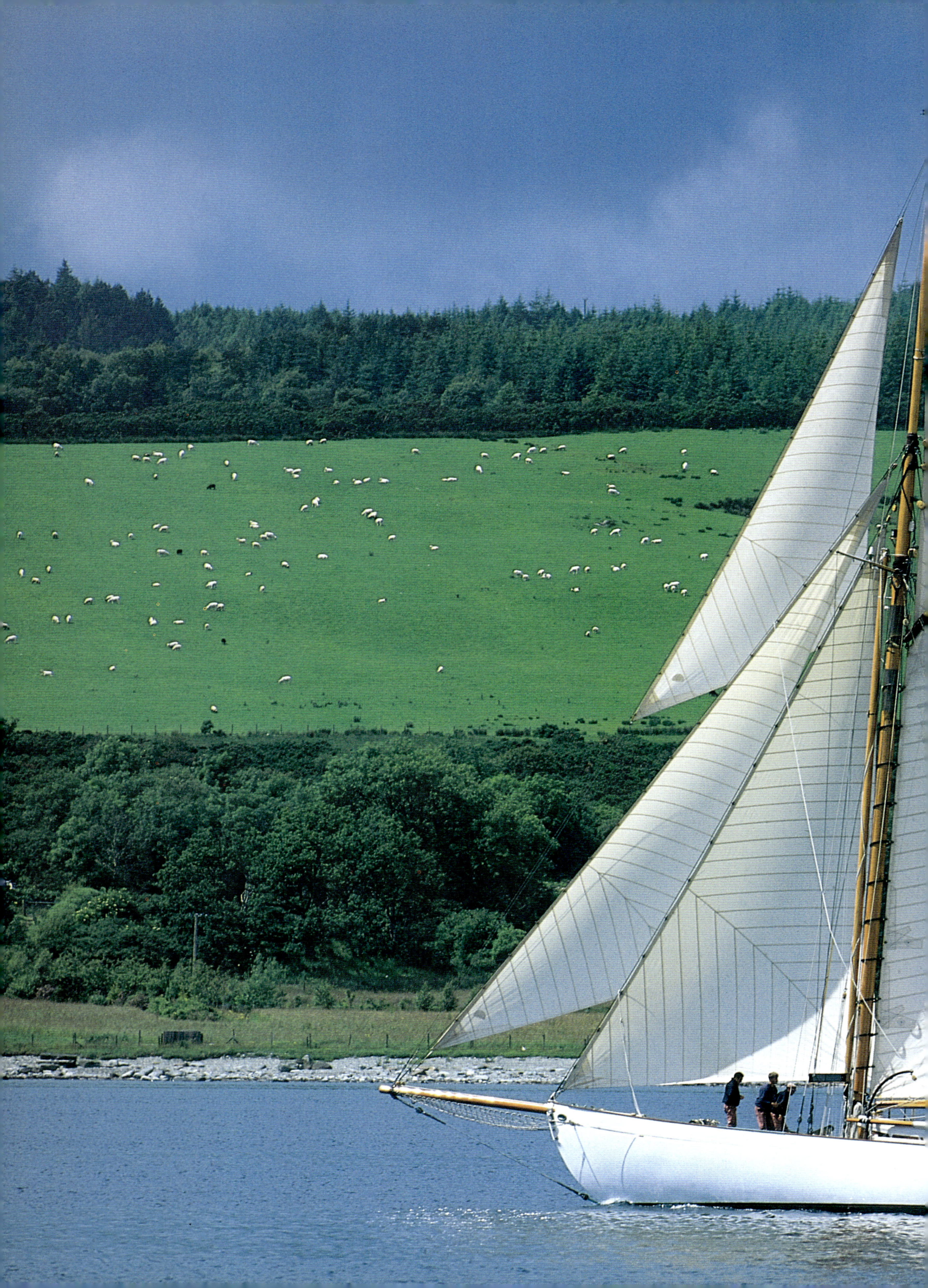

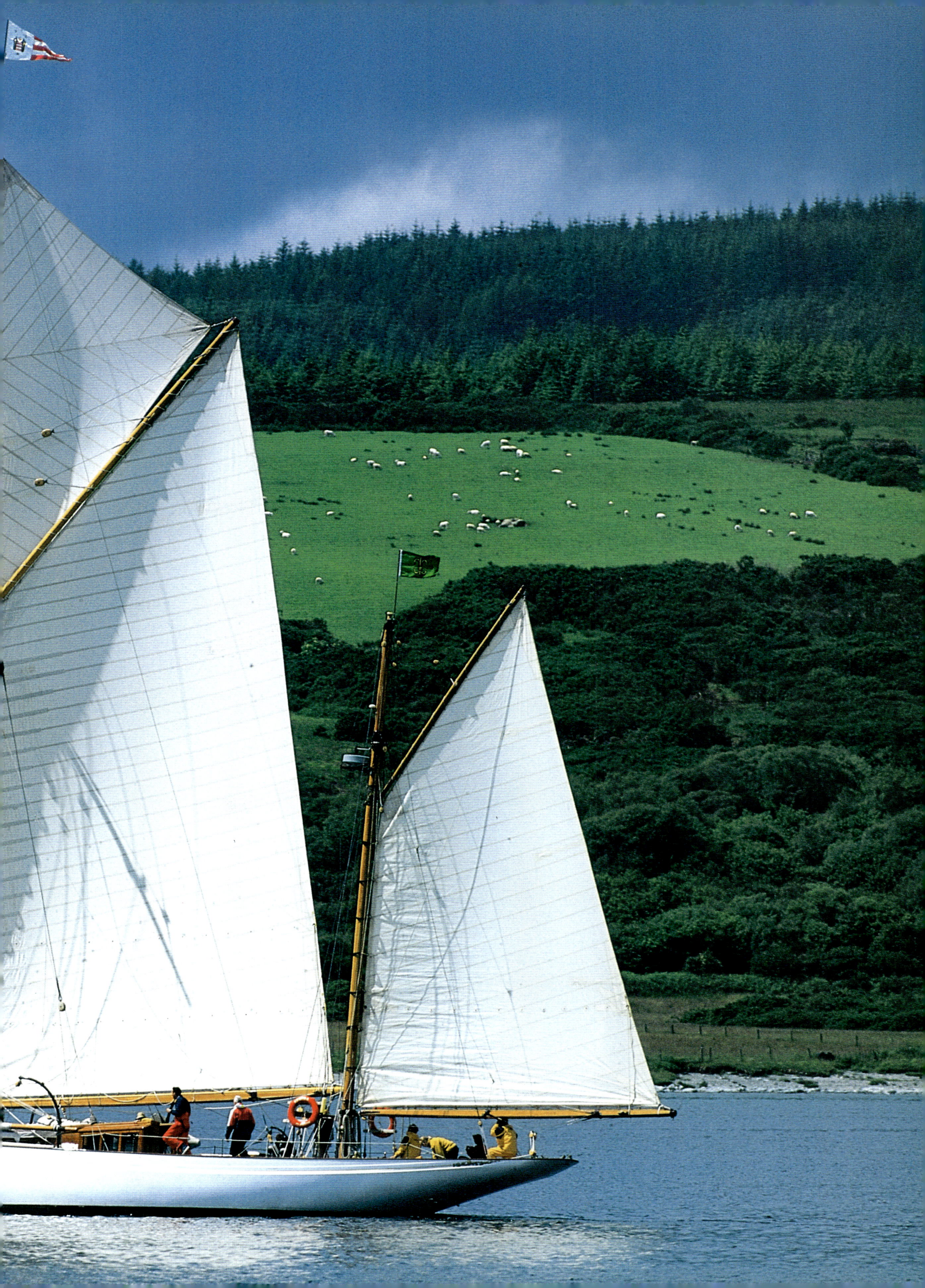

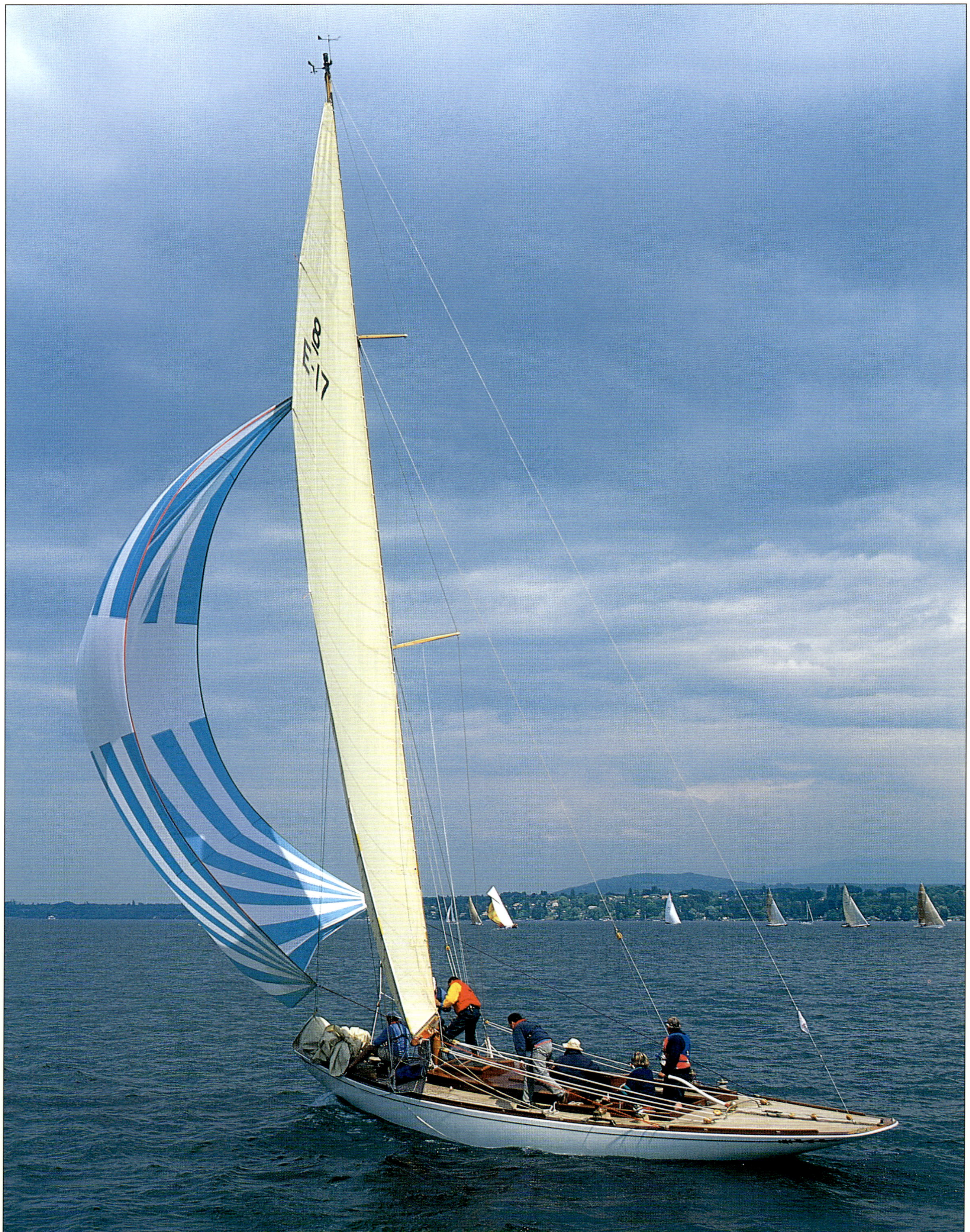
E-17

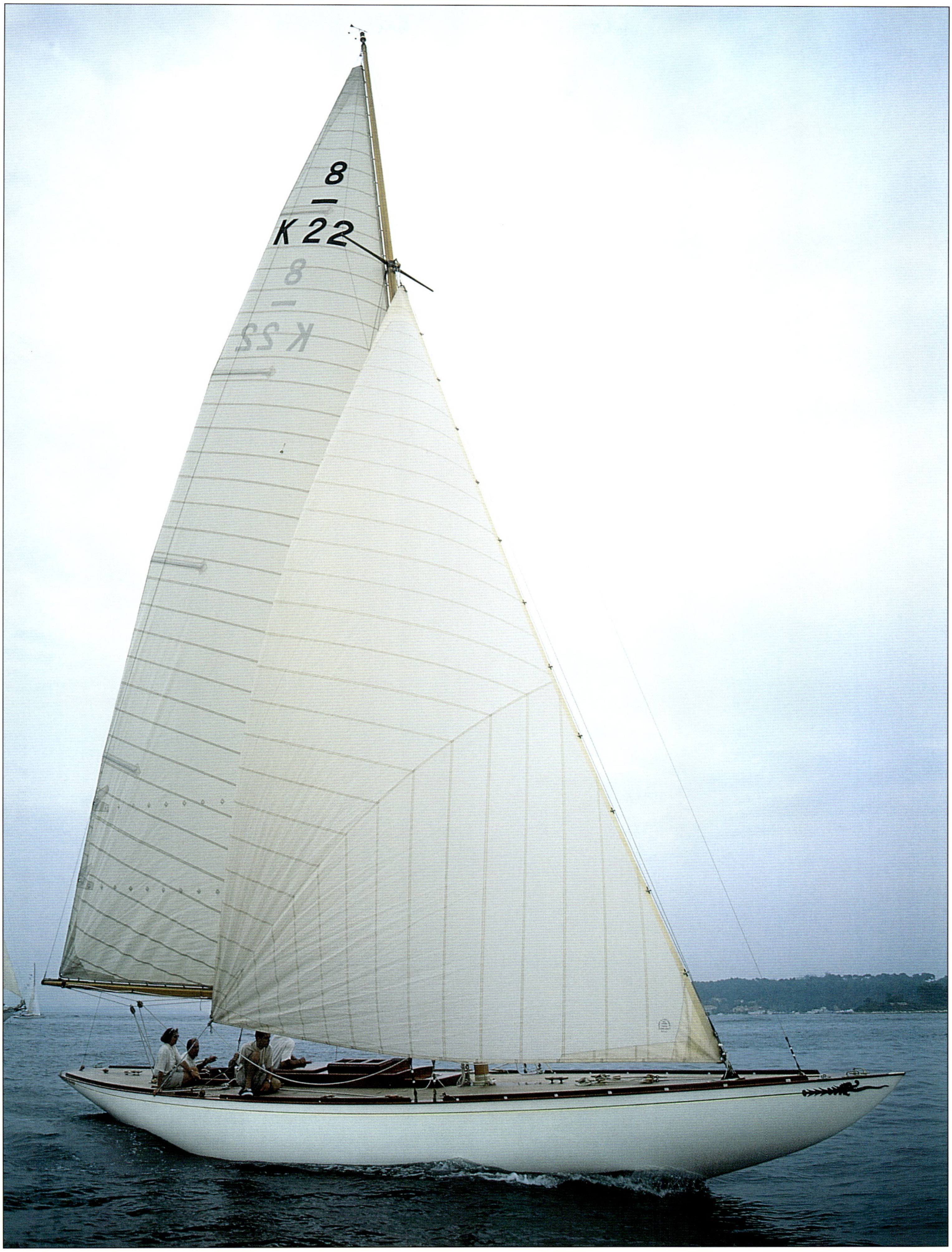
8
K22

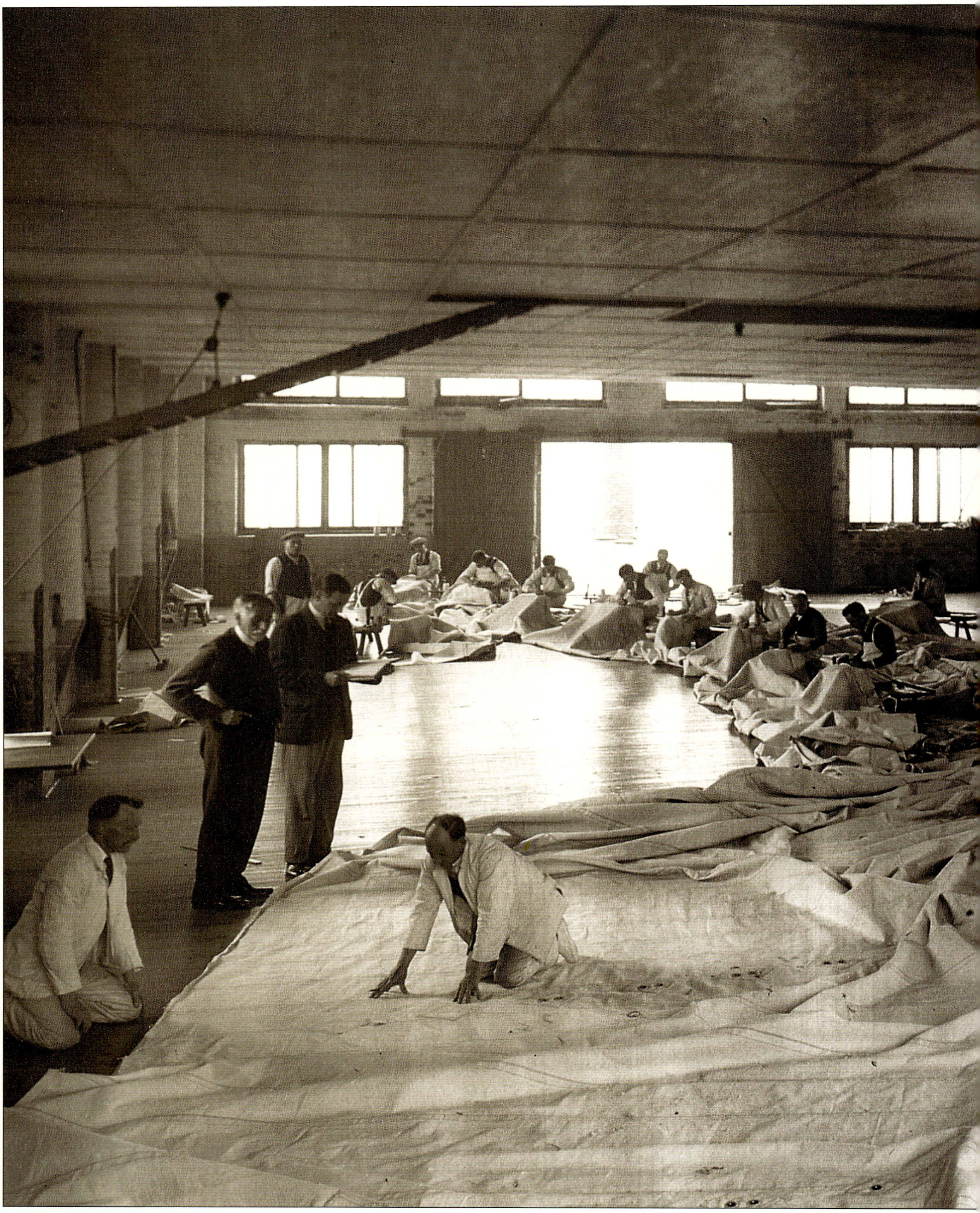

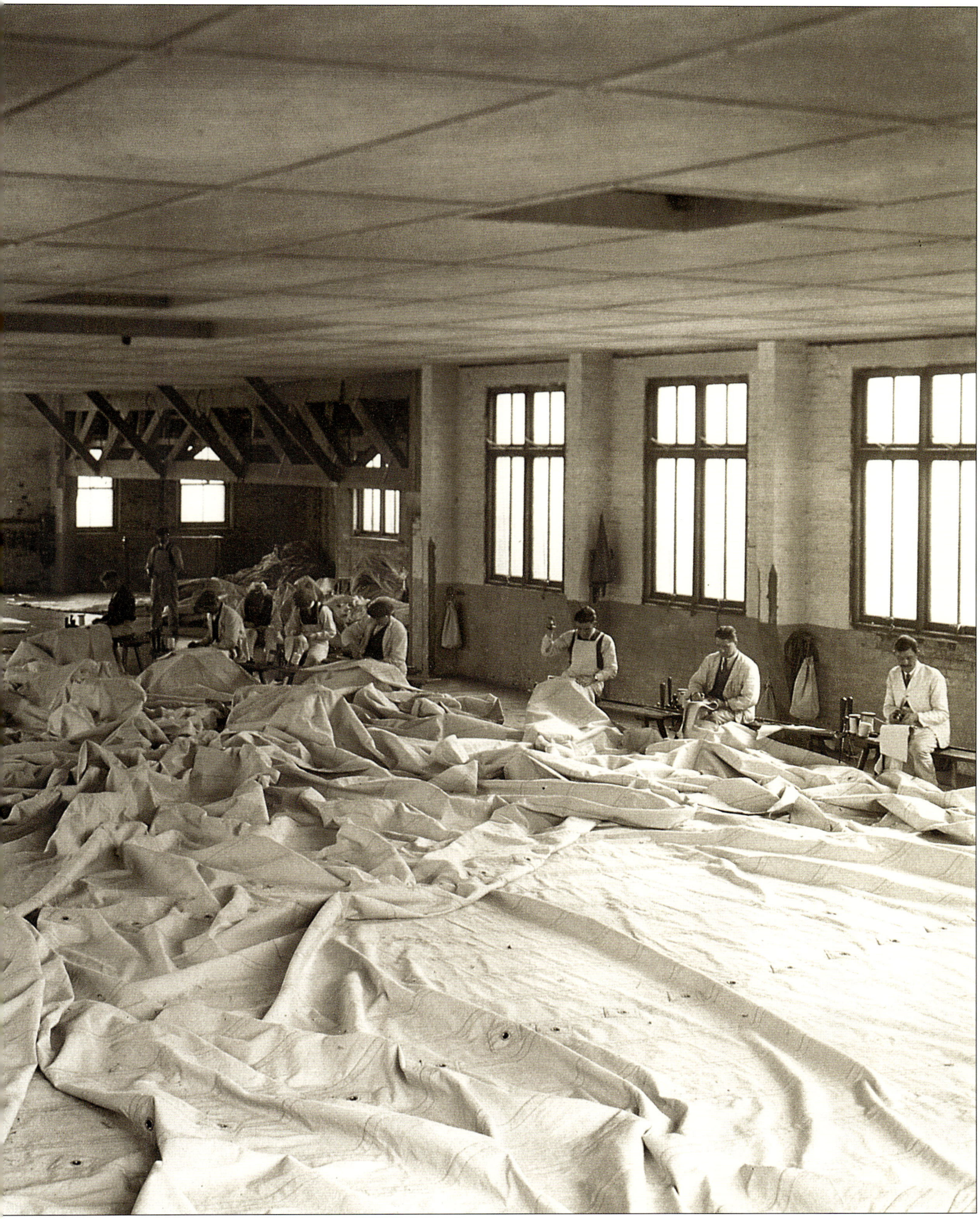

Given the new line up in Cowes and Tom Ratsey's increasing age, James Lapthorn IV became increasingly influential. As earlier, he was greatly assisted in this by his proximity to the successful Charles E. Nicholson. In 1921 Nicholson converted *Nyria* to the Bermudan rig;this was the first Big Class yacht to dispense with gaff rig. Lapthorn made the mainsail; it was a great success and Bermudan sails became the greatest single development in yacht rigging in the twentieth century. Tom Ratsey of course lamented the development and as late as 1928 when two new Bermudan Big Class cutters were built he condemned them with little justification *'Hurray the Bermudas are no good for ordinary weather, I prophesy that both Astra and Cambria are re-rigged as [gaff] cutters for next season.'*[40] When Sir Thomas Lipton challenged again for the America's Cup in 1930 Tom Ratsey took pleasure in rather pedantically reporting his contribution to the first Bermudan rigged challenger: *'Sailed in Shamrock V and was very successful in suggesting an alteration to the Gosport mainsail which resulted in marvellously rectifying the serious hard spot in the Gosport sail which they had failed to rectify.'*[41] With Lapthorn now the dynamo of the firm he did not want to travel to America with the challenger but despite his smug contribution neither did Tom Ratsey wish to be

Previous Page: In 1931 *Britannia* was converted to the Bermudan rig. The new rig was designed by C. E. Nicholson and the new spars built in Gosport. The new sails would logically have been built in Gosport but having made all of *Britannia's* sails since she was first launched in 1893, Tom Ratsey overcame his disapproval insisting that his Cowes loft would always make *Britannia's* sails, even if they were Bermudan. Tom Ratsey is on the left overseeing the new mainsail./ *Beken of Cowes*

Above: The launch of *Shamrock V* from Camper & Nicholsons yard in 1930. The first of the British J class, she was Sir Thomas Lipton's last challenger for the America's Cup. / *Franklin Ratsey-Woodroffe*

Left: After the adoption of Bermudan main sails, spinnakers became one of the main vehicles for experimentation. One theory suggested that by letting some wind through the sail driving power would actually be increased. Tom Ratsey experimented on *Dolly Varden* but of course she remained gaff rigged. / *Beken of Cowes*

Right: *Shamrock V* on the Clyde. A rare photograph of Sir Thomas Lipton actually under sail on one of his yachts, he is standing right aft talking to his sailmaker James Stanley Lapthorn IV. / *James F. Lapthorn*

Over 1: The ketch *Thendara* designed by Alfred Mylne in 1937 is the largest of his sailing yachts to survive and is seen her at the Nioulargue in 1994, the first regatta she competed in following her restoration. / *Franco Pace*

Over 2: *Thendara* in a building mistral at the 1994 Nioulargue. / *Franco Pace*

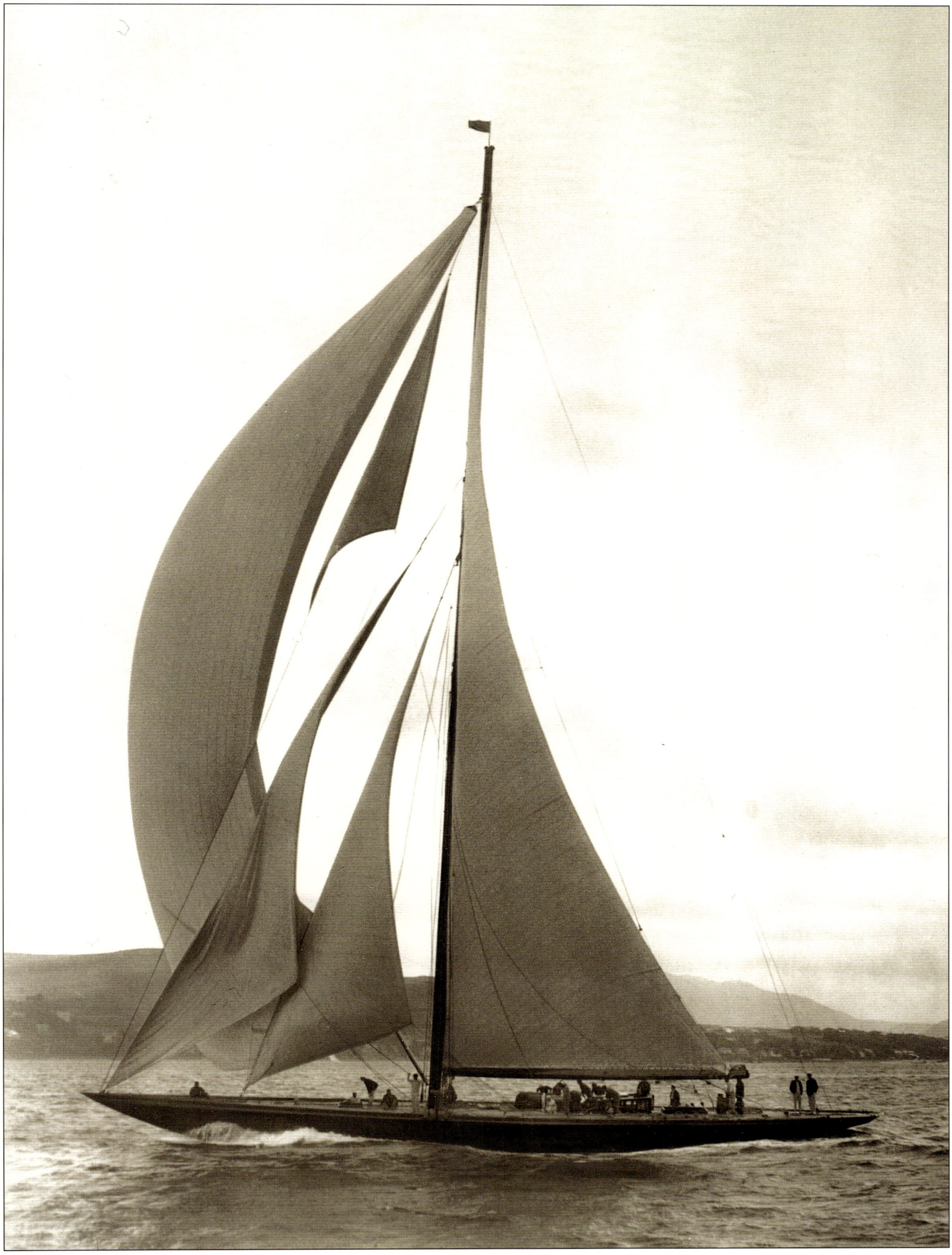

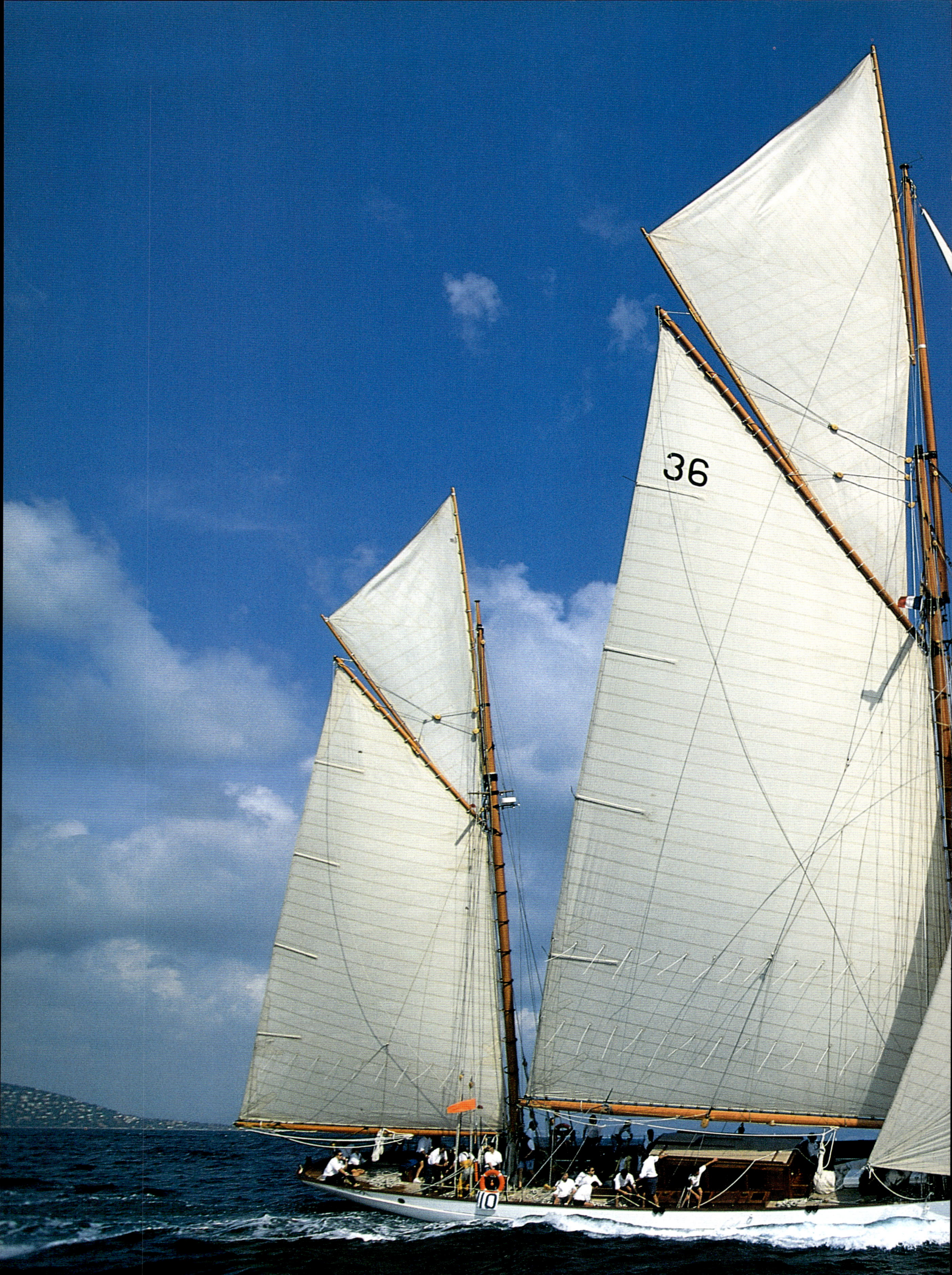
36
10

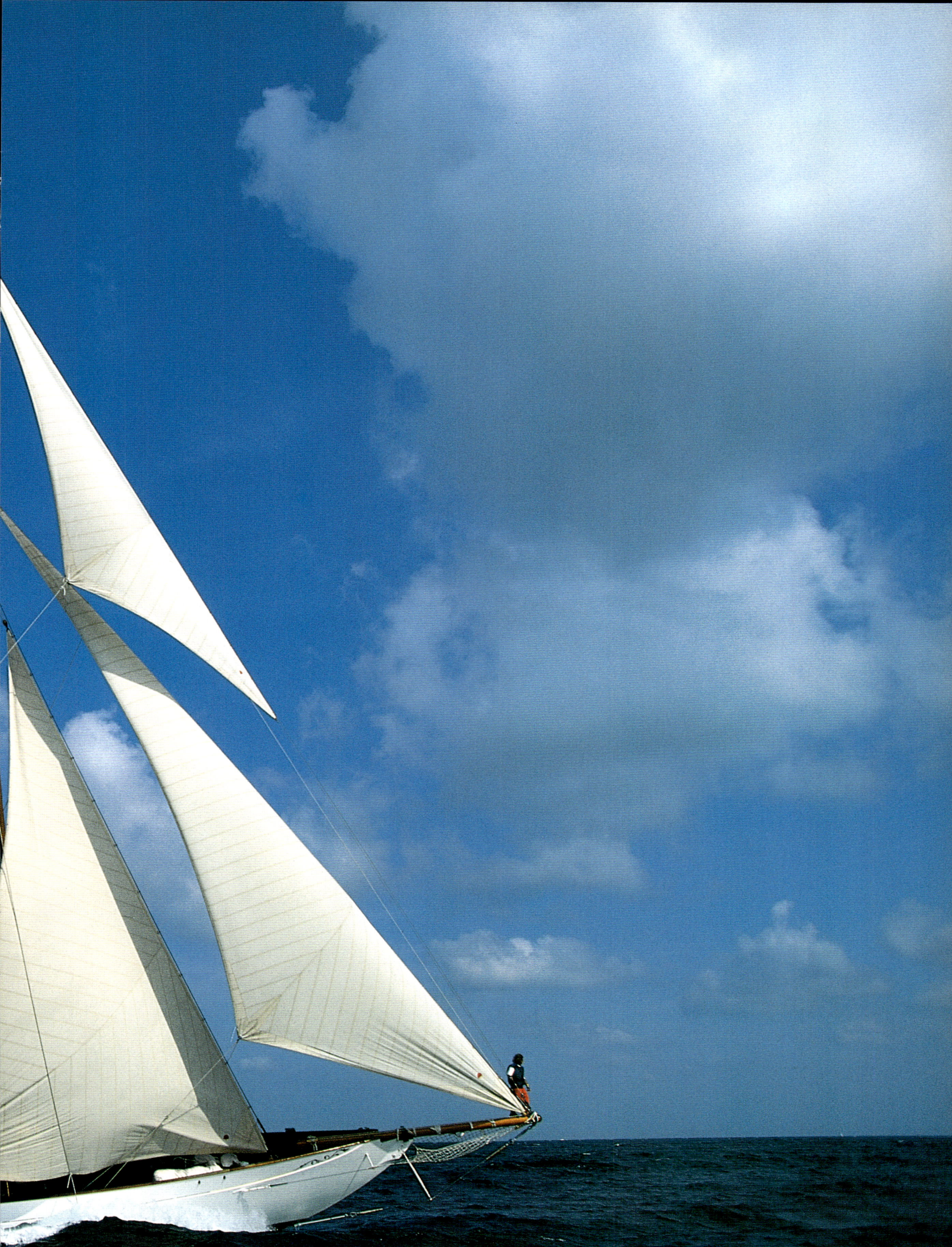

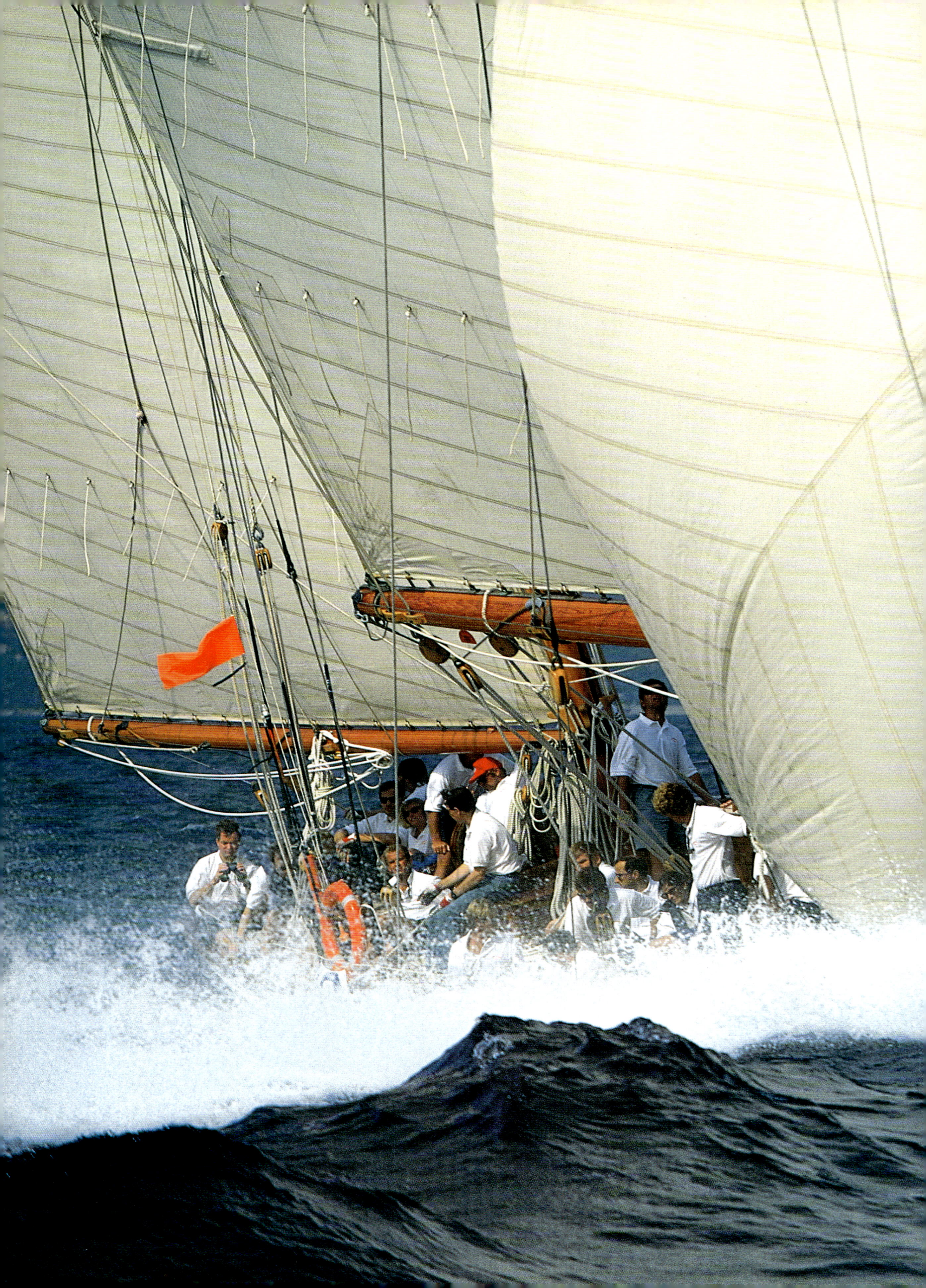

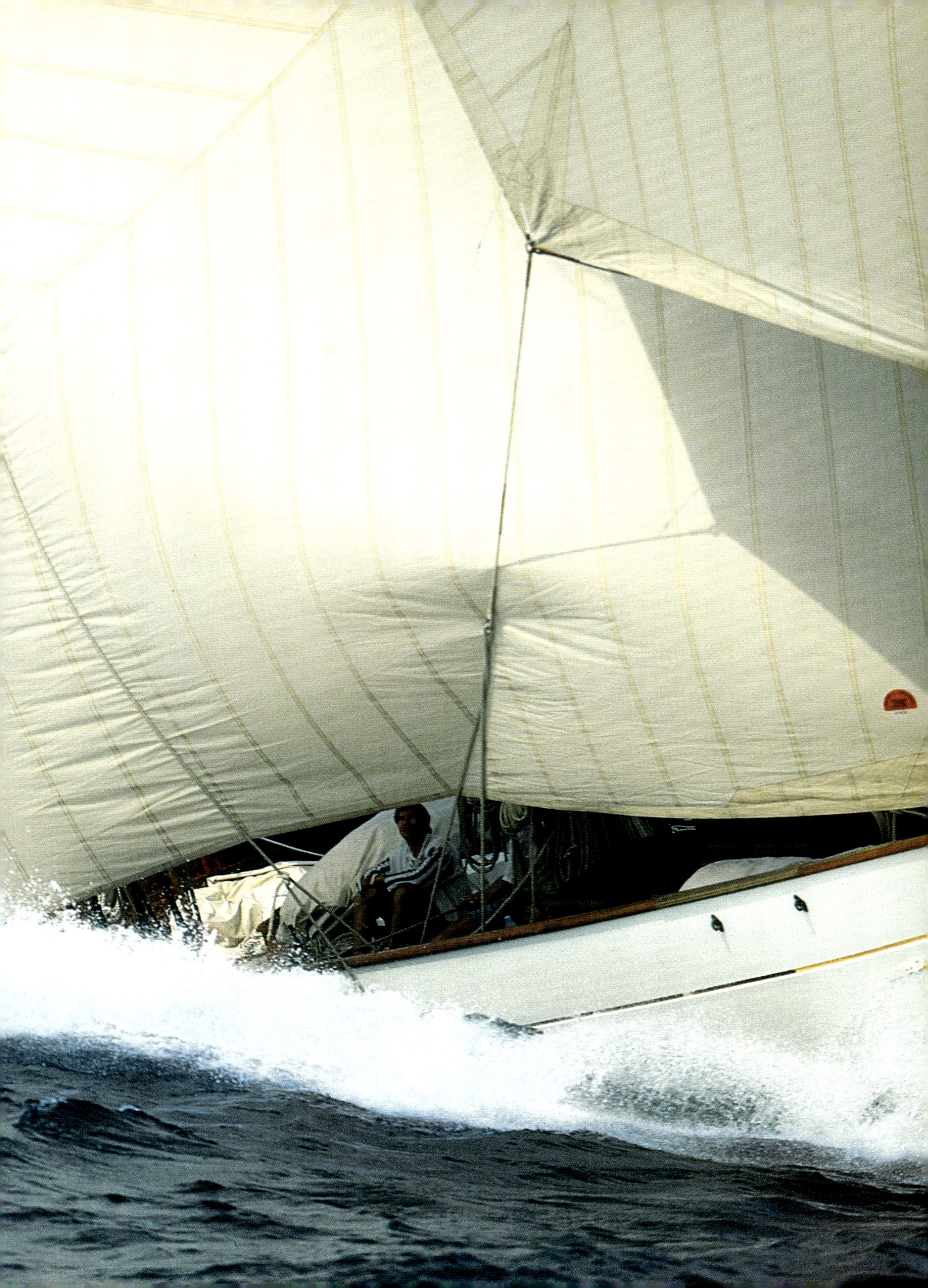

involved. In the event he fulfilled the role he had begun over fifty years before, this time accompanied by his son Chris.[42]

Having been responsible for all *Britannia's* sails since she first came out in 1893, her conversion to Bermudan rig in 1931 must have caused Thomas W. Ratsey some soul searching but his loyalty to the King was greater than to his principles. *Britannia's* new mainsail was cut at the Cowes loft under Ratsey's supervision and C. E. Nicholson was delighted with the result. The payback for Ratsey was immense; he was a close friend of the King's sailing master, Sir Philip Hunloke, and had an open invitation to sail on *Britannia*. It was a privilege he had enjoyed many times but at the age of 80 in 1931 it was one which he increasingly chose to forego. A typical entry in his log for that year reads: '*I did think of Saturday aboard the Britannia but it was a long way to row to her so I shall put it off.*'[43] Rather, Ratsey spent an increasing amount of time on his 1872-built cutter *Dolly Varden*. He lived aboard in the summer and sailed in the Solent nearly every day cadging tows back to Cowes whenever the wind failed.

Above: Tom Ratsey never fully retired and Ratsey & Lapthorn's Cowes loft was his fiefdom. / *Beken of Cowes*

Opposite Above: Only the sewing machines betrayed technological progress in Ratsey & Lapthorn's eighteenth century Cowes loft. / *Beken of Cowes*

Opposite Below: Tom Ratsey (left) relaxing with friends in *Dolly Varden's* cockpit. The who's who of the yachting world visited Tom Ratsey and guests during his final summer in 1934 included the King and Queen. / *Franklin Ratsey-Woodroffe*

Over 1 Left: With every stitch of canvas set, the 1931 Fife-designed schooner *Altair* drifts gently towards the finish line at the 1992 Nioulargue. / *Franco Pace*

Over 1 Right: An aerial shot of *Altair* on the wind at the 1992 Nioulargue. / *Franco Pace*

Over 2: *Altair's* arrival at the 1989 Nioulargue was breathtaking. Her restoration, including hand stitched Ratsey & Lapthorn sails, was so authentic that it set a bench mark for all the projects that followed. / *Franco Pace*

Over 3: Setting a traditional spinnaker inside her forestay, *Altair* heads for St Tropez in the last of the wind and light at the 1992 Nioulargue. / *Franco Pace*

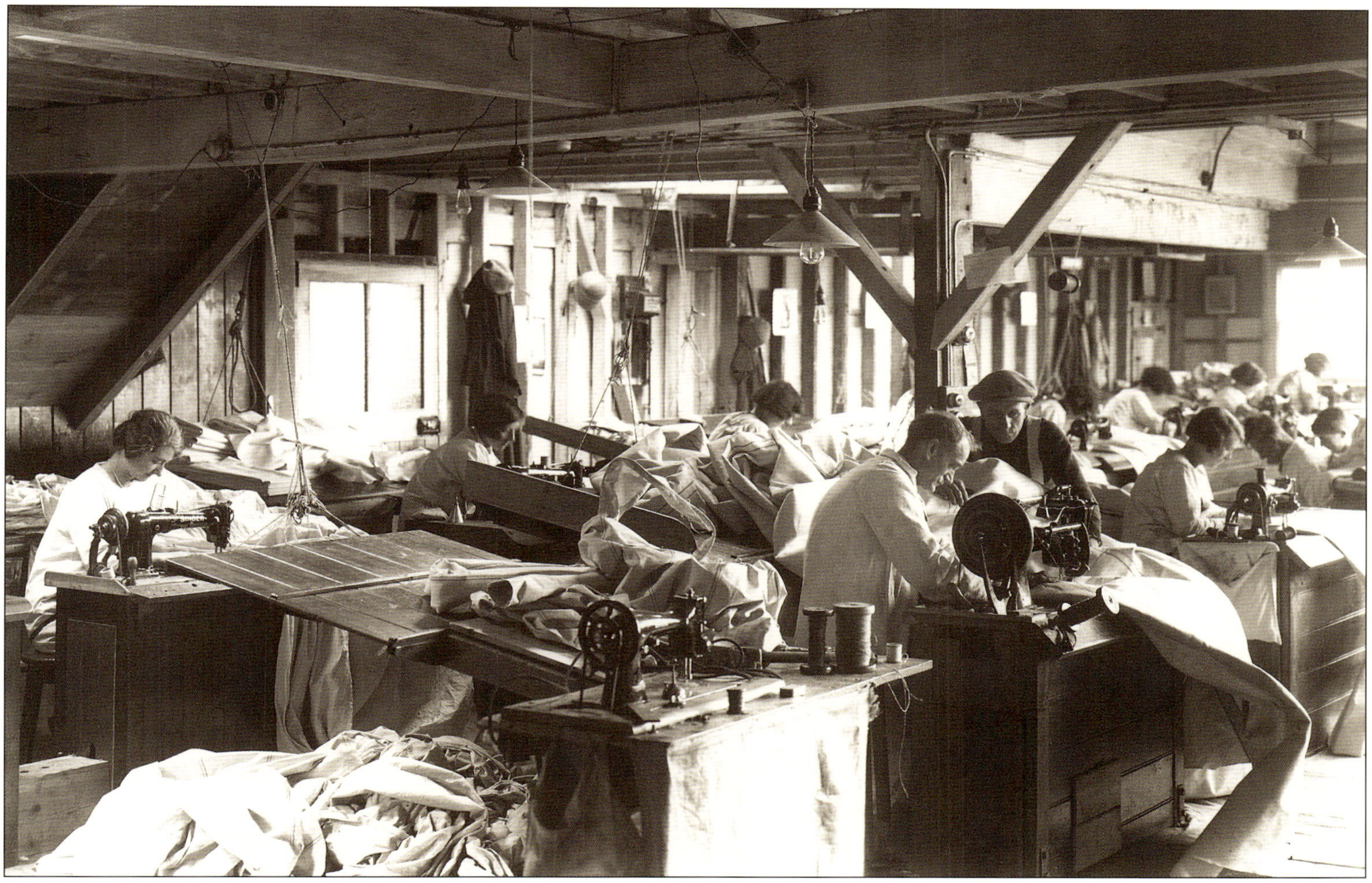

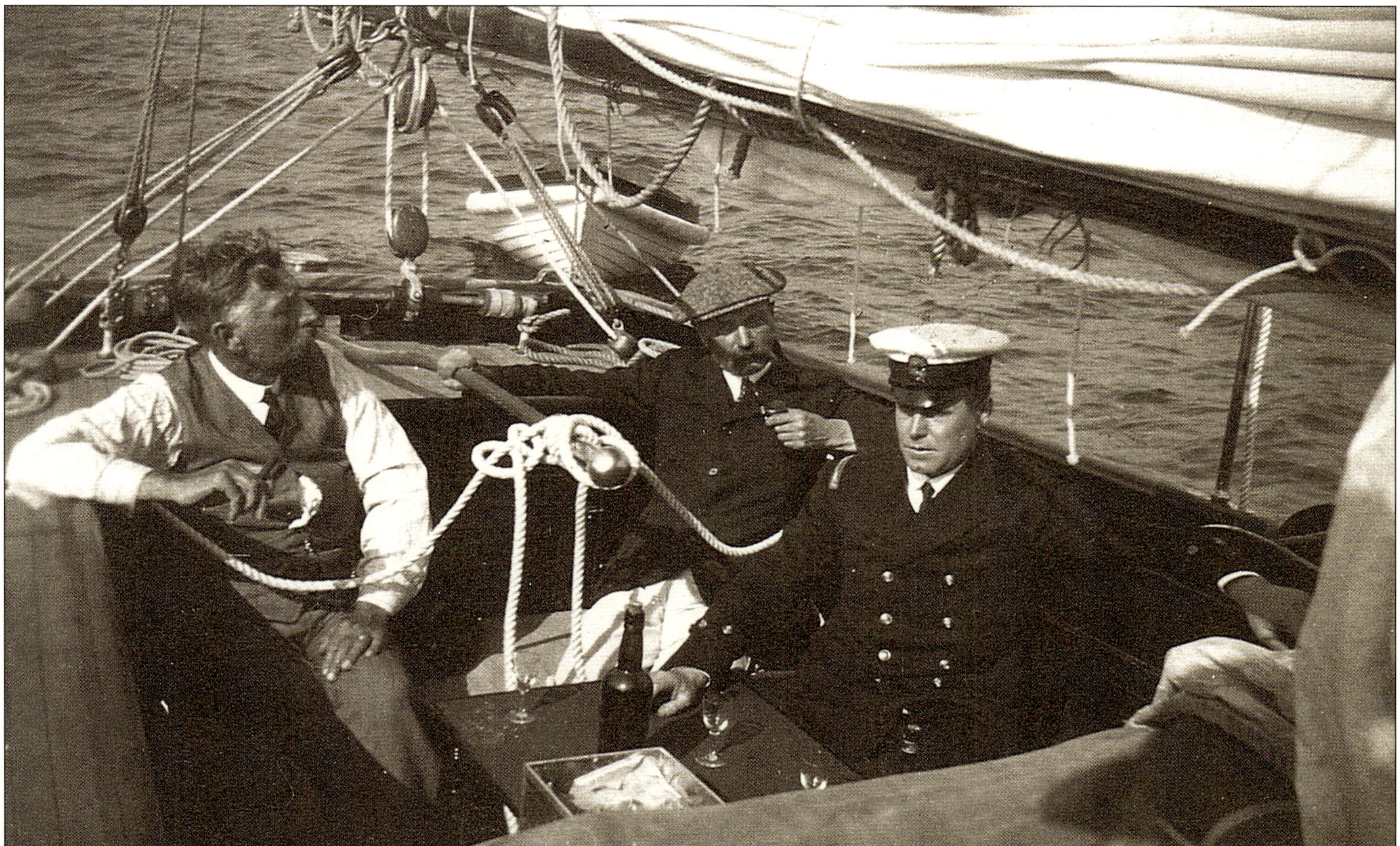

116

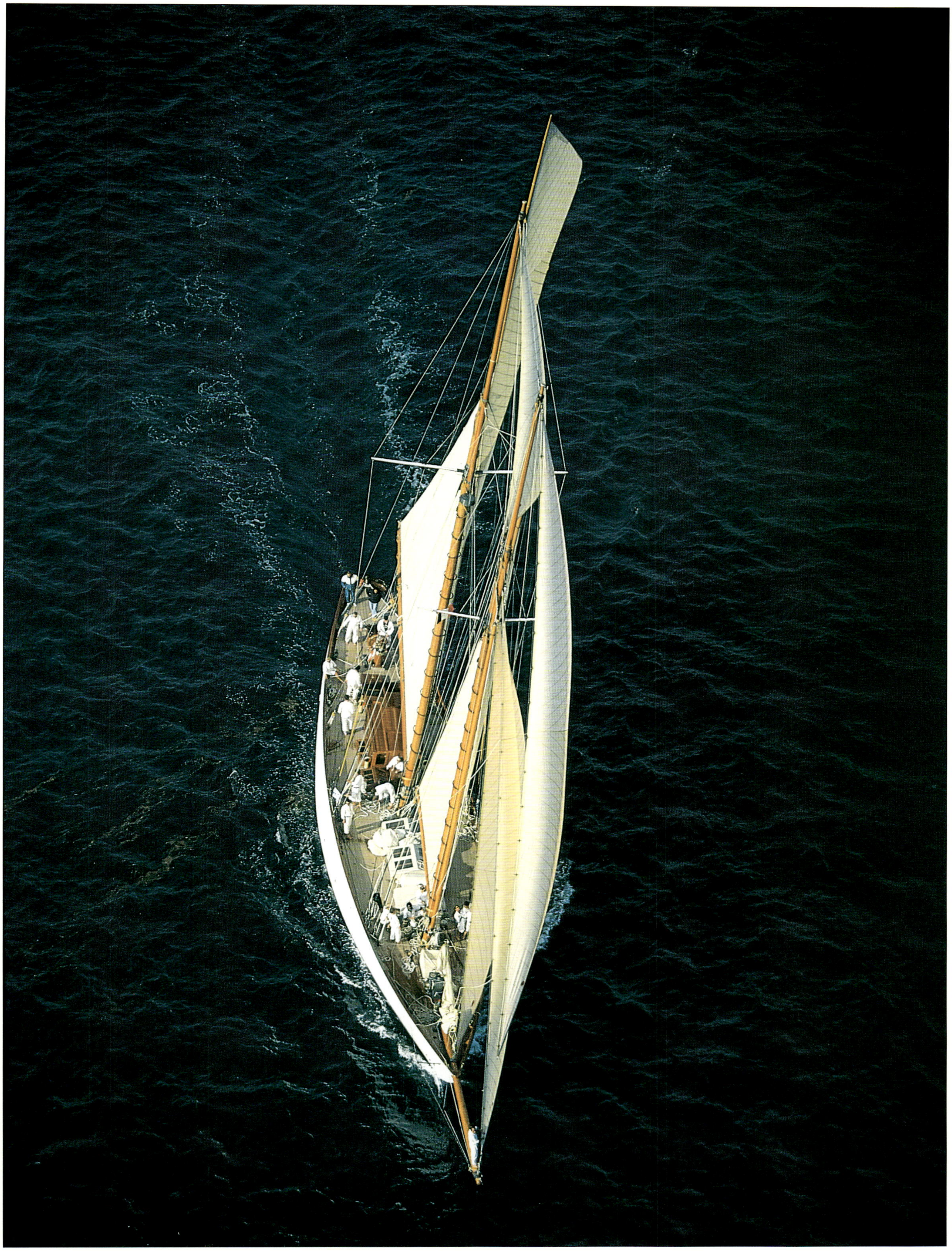

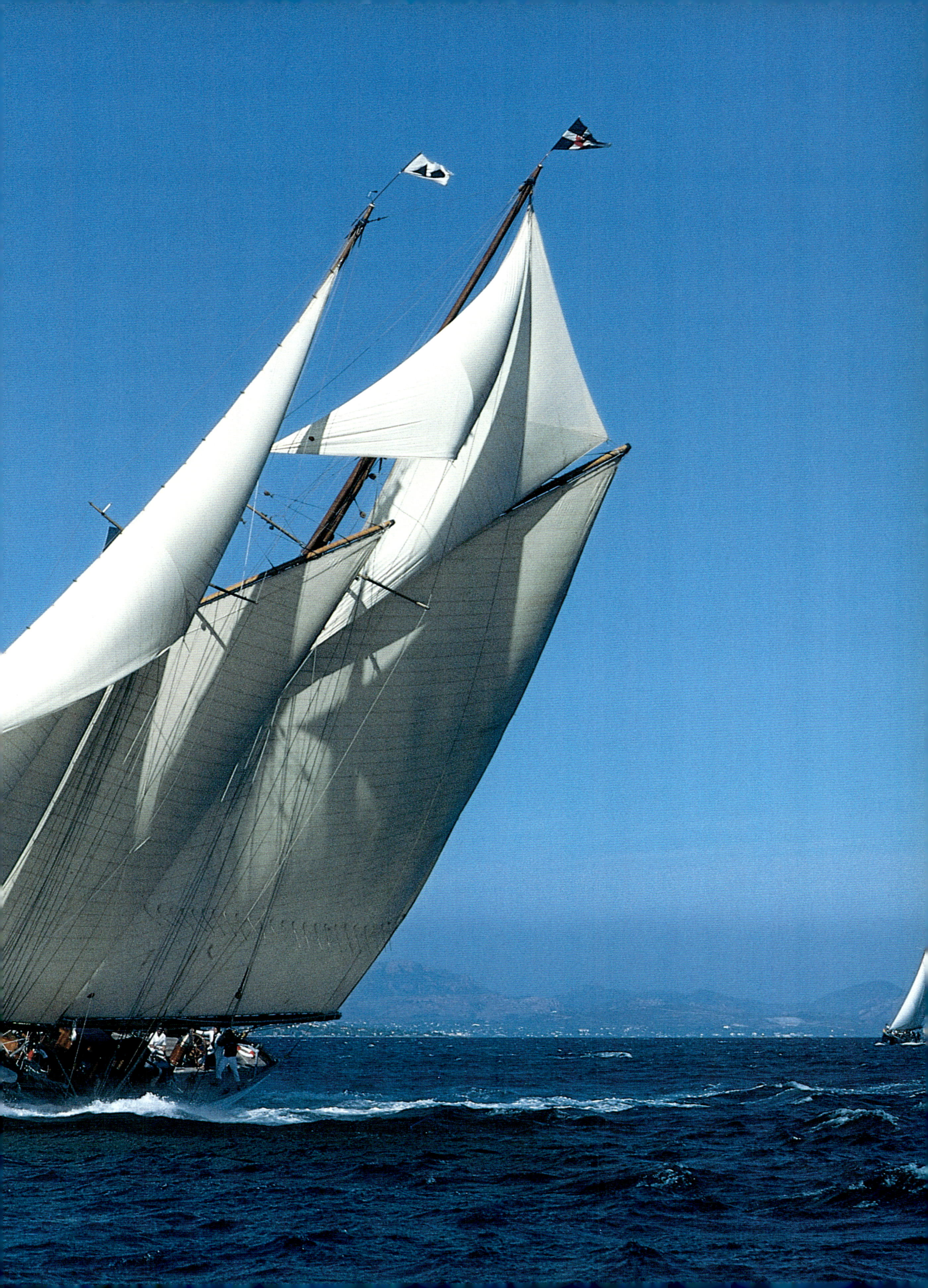

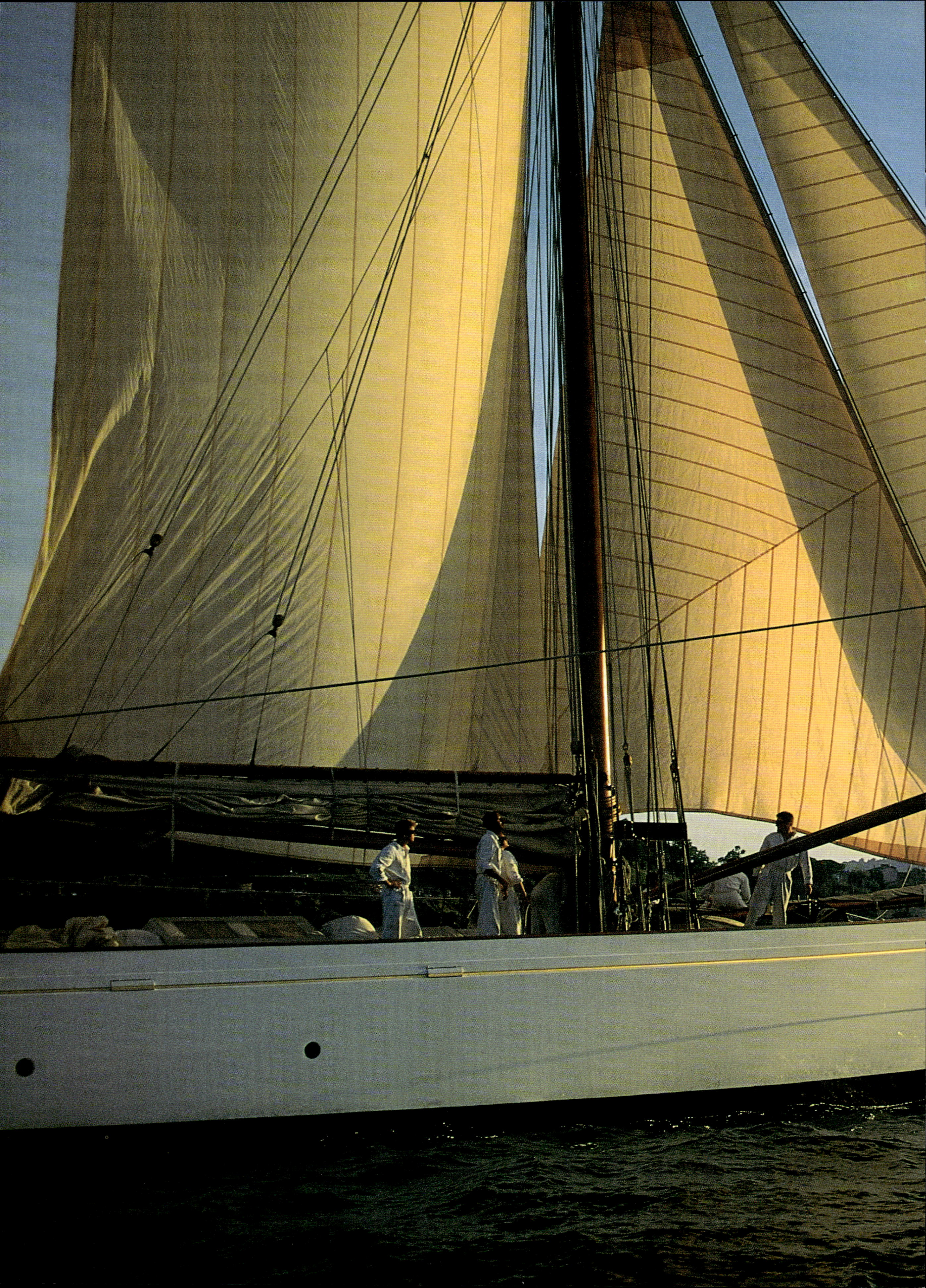

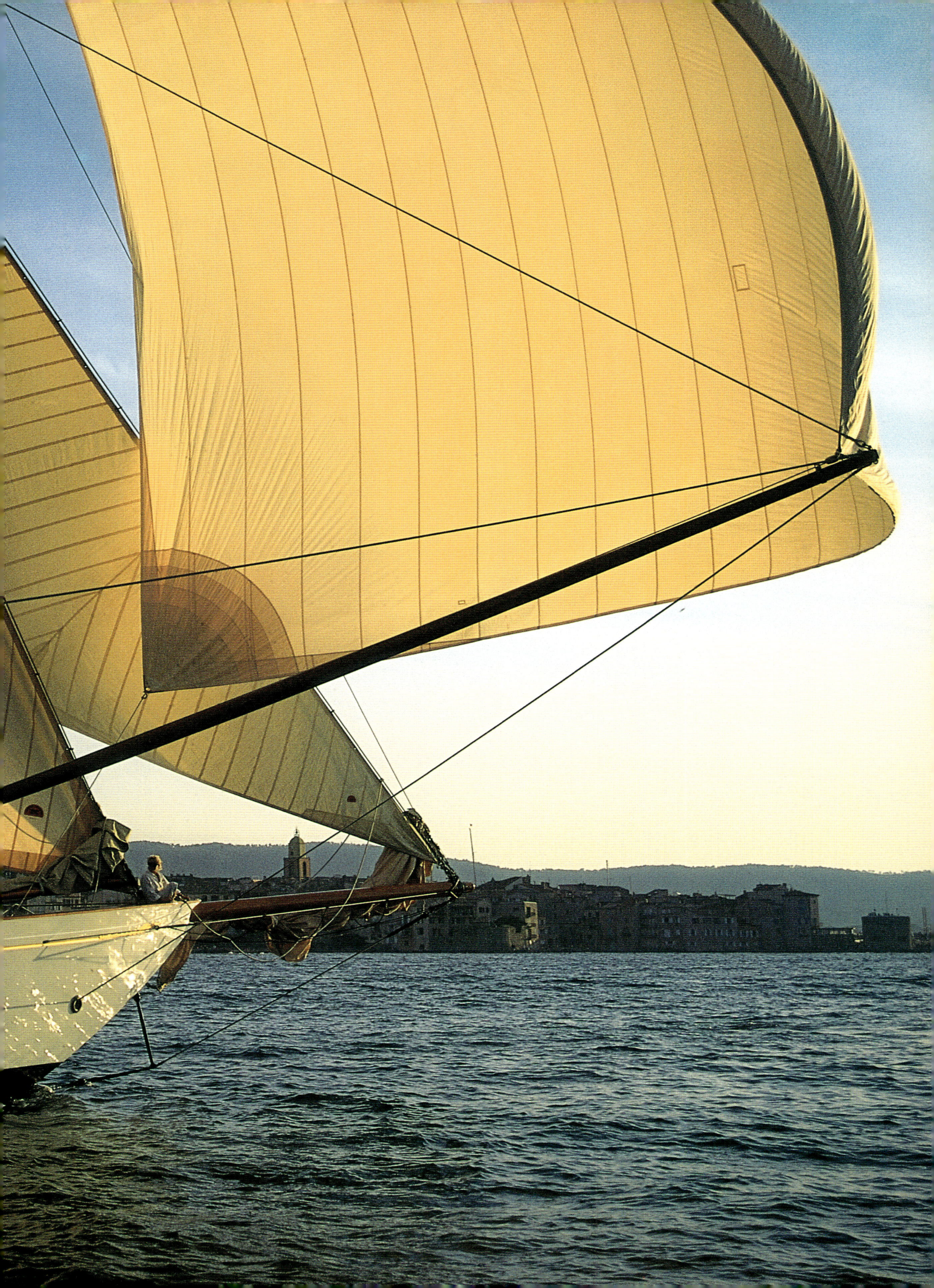

In his logs Thomas W. Ratsey recorded the passing of many of his friends and contemporaries in yachting. Of Charles Bevis, who had skippered *Sybarita*, *Maymon*, *White Heather* and *Lulworth* he wrote '*a very fine man who could get more out of an unsuccessful boat than anyone I ever knew.*'[44] In October 1931 he simply noted '*Clocks back the hour, so the season is ended once again. I am sorry, Sir Thomas Lipton died last night, he did a lot for yachting and his place will be hard to fill.*'[45] The logs, however, are not just a collection of epitaphs and neither do they contain much on navigation, they are mostly an old man's erratic and rather sentimental jottings. Additionally they are a veritable who's who of international yachting. Ratsey had become the grand old man of yachting, someone to meet; distinguished guests on *Dolly Varden* were frequent. In 1933 he had a fall on board *Dolly Varden* that left him crippled but he had himself winched aboard for the 1934 season. The King and Queen called on Ratsey one day whilst he was dozing in the saloon. He was woken by one of the crew '*Sir, the Royal barge is coming alongside*' to which he responded '*My God, where are my teeth?*' The King came aboard and spent about 20 minutes chatting to Ratsey whilst Christopher who was soaked having just finished a dinghy race sat on the side deck with his feet on the royal barge entertaining the Queen. The informality was no challenge to Ratsey, his nephew G. Colin Ratsey recalled the style of Tom Ratsey's relationship with the King:

> The trouble was when the *Britannia* finished a race the King would go down below and all the other guests would stay above because they seemed to be frightened of him. Not a bit so with Tom. He went below and chatted with the King, and they usually had a glass of sherry together, so they became bosom pals.[46]

Tom Ratsey died in March 1935. Lady Cynthia Colville wrote in *The Times* that he '*touched life at many points and few men will be regretted by so many and varied friends. He stood for an ideal in our social, commercial and sporting life which is pleasant to regard as peculiarly English.*'[47]

Above: *Dolly Varden* under a characteristically immaculate suit of sails. / *Beken of Cowes*

Below: In 1929 Tom Ratsey travelled to America to watch the races for the Seawanhaka Cup. When *Caryl* went two races down in the five race series against the American *Gypsy* Ratsey invoked his lucky sock and wearing it inside out predicted a British victory. *Caryl* won in what he described as '*the most marvellous race I ever witnessed*' and the lucky sock was claimed by the victor's mother. / *Anne Butler*

Thomas W. Ratsey's reluctant conversion to the Bermudan rig aside, Ratsey & Lapthorn were not challenged by evolution in sail design through the inter-war period. If the Gosport loft had led the way with *Nyria* in 1921, they were certainly outdone by the sheer volume of large sails and innovations that the New York loft introduced through the 1930s. The new large premises gave them a great advantage over their counterparts in Gosport who made large main sails in nine sections only seeing the final shape when the sail was first set. Such advantages allowed the New York loft to successfully make all the sails for the potential defenders and trial horses of the 1930 America's Cup. The value of the orders for *Enterprise*, *Weetamoe*, *Yankee*, *Whirlwind*, *Resolute* and *Vanity* totalled in excess of $500,000; 36,000 square feet of working sails, and weighed a total of 12 tons. It remains the greatest output of any single sail loft in a period of under twelve months.

Realising that frenzied America's Cup activity in Newport RI would require him to have a base there, George E. Ratsey built the Alden-designed schooner, *Zaida*, but left the interior virtually empty. He intended her as a floating office and fitted only a dividing curtain so that two meetings could be held at the same time. His son G. Colin Ratsey recorded their first day in Newport: *'One group was sent forward and the curtain was pulled, and the other group went aft. The result was, at the end of the day, some stupendous orders had been placed, all in secrecy, so the boat almost paid for itself that day.'*[48] Besides the flurry of orders linked to the America's Cup, some can be attributed to further improvement in Haywards sail cloth which originated in America. In 1927, a Boston cotton broker contacted the firm suggesting that Sudanese Sekel cotton might prove superior than the Egyptian cotton then in use. Haywards ran up samples and the cloth was better than anything previously seen. Of course it came at a premium and only the successful defender *Enterprise* used it in the 1930 Cup races.

Despite the amenities of *Zaida*, George E. Ratsey tired of the Newport scene and sent his son G. Colin to *'dance attendance'* on Harold Vanderbilt, head of the *Enterprise* syndicate. The young Ratsey was put up on board Vanderbilt's motor yacht *Vara* along with *Enterprise*'s designer W. Starling Burgess. It was during dinner after an exhausting day of pre-Cup practising that Burgess *'suddenly jumped up, got a piece of paper and drew out the Park Avenue boom, which was one of the things that helped keep the*

Above: Initially the New York loft was run on a rota system with different members of the Ratsey family travelling out for six month stints. This system survived until World War I when George E. Ratsey (right) assumed control. He was joined in 1919 by his eldest son Ernest A. Ratsey and when his health failed during World War II his second son G. Colin Ratsey joined the New York branch. / *Rosenfeld Collection, Mystic Seaport Museum*

Over 1: To defend the America's Cup in 1930 four new J class yachts were built and the 1914 defenders *Vanitie* and *Resolute* were re-rigged. All six yachts were outfitted by Ratsey & Lapthorn's New York loft. Here staff show the mainsail built for the J class *Yankee*. / *Rosenfeld Collection, Mystic Seaport Museum*

Over 2: *Weetamoe, Enterprise, Resolute, Yankee* and *Vanitie*, five of the six big cutters that raced in American waters in the summer of 1930. *Enterprise* went on to defeat *Shamrock V* in that year's America's Cup contest but all flew Ratsey & Lapthorn sails. / *Rosenfeld Collection, Mystic Seaport Museum*

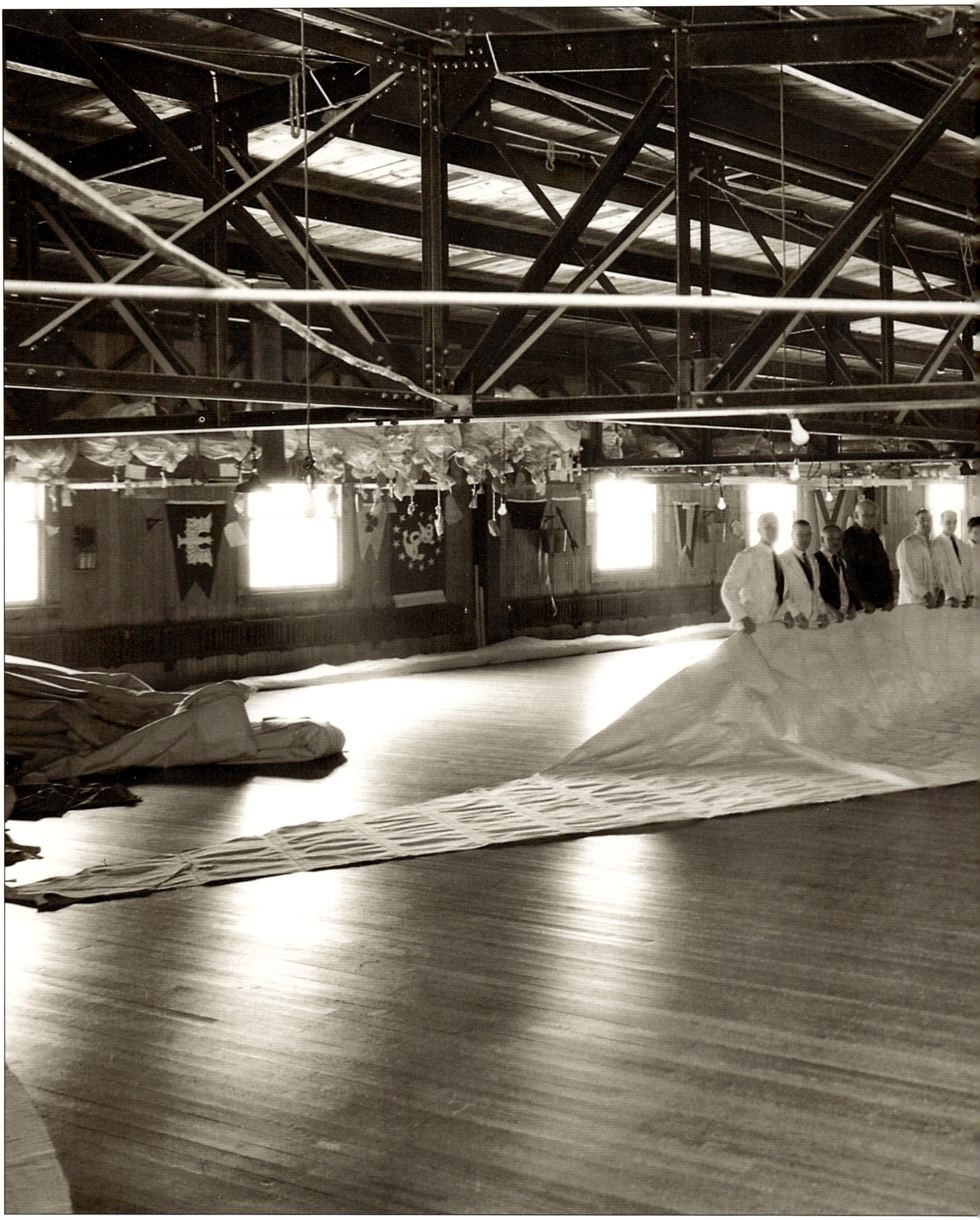

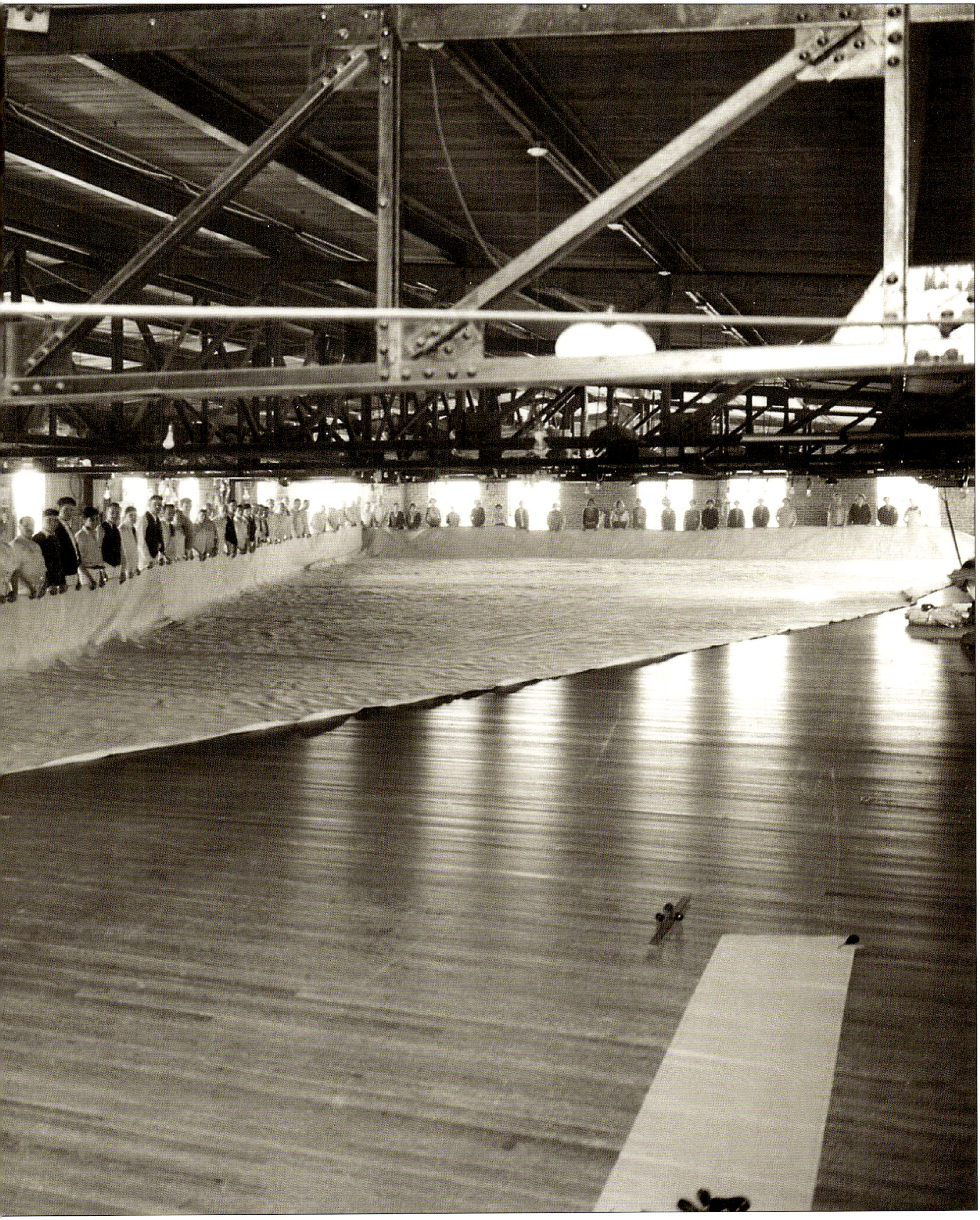

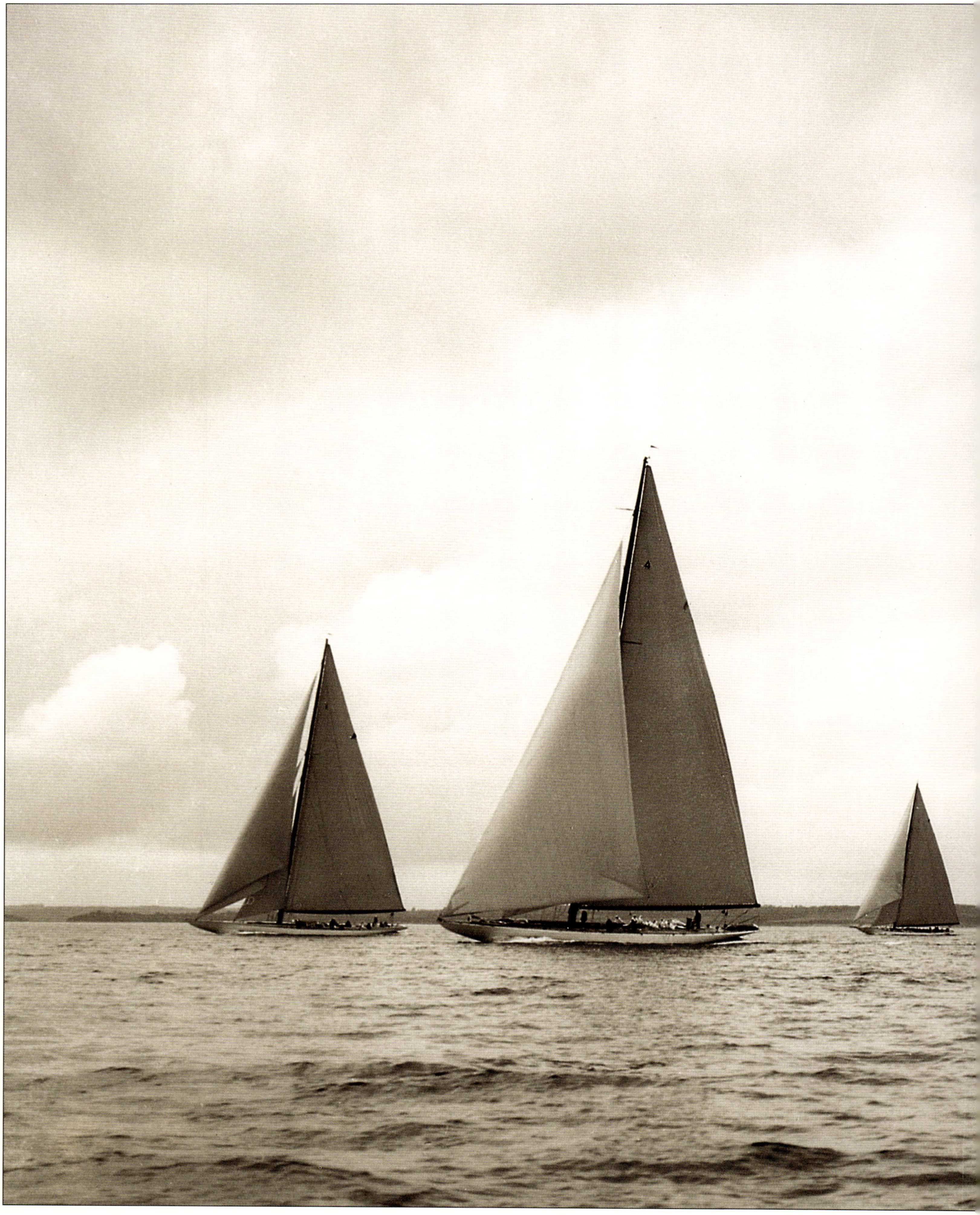

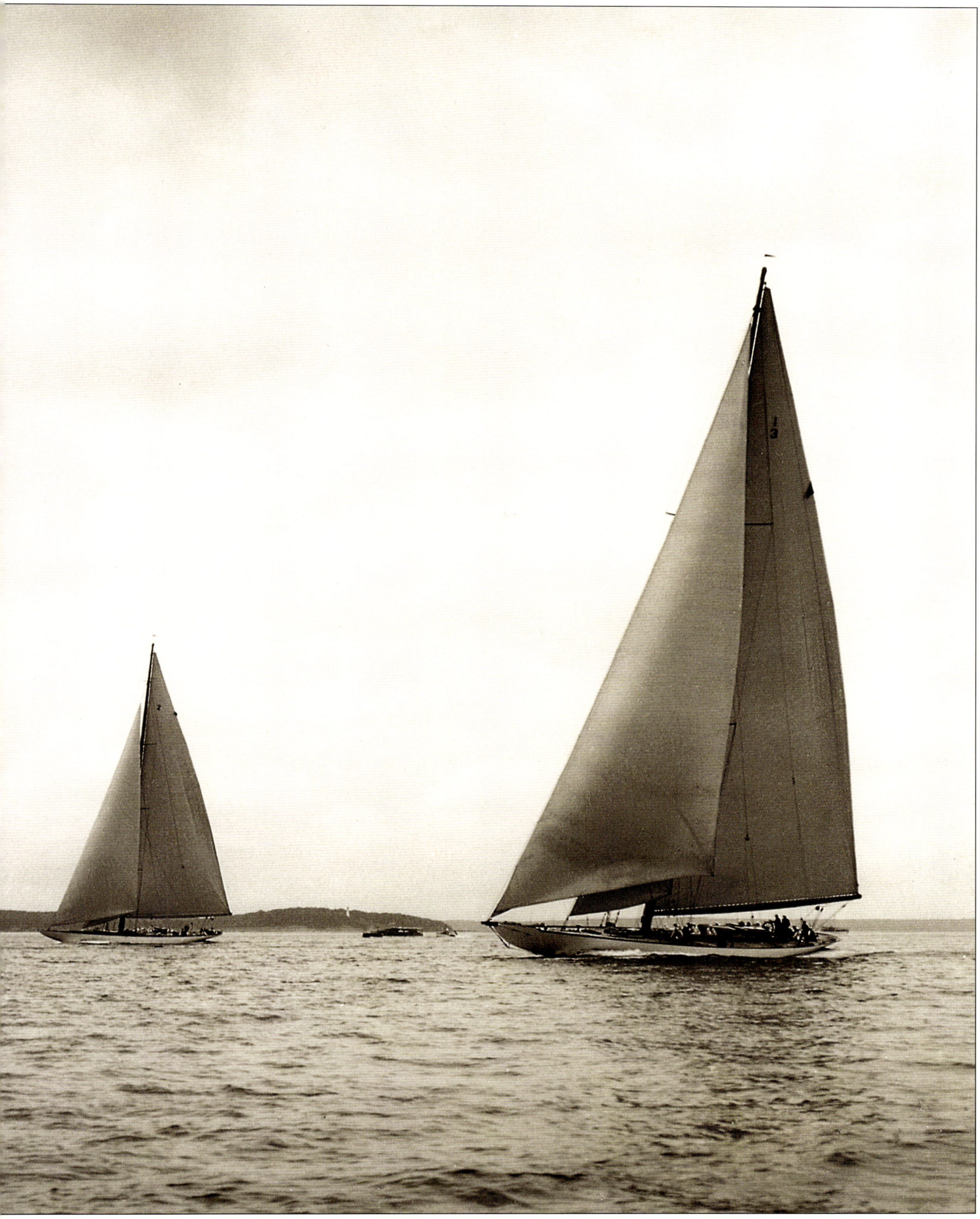

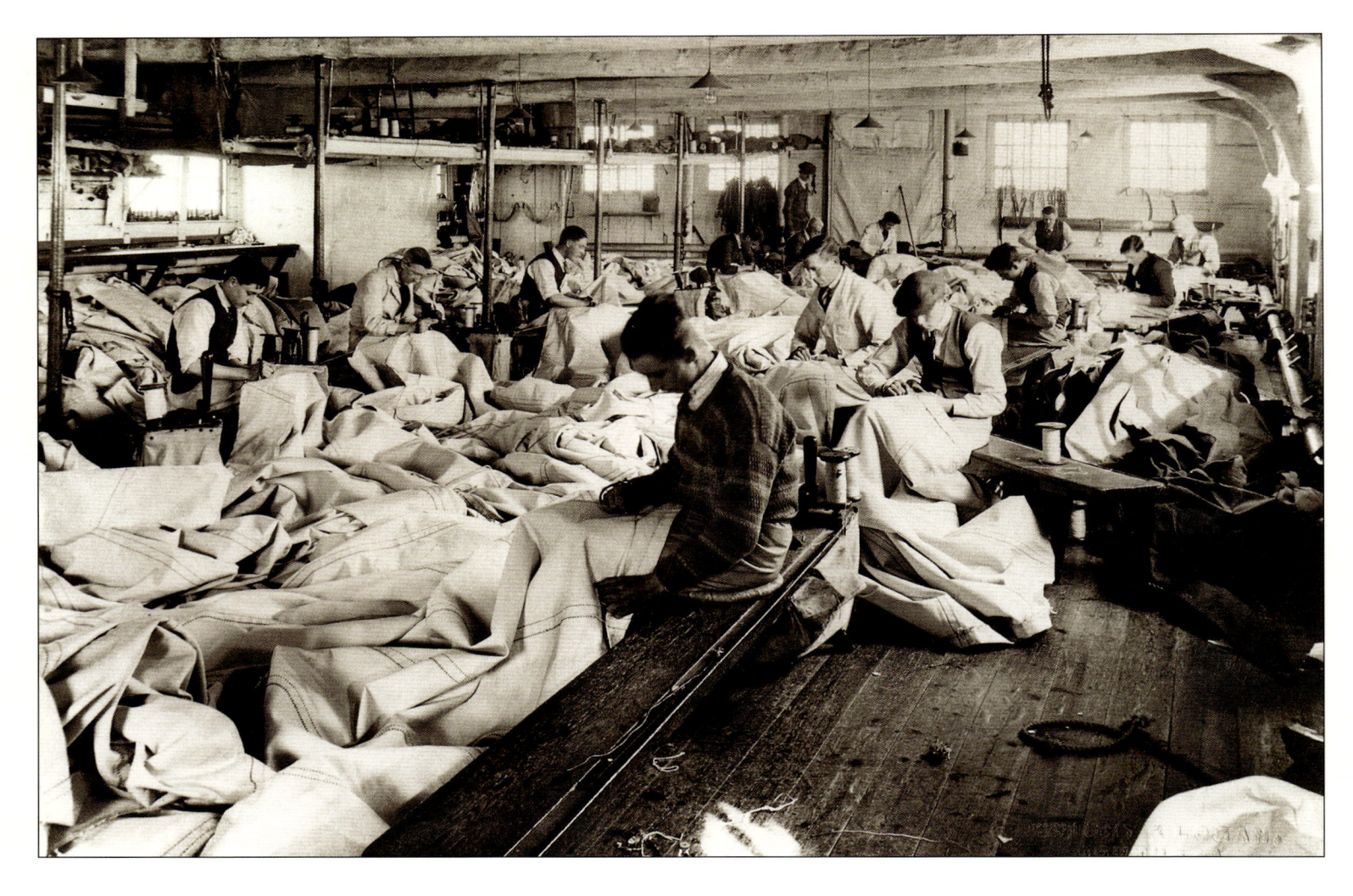

America's Cup.'⁴⁹ The idea was simple; the new boom was built with a triangular section 18' wide on the top. Across it there were tracks with slides allowing the sail to slide from side to side when the yacht tacked. By placing pegs in the tracks to limit the sail's movement, the perfect aerofoil shape could be created for all wind strengths. Another New York loft development of the period was the Cunningham. In 1927, whilst racing his 6 Metre *Lucie*, Briggs Cunningham decided that he wanted the luff of his main sail shortened. With no advance warning his chauffeur arrived at the New York loft with the sail at around 5 pm. There was little that could be done overnight but the foreman George Graham suggested making a hole in the sail about 9 inches' above the tack allowing the sail to be pulled down and thus shortening the luff. The resulting bunch at the foot did not harm the sail's performance. *Lucie* won the following day, and the Cunningham has been in use ever since.

The most significant developments in the 1930s were in the type of foresails used and these came to a head in 1934. The British challenger *Endeavour* introduced the double clewed jib. The idea was to increase the luff of the sail without the consequent increase in sail area which would make the sail difficult to handle. C. E. Nicholson had the initial idea but *Endeavour's* owner Sir Thomas Sopwith perfected it in wind tunnel tests before James Stanley Lapthorn IV made it. The sail was a great success and all involved thought it their idea; Lapthorn noted: '*Sopwith gets the credit for this and we let it go at that, for after all he took the risk and it was done at his expense. It is the old story, the sailmaker has got to make it practicable and the result is generally very different from the first suggestion, but that is all forgotten... I always feel the sailmaker gets very little credit for his work. The slow boat always has bad sails, while in a fast boat the sails do not count.*'⁵⁰

Above: Making *Endeavour's* sails in the cramped conditions of the Gosport loft in early 1934. With large sails such as those used on the J class, it was impossible to lay out the whole sail and the finished sail was only fully seen when hoisted. In 1936 when *Endeavour II's* sails were being built Sir Thomas Sopwith obtained the use of a navy sports hall in a bid to further improve the firm's cutting ability. / *Mystic Seaport Museum*

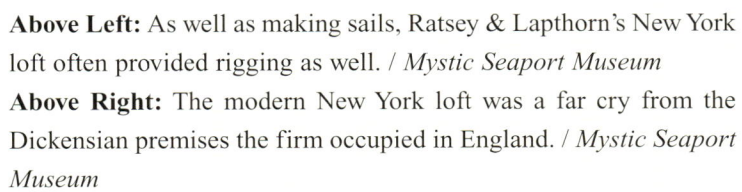

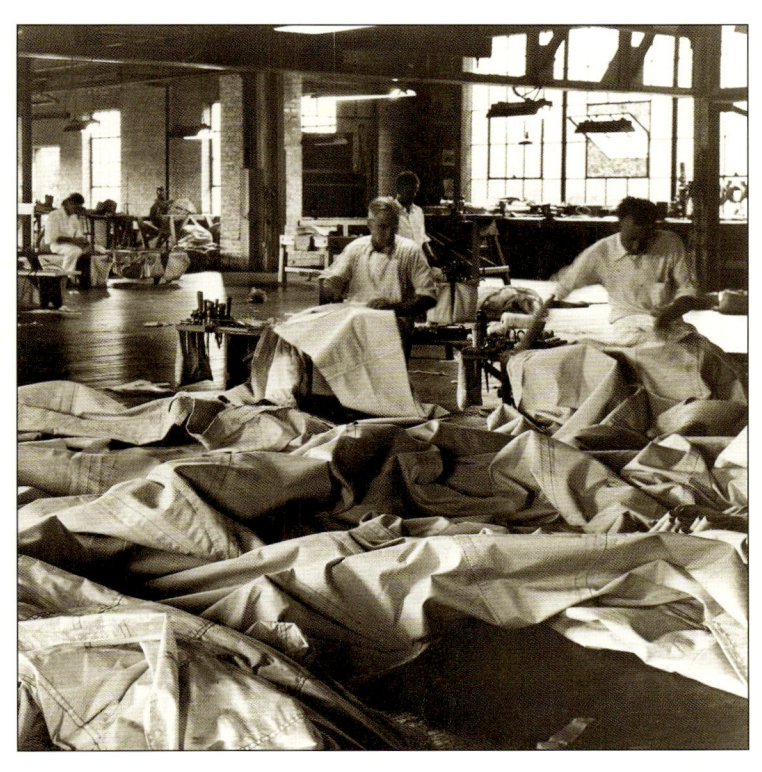

Above Left: As well as making sails, Ratsey & Lapthorn's New York loft often provided rigging as well. / *Mystic Seaport Museum*

Above Right: The modern New York loft was a far cry from the Dickensian premises the firm occupied in England. / *Mystic Seaport Museum*

Below: George E. Ratsey acquired the John Alden-designed schooner *Zaida* to act as a floating office in Newport during the run up to the 1930 America's Cup. Rather than having conventional cabins, she was fitted up with meeting rooms forward and aft. / *Rosenfeld Collection, Mystic Seaport Museum*

In the event the success of the double clewed or quadrilateral jib played little part in the outcome of the America's Cup races. Trials with the Gosport loft's secret sail in England had been seen by American yachtsman Sherman Hoyt and Vanderbilt's defender *Rainbow* was similarly outfitted. On the other hand, British attempts to duplicate American innovations were less successful. In 1934 large genoa jibs were not in common use in England but aware that they were in America, Sopwith ordered one from Lapthorn. Beecher Moore, in charge of *Endeavour's* sail locker noted that '*It was made of what seemed to be storm canvas, almost impossible to get into our locker since it would not fold, it was very difficult to set and only filled properly when the wind was too strong to set it.*' On board *Endeavour*, G. Colin Ratsey was representing the sailmakers, an apparently acceptable solution since the races fell during the six months of the year that he was based in England. However, with his father and elder brother running the New York loft he could also rely on their loyalty. The order for a new genoa for *Endeavour* was given only three days before the first race and the seemingly impossible was only achieved by Ratsey & Lapthorn cutting the sail in New York and installing sewing machines in a covered railway wagon so that they could assemble it on the way to Newport.

Above Left: George E. Ratsey at the helm of *Zaida* with his other yacht, *Golliwog*, astern. / *Mystic Seaport Museum*

Above: Under sail in January 1935, George E. Ratsey ice yachting on Peach Lake, NY. / *Mystic Seaport Museum*

Opposite Above: George E. Ratsey (left) along with Sherman Hoyt 'dancing attendance' on Harold Vanderbilt (right) aboard the 1934 America's Cup defender *Rainbow*. Note the conventional flexible boom. / *Rosenfeld Collection, Mystic Seaport Museum*

Opposite Below: The Park Avenue boom was designed by W. Starling Burgess, by allowing the foot of the mainsail to slide across tracks on the top of the boom a perfect aerofoil shape could be created. According to G. Colin Ratsey, the idea occurred to Burgess half way through dinner on Vanderbilt's motor yacht *Vara*. It was one of the features that helped *Enterprise* retain the America's Cup in 1930. / *Rosenfeld Collection, Mystic Seaport Museum*

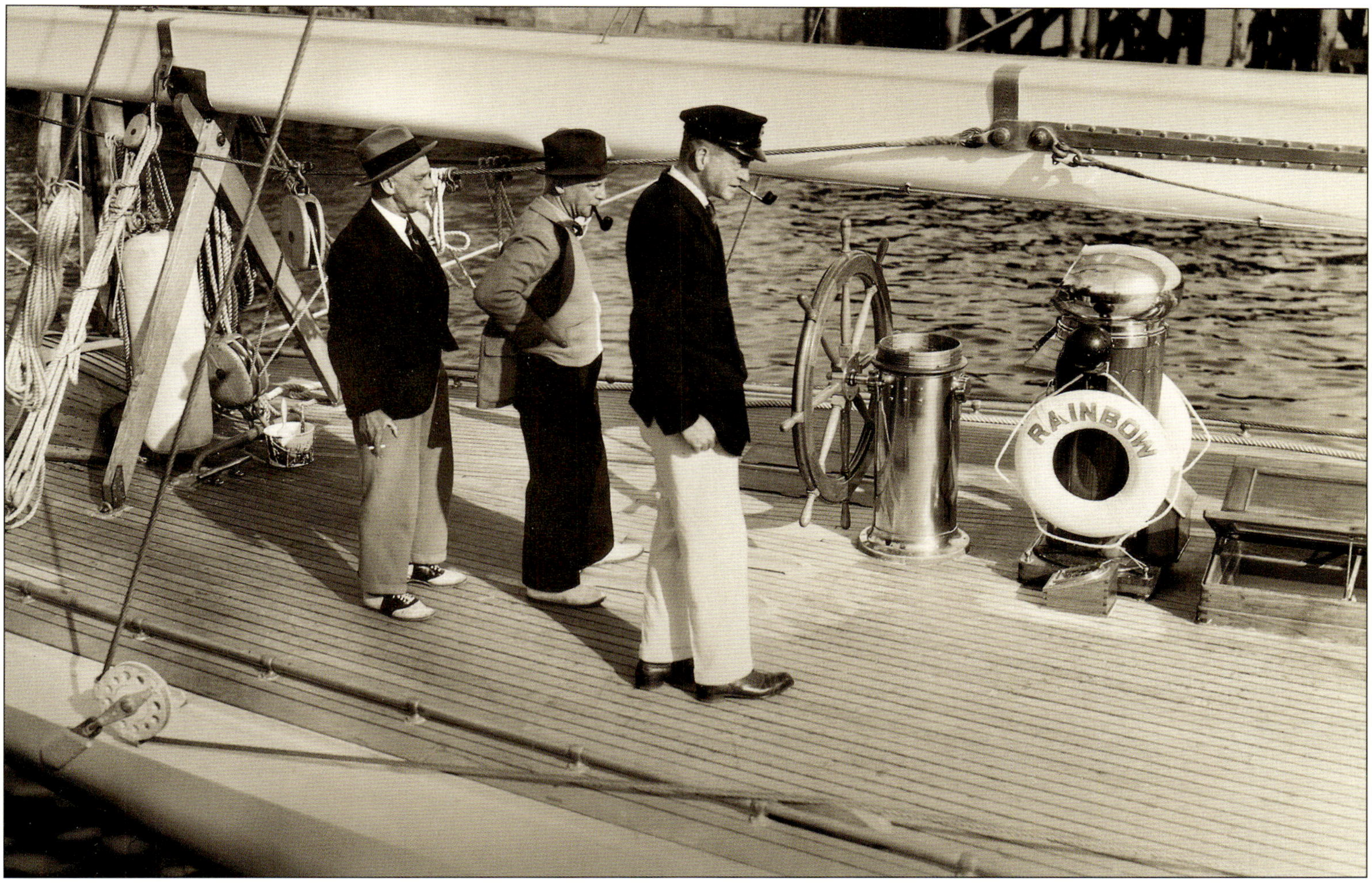
RAINBOW

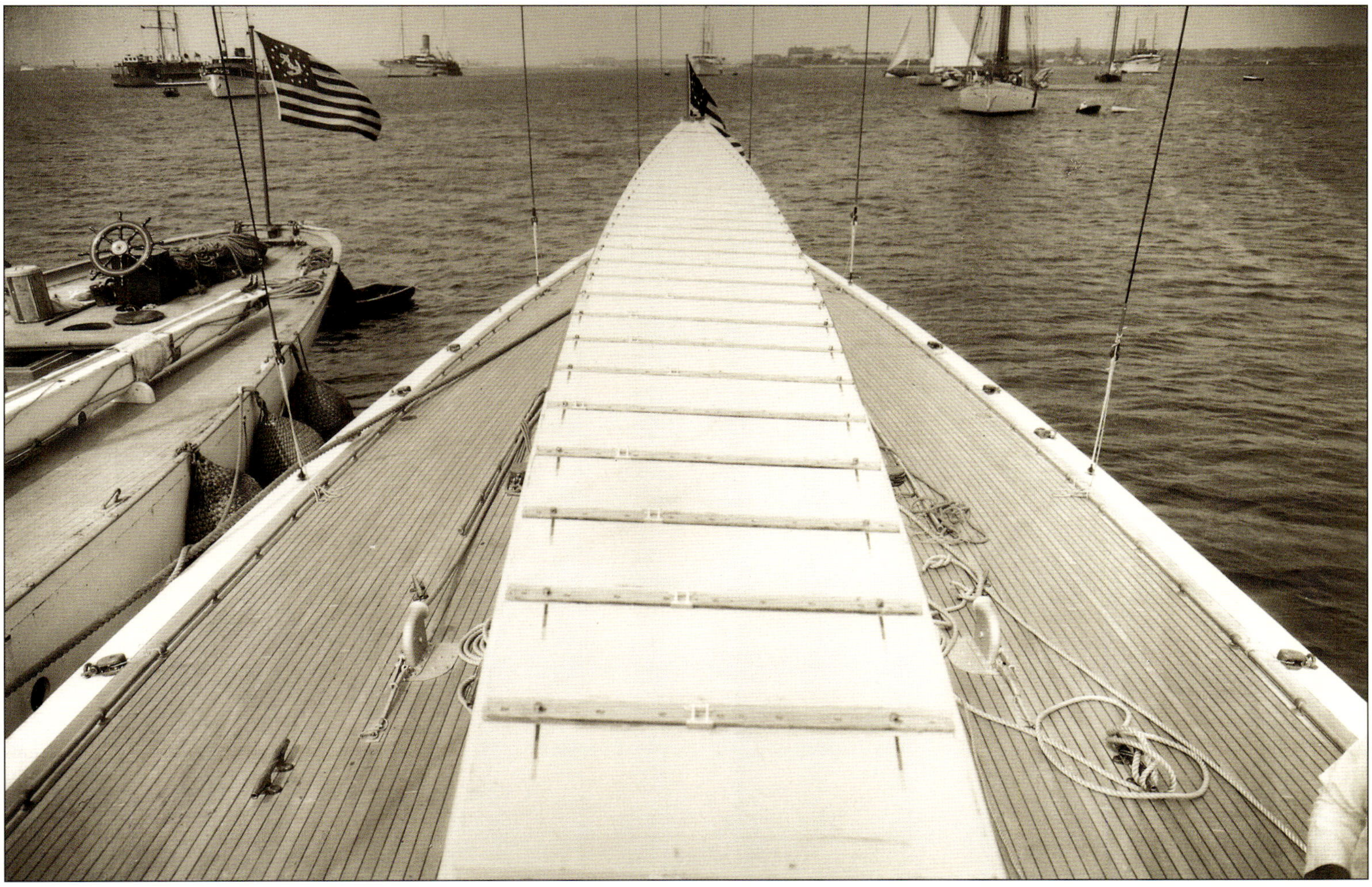

Above: *Endeavour's* amateur crew for the 1934 challenge. The Sopwiths are standing third and fourth from left, G. Colin Ratsey is standing fourth from right. / *Author's Collection*
Left: James Stanley Lapthorn IV (1881-1973) the mainstay of the Gosport loft through the inter-war years and champion of the Bermudan main sail. / *James F. Lapthorn*
Opposite: The two *Endeavours* (*Endeavour II* on left) on the Solent, note the quadrilateral jibs. / *Beken of Cowes*
Over: *Ranger*, the fastest of the J class defeated *Endeavour II* in the 1937 America's Cup series. Note the genoa. / *Rosenfeld Collection, Mystic Seaport Museum*

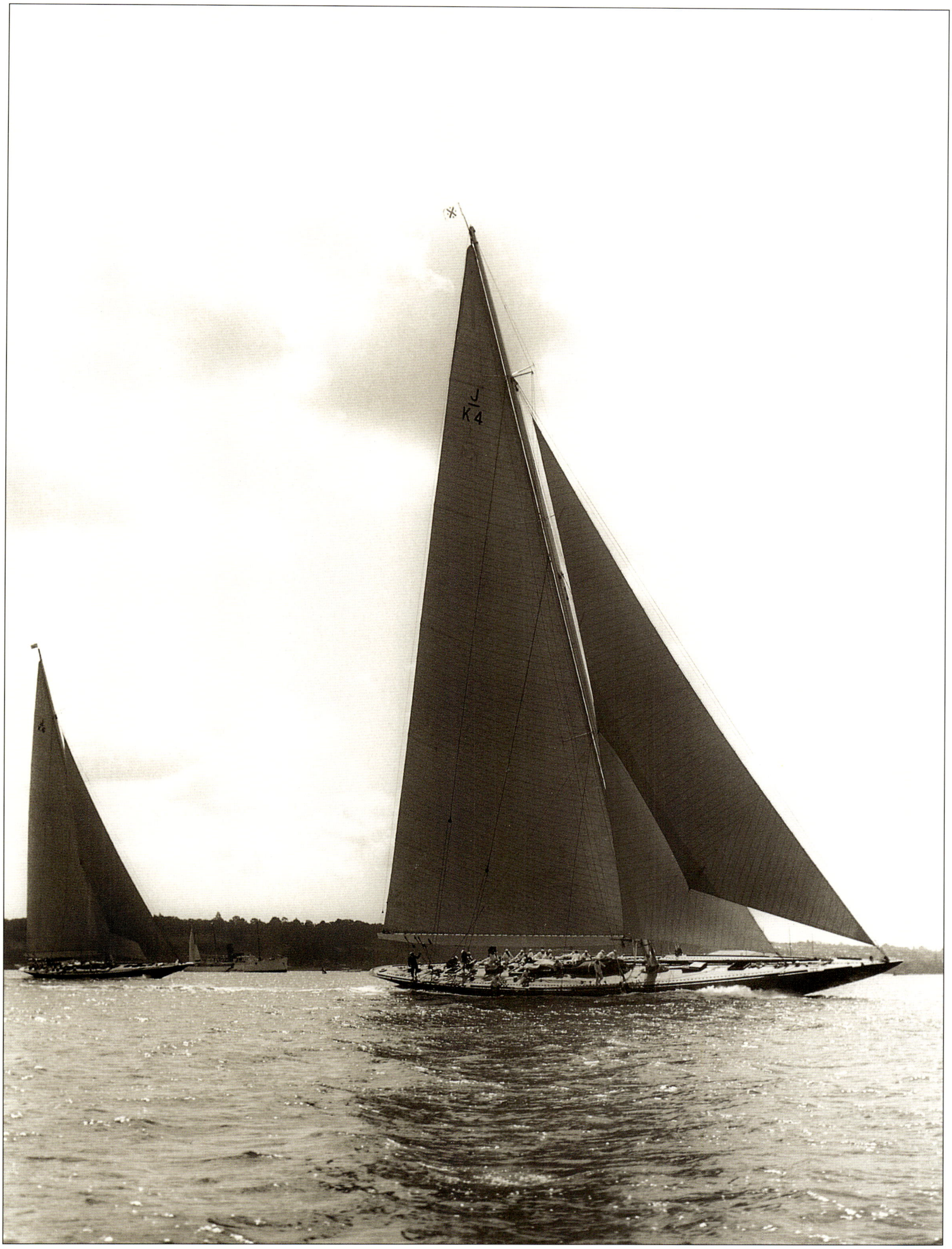
J
K 4

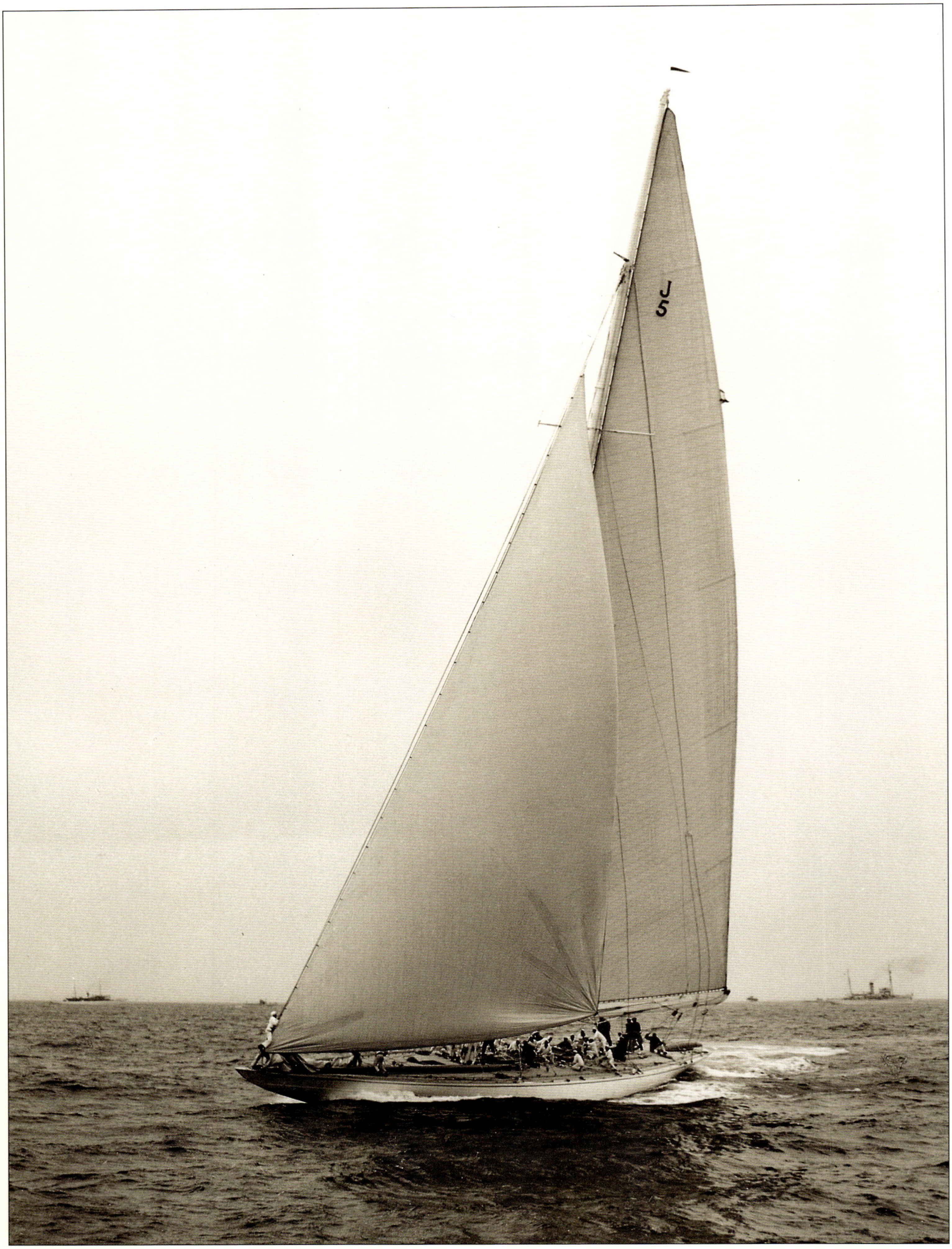
J
5

James Foster Lapthorn V joined his father at the Gosport loft in 1936, just as the days of Big Class racing were drawing to a close. George V had died, *Britannia* was scuttled and the J class was almost over. Sir Thomas Sopwith challenged a final time for the America's Cup in 1937 with *Endeavour II* and the Gosport loft built its final set of J class sails. In Cowes Franklin Ratsey Woodroffe, Muriel Ratsey's son, began his apprenticeship in 1937. He was not initially destined for service in the family firm, but the death from pneumonia of his older brother Roger in 1931 dictated his future. If the young newcomers had missed the glory days they may have been partly compensated when Chris Ratsey spent the fruits of the profitable years on commissioning William Fife to design and build the ocean racer *Evenlode*. With a family and loft crew *Evenlode* followed in the wake of *Dolly Varden* chalking up an impressive list of victories in the years immediately preceding and following the Second World War.

Unlike the situation in 1914, the cessation of yachting in 1939 only confirmed a general decline in the sport. Franklin Ratsey Woodroffe escaped from the Cowes loft to the Royal Military Academy at Sandhurst which he followed with a distinguished career in the West Lothian Regiment. His recently retired namesake and uncle, Franklin Ratsey, rejoined the navy becoming a captain on the North Atlantic convoys. In Gosport James Lapthorn IV remained at work but James V joined his brother, Peter R. Lapthorn, who was already serving in the navy. From on board *HMS Hood*, the largest battleship in the British fleet, Peter Lapthorn wrote to Ernest A. Ratsey in New York expressing his relief at America's joining the war effort: *'First of all let me thank you in America for the help which you are giving us over this side of the herring pond. We are damn grateful for it, for at present we are not in a very enviable position.'*[51] The war brought an end to some of the inter-loft rivalries as all worked on a wide range of naval and government contracts; sadly it also saw the destruction of the firm's two British lofts.

Below: The end of the Big Class. On the afternoon of 8 July 1936, *Britannia* left Cowes for the last time. King George V had left instructions that she was to be scuttled after his death, within a year Big Class racing died out. / *Franklin Ratsey-Woodroffe*
Over: *Solway Maid*, the last of Fife's designs to leave his yard, she did not sail until after the Second World War. Here *Solway Maid* is seen in a stiff breeze at the 1998 Cowes Classics. / *Franco Pace*

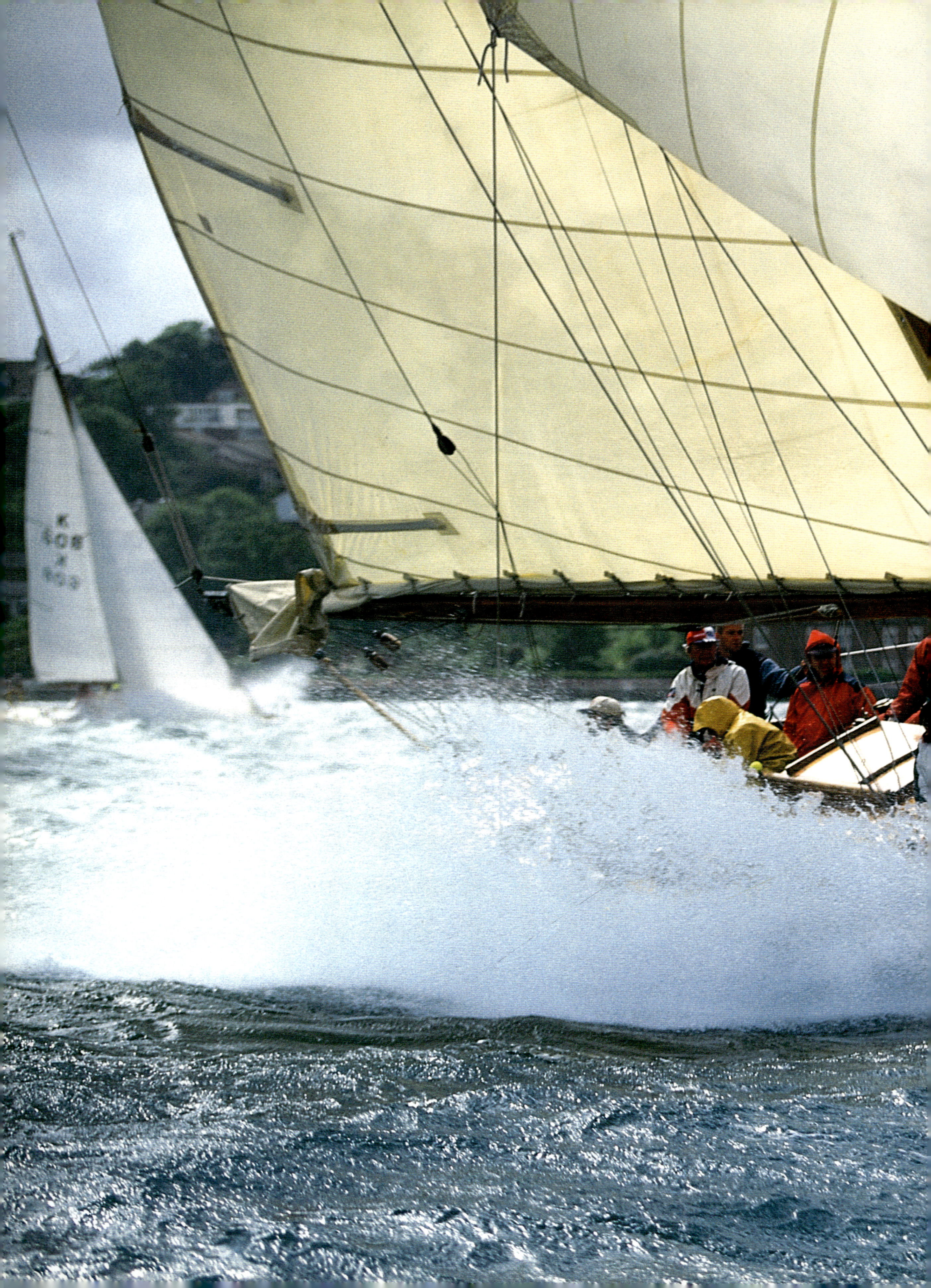

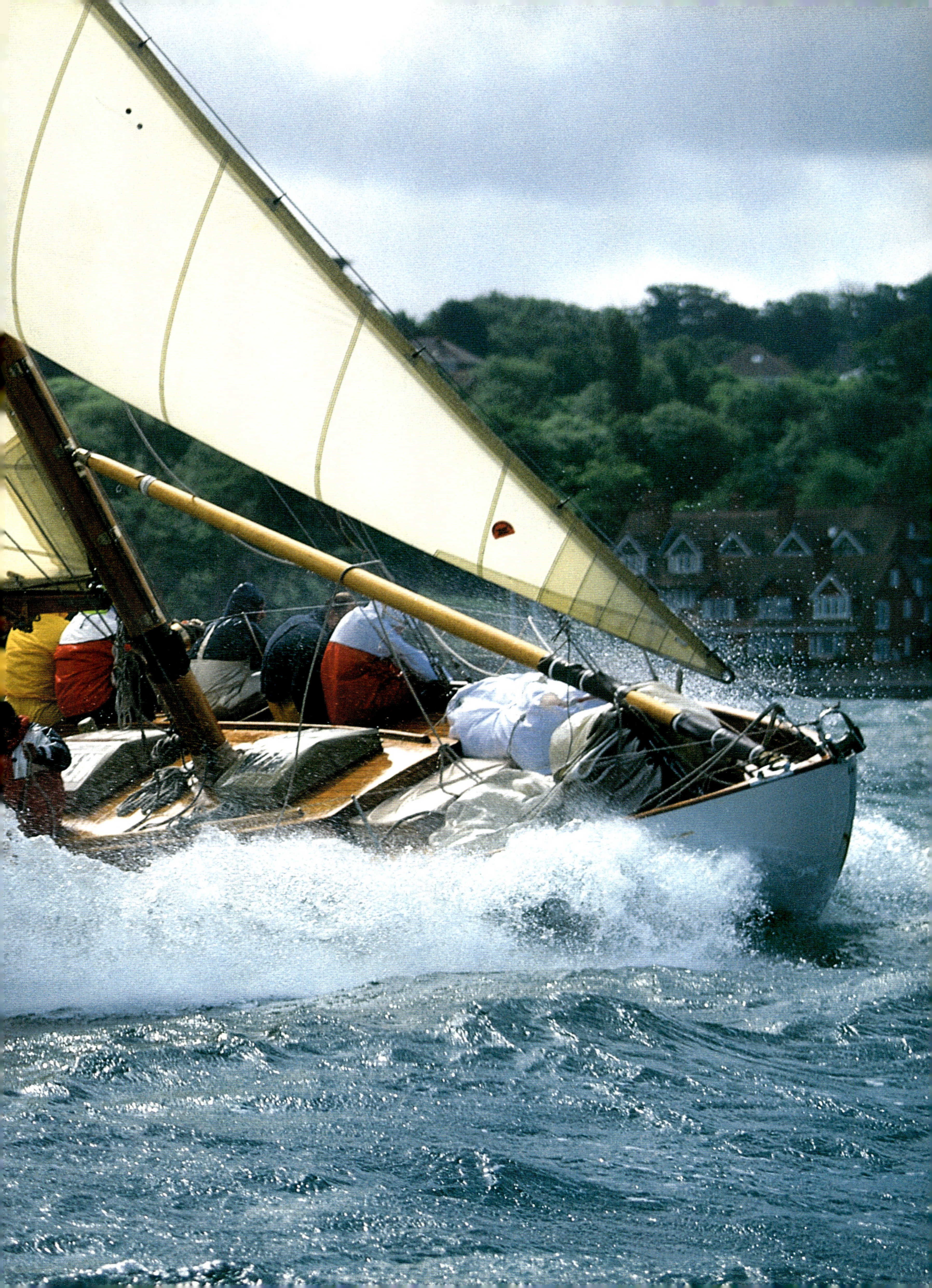

Both Gosport and Cowes were adjacent to high risk naval centres. In January 1941 the Gosport loft was fire bombed and James Lapthorn IV sent telegrams to Cowes and New York, '*Sail loft completely gone. All safe.*' Transferring their business to a local church hall, Lapthorn was able to report '*One week and we are up again-Not so bad! Bet it would make little ole Hitler mad.*' From then on the makeshift loft specialised in canvas hangers for planes but also undertook a wide range of other canvas work. Away from Gosport, Peter R. Lapthorn was lost aboard the *Hood* when she was sunk trying to prevent the *Bismarck* breaking out to the North Atlantic. In Cowes, Chris Ratsey had moved the firm from its two eighteenth century lofts on the High Street soon after taking over from his father. The modern loft was virtually next door to the John Samuel White yard and when this was bombed in May 1942, the new loft was completely destroyed. The loss was less serious than that at Gosport since the firm simply retreated to its former premises.

Above: Sailmaking in the new Cowes loft, T. Christopher Ratsey overseeing from the balcony. These new purpose built premises were destroyed during World War II. / *Beken of Cowes*

Opposite: Chris Ratsey commissioned William Fife to design and build *Evenlode* for the 1937 season. She was one of the last of Fife's great designs to be built and was cherished by the Ratsey family until 1960. / *Beken of Cowes*

Escaping destruction, the war time activities of the New York loft are far better documented than those of their British counterparts. Soon after the bombing of Pearl Harbour George E. Ratsey's health began to deteriorate and he died on Christmas day 1942. To fill the vacuum his eldest son Ernest A. Ratsey persuaded the British government to allow his younger brother G. Colin Ratsey to emigrate. The day-to-day war time business of the New York loft was the manufacture of canvas covers and tents of which they made hundreds of thousands. G. Colin Ratsey's role was to assist in the design of airborne lifeboats for the navy and army departments of the Bureau of Aeronautics. Many airmen who ditched their planes were being lost because sea born recovery could not be dispatched in time. In Britain the dinghy designer Uffa Fox had conceived and designed 20 foot lifeboats that could be carried under aeroplanes in much the same way as torpedoes and parachuted to the stranded airmen. G. Colin Ratsey, who knew Uffa Fox well, having sailed dinghies both with and against him, was familiar with his brainchild. Having designed the rig of the American version, he described the first trial of the army boat:

Coming over the horizon was the B17 with the life boat strapped to the bomb rack under the belly. We watched carefully because she was flying at some 4 or 5,000 feet altitude. Suddenly, the boat

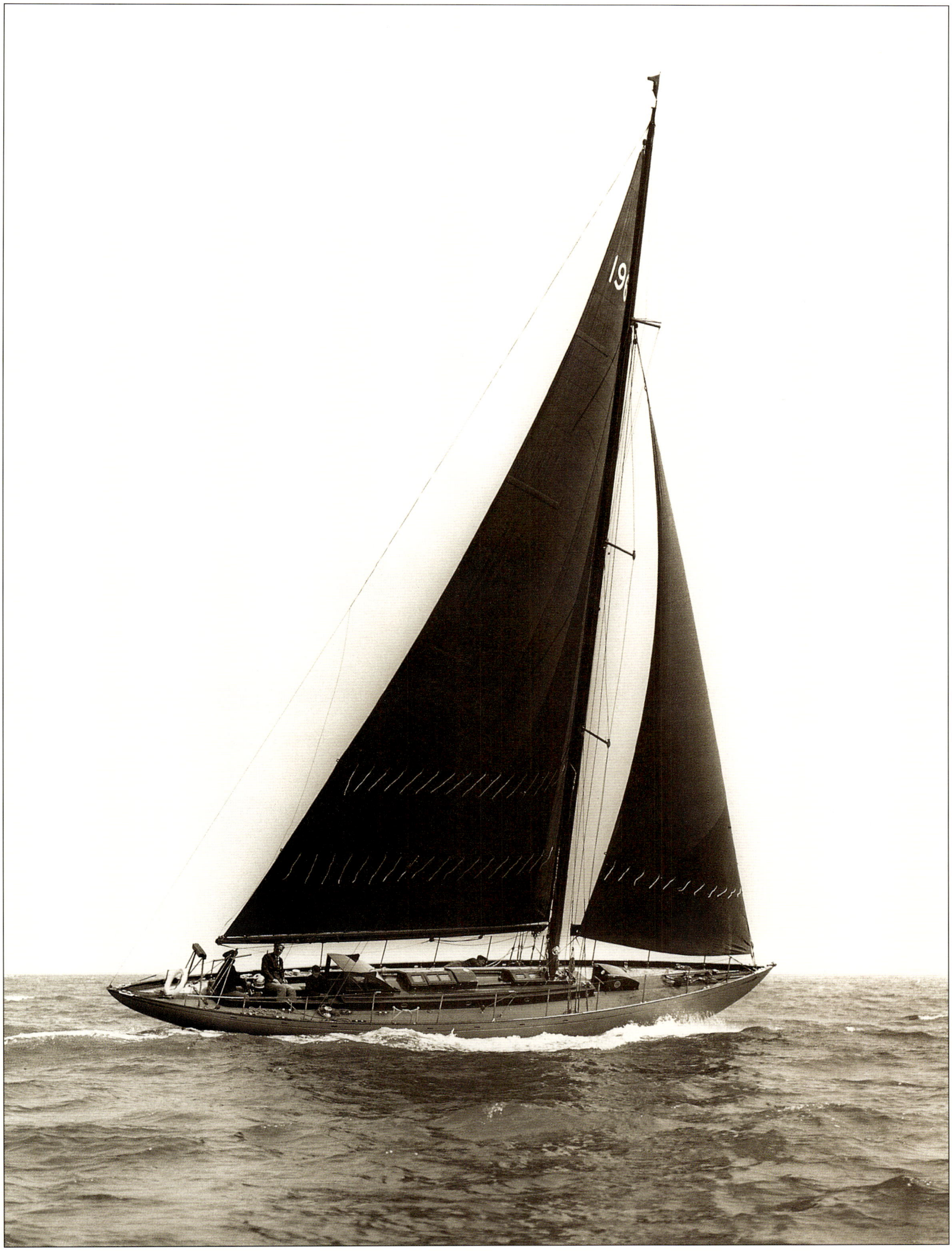
19

came away from the plane and did a nice dive to start with, clear of the plane but no parachute appeared. The boat came tumbling down, over and over, until she hit the water and exploded into very small pieces. It was only when we returned to land that it was discovered the crew had forgotten to hook up the static line which pulled the parachutes out of their packs as the boat dropped.[52]

Teething troubles aside the project was successful but the US Navy did not like the hull of the army's boat and asked Ratsey to improve it. To do this he enlisted Bill Luders to design a new hull and hundreds of the navy type were eventually built.

Above: G. Colin Ratsey pioneered the development of airborne life boats in America during World War II. The boats were used to rescue stranded airmen who could not be picked up by other means. / *Mystic Seaport Museum*

Left: Quay Lane, Gosport on the morning of 11 February 1941. Ratsey & Lapthorn's loft stood at the far end and was totally destroyed. / *Author's Collection*

Immediately after the war the Lapthorns began to plan their new loft. They were ambitious but in the austerity years with ongoing rationing and materials control as well as new taxes on such luxuries as yachts they had to use all their influence as major employers in Gosport to obtain the required permits. When they succeeded, they emulated the New York loft and built the largest sail loft in Britain. With three 150' by 45' floors it was an unjustifiably optimistic building that clearly drew on the Big Class era for its inspiration. Although the firm's destroyed premises in Britain were a serious problem, they were still dependent on Hayward's for their cloth and the weavers facilities had been ruined when taken over for military purposes. G. Colin Ratsey visited the site in 1945:

> I found the whole factory stacked with ammunition... Haywards had tried to move the ammunition but, due to the government red tape, it stayed there for several years... Most of the machinery had been pushed into the fields to make way for the ammunition.[53]

A quality supplier of sail cloth had always been vital to the well being of Ratsey & Lapthorn. Not only was the firm now forced to scout around amongst suppliers of second rate cotton duck but even this was now being superseded by synthetic materials. On rejoining the firm after World War II Franklin Ratsey Woodroffe asserted his family connection with the firm by making increased use of his middle name and eventually changed his surname to the hyphenated Ratsey-Woodroffe; it was he who first addressed the cloth issue. Although Stephen Ratsey, Chris' son and the heir apparent served his apprenticeship in the firm his relationship with it was always difficult. He suffered from a drink problem and left Ratsey & Lapthorn, setting up sailmaking lofts in Ireland, Bristol, Cowes and eventually Southampton before his early death in 1988. At Cowes it was Franklin Ratsey-Woodroffe who became Chris Ratsey's number two.

In the 1952 Olympics Franklin Ratsey-Woodroffe crewed on the 6 Metre, *Titia* which achieved only 9th place amongst the 11 competing nations. The successful boats all had synthetic sails and he became convinced that the firm would need to adapt to this new cloth if it were to remain successful. However, his uncle and superior Chris Ratsey thought it was only a passing trend and refused to even meet the ICI representative to discuss the possibilities of Terylene. Consequently the Cowes loft persevered with second rate cotton. By the time of the revival of the America's Cup in 1958, the

Above: The rebuilt Gosport loft on Portsmouth Harbour was the largest sailmaking loft in the Britain but it was rarely used to capacity. / *The Gosport Museum*

Below: James F Lapthorn, who spearheaded the Gosport loft's revival after the Second World War and ran it until its final closure in 1971 when he transferred to the Cowes loft. / *James F. Lapthorn*

Over: *Madrigal* was William Fife's last design, she is seen here on her first sail after restoration in 1997. / *Franco Pace*

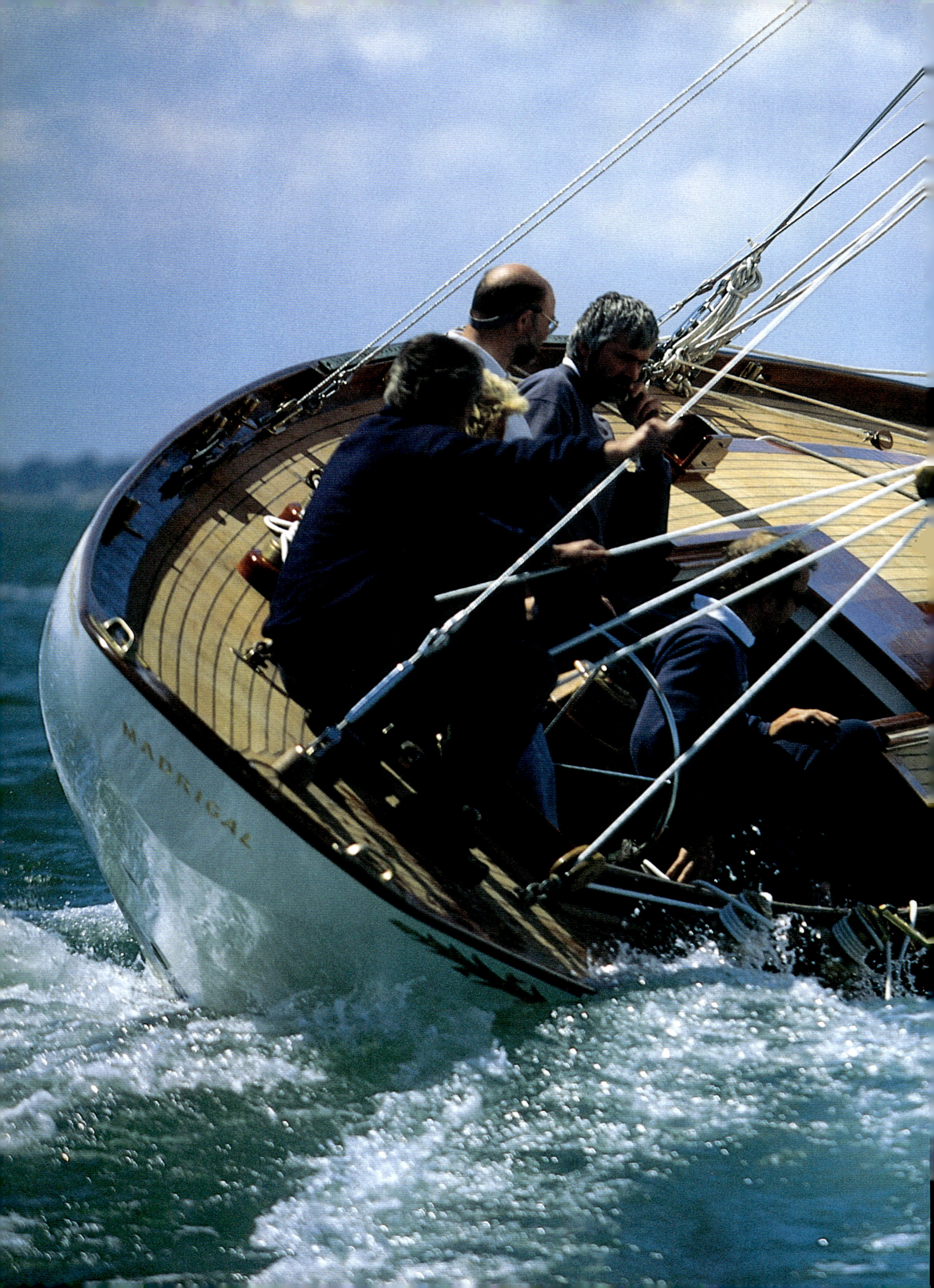
MADRIGAL

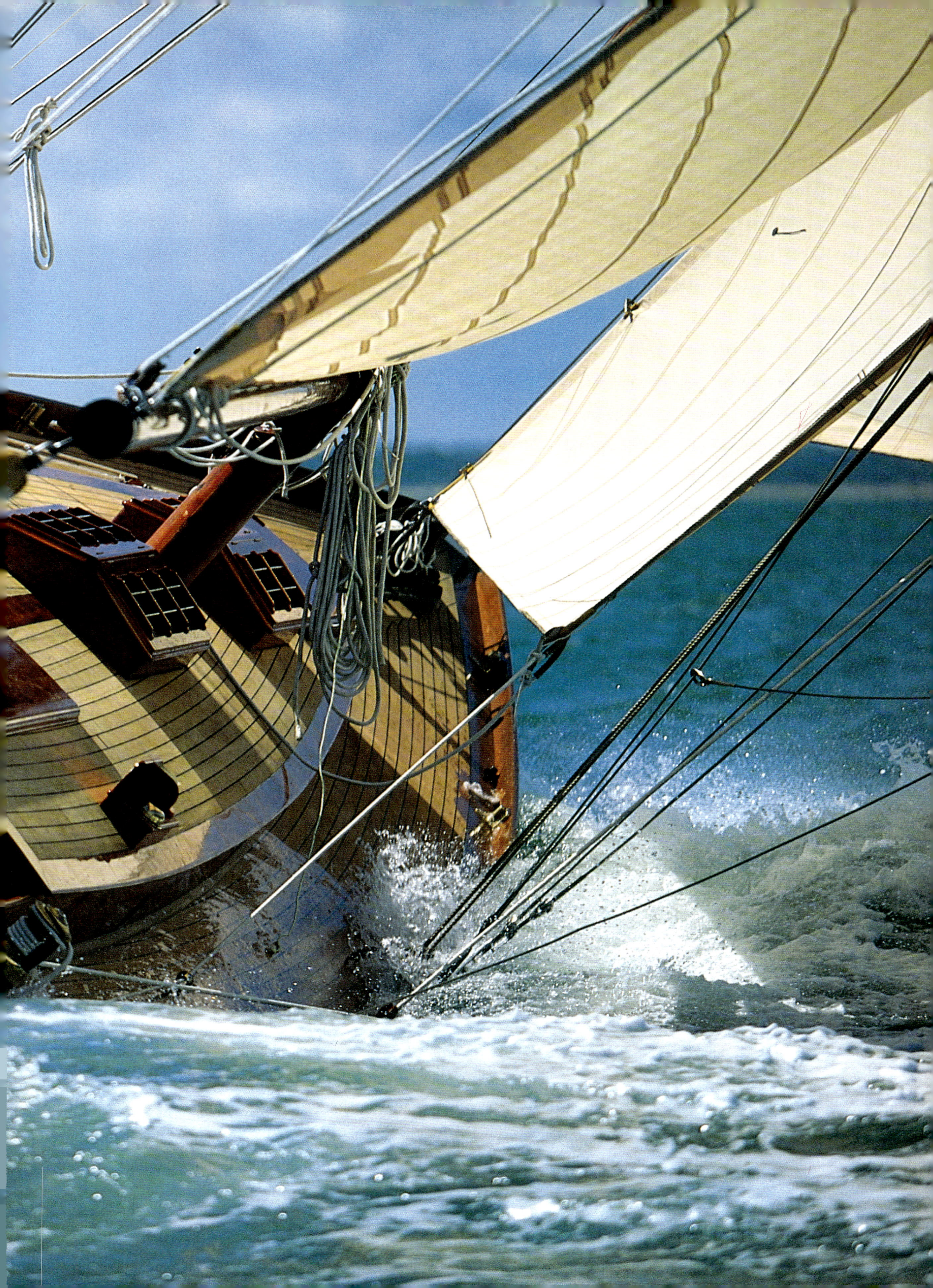

death knell of natural fibres for sails had been sounded. The rules governing the contest dictated that competing yachts should be built and equipped in their country of origin and consequently the Royal Yacht Squadron challenger, *Sceptre*, used cloth woven in Britain. Predictably *Sceptre's* sails were mostly made at Ratsey & Lapthorn's Gosport loft but poor cloth and inexperience in cutting synthetic materials made for a poor suit that was only disguised by *Sceptre's* many other disadvantages. G. Colin Ratsey was deputised from the New York loft to take care of alterations but he was not able to make any substantial improvements. Back in England Chris Ratsey's retirement the same year marked the final passing of the cotton sail era.

On assuming the leading role Franklin Ratsey-Woodroffe was dedicated to again obtaining a supply of quality material. Working with Haywards some progress was made, but with sail cloth representing only a marginal activity for the firm, it allocated very few resources to developing the specialist fabrics required. In the event a range of suppliers was used but Owen Aisher's 1964 America's Cup challenge proved again that the firm had still not caught up with American weaving technology. *Kurewa's* sails were well cut but the cloth stretched and Franklin Ratsey-Woodroffe, who had travelled with the challenger, spent his nights restoring their shape. The experience spelled disaster for the firm and obtaining no support from British weavers, Ratsey-Woodroffe elected to weave his own cloth. Resistance within the firm to this departure from their traditional business was strong but by co-opting Owen Aisher onto the board, Ratsey-Woodroffe imposed his will. Immediately his step-son Mark was despatched to Lancashire to learn how to weave and the venture was launched around one second hand loom. The first quality cloth was produced in 1966 but to finance the required investment in plant Ratsey & Lapthorn Ltd sold its holding in the New York loft, finally making it wholly independent.

Above: The launch of Franklin Ratsey-Woodroffe's ocean racer *Misty* at Clare Lallows yard in 1959. Franklin Ratsey-Woodroffe is in the centre with Clare Lallow to the left. / *Franklin Ratsey-Woodroffe*

Opposite: Franklin Ratsey-Woodoffe's *Lothian* was named after the regiment with which he fought and gained a Military Cross during the Second World War, she was launched from Clare Lallows' Cowes yard in 1952. / *Beken of Cowes*

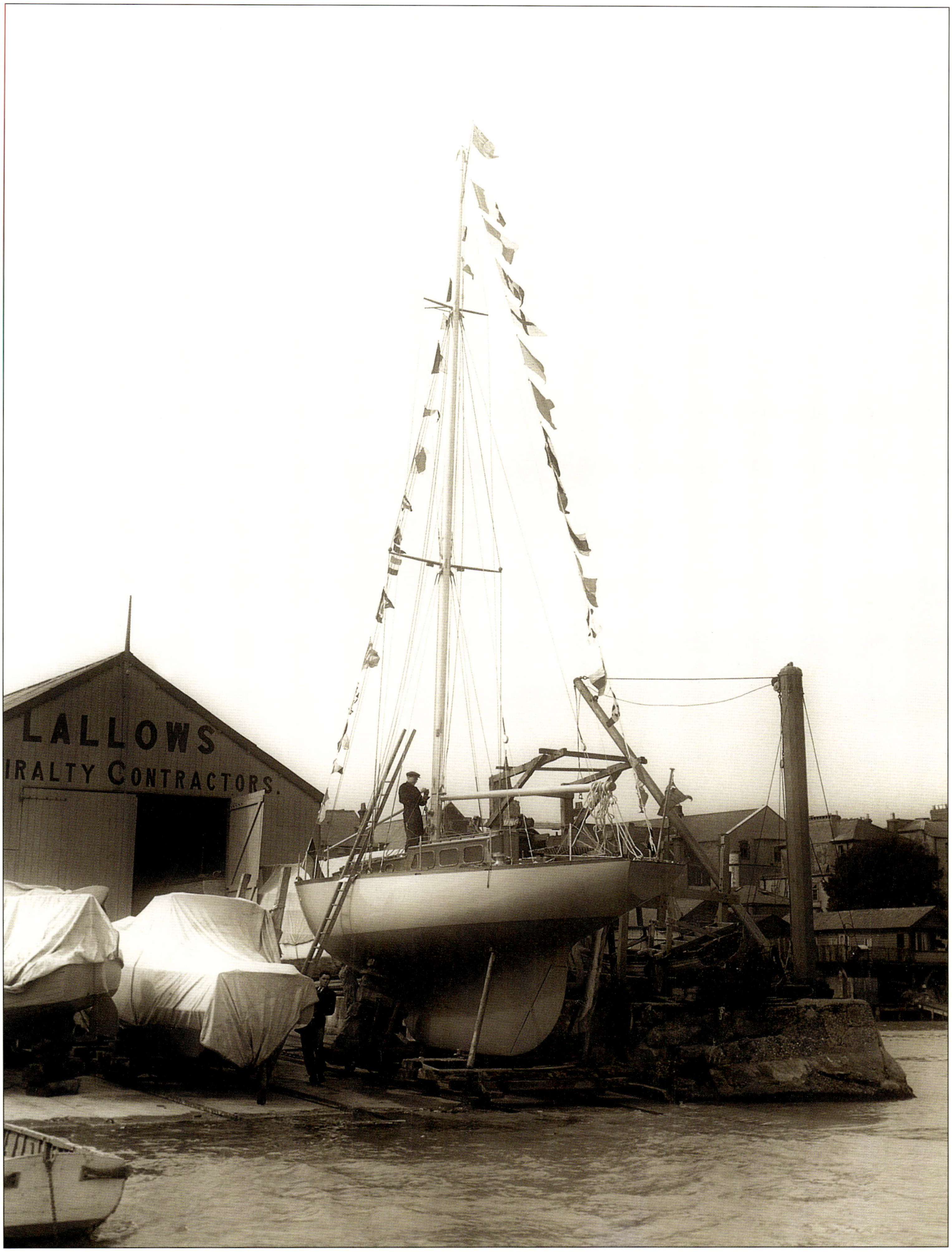
LALLOWS
IRALTY CONTRACTORS.

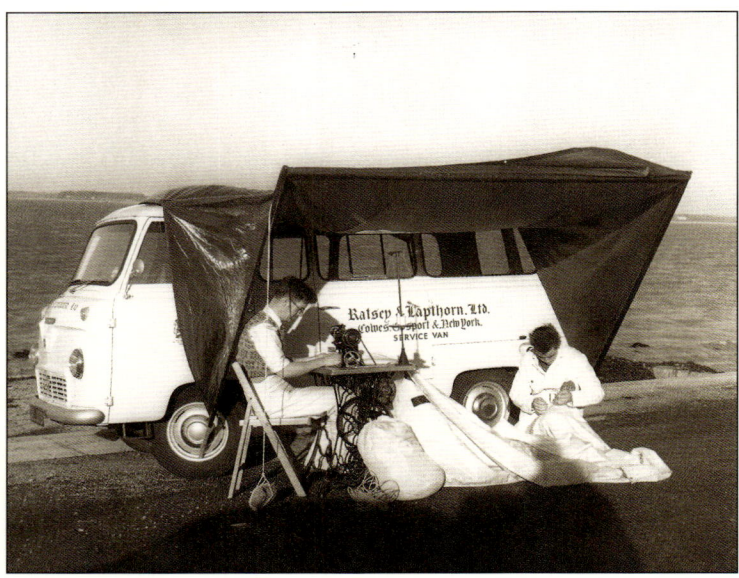

Above Left: Experimenting with 12 Metre mainsails ashore prior to the 1964 America's Cup. The mast was set up by Harry Spencer then skipper of *Norsaga* (ex *Trivia*). / *Beken of Cowes*

Above Right: Franklin Ratsey-Woodroffe crewed on the 6 Metre *Titia* in the 1952 Olympics. A poor result against yachts equipped with synthetic sails convinced him that the days of cotton sails were over. / *Beken of Cowes*

Below Left: In the late 1950s Ratsey & Lapthorn's mobile service van helped maintain the standard of customer care that clients required. / *Beken of Cowes*

Opposite: The British 12 Metre *Sceptre* did not distinguish herself in the in the first post-war America's Cup challenge. Despite adopting synthetic fibres, a lack of experience with these and the then poor quality of British made cloth further disadvantaged the unpromising challenger. / *Beken of Cowes*

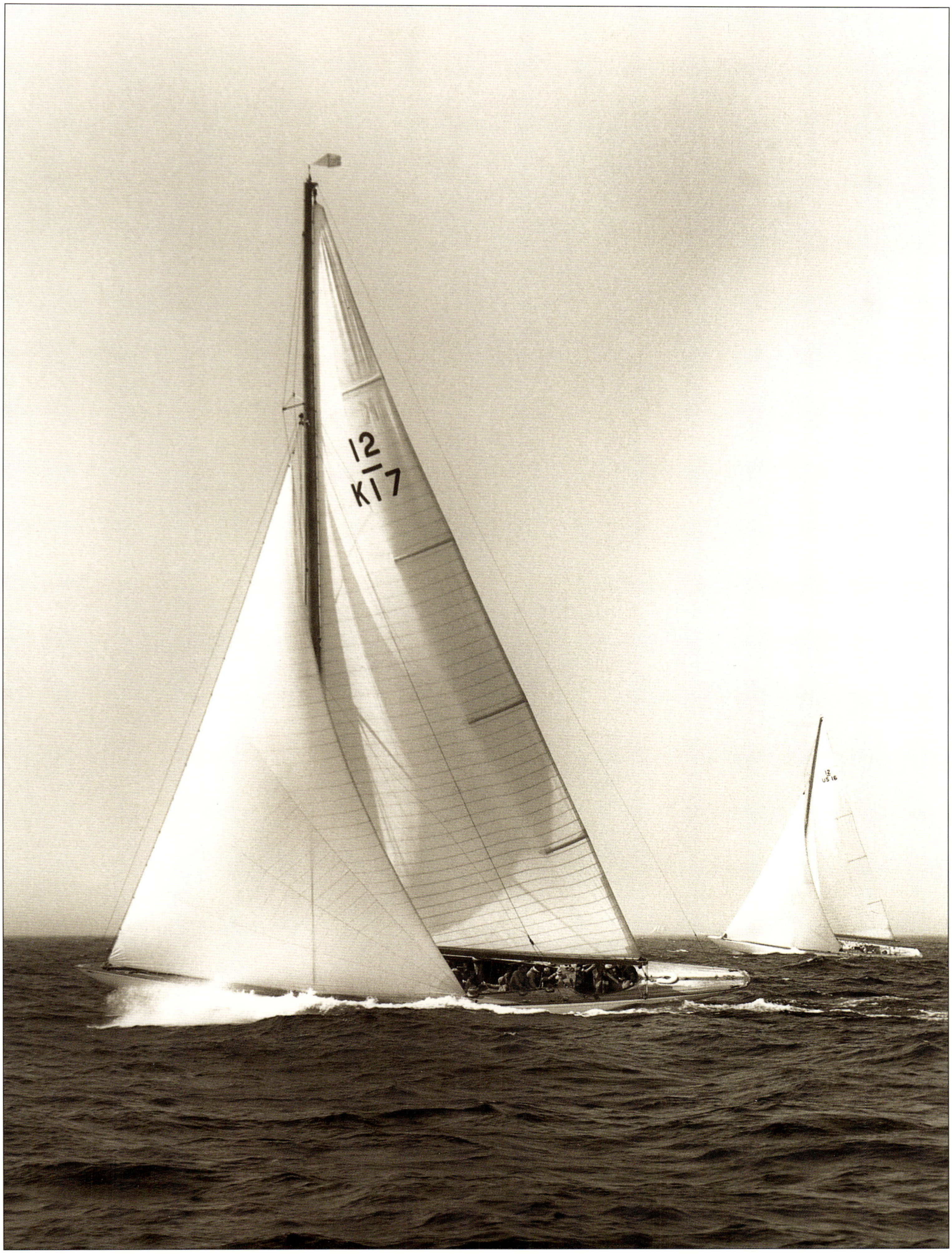

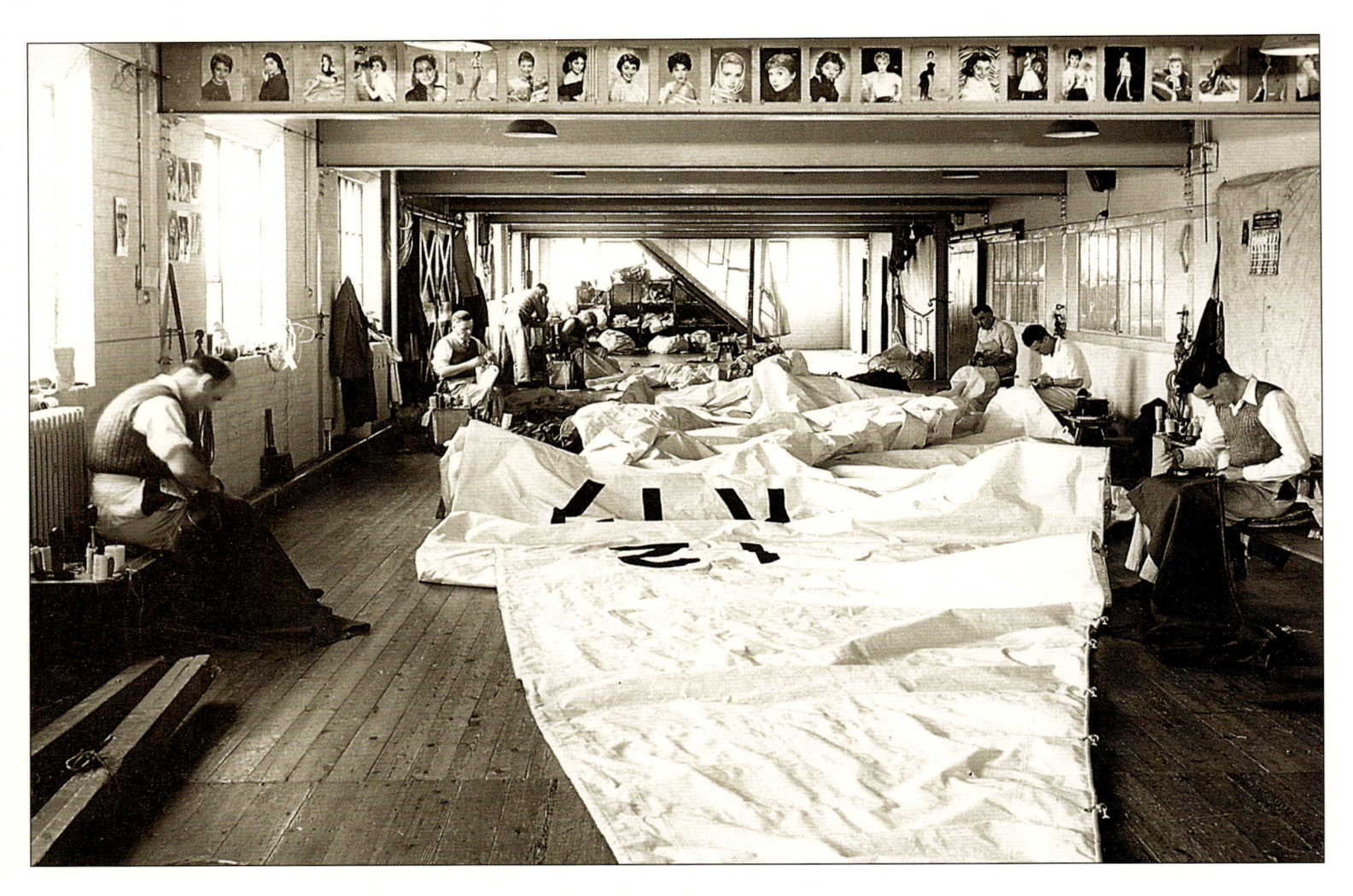

Above: *Sceptre's* main sail approaching completion at Ratsey & Lapthorn's Gosport loft. / *James F. Lapthorn*

Below Left: The 1964 British 12 Metres *Kurewa* and *Sovereign* suffered from much the same problems as *Sceptre* and *Sovereign* stood little chance against the American defender *Constellation*. It was with the arrival of *Kurewa's* owner, Owen Aisher, onto Ratsey & Lapthorn's board that company began to weave its own synthetic cloth. / *Beken of Cowes*

Opposite: In 1956 Stavros Niarchos lent his three masted schooner *Creole* to serve as the British entry in the first tall ships race. John Illingworth was in command and designed the world's largest spinnaker. The sail was built by Ratsey & Lapthorn at their Gosport loft, one of the few occasions when that building's ambitious proportions were justified. / *James F. Lapthorn*

Over: The 12 Metre *Freedom* successfully defended the America's Cup in 1980 but her high-tech sails were beyond the capacity of Ratsey & Lapthorn's New York loft. / *Franco Pace*

To finance their independence, the New York-based Ratseys, now including Ernest A. Ratsey's son Colin, formed a partnership with Jack Sutphen. With no background in sail making it was anticipated that Sutphen would mainly assist the loft at a managerial level, but the firm's strategy through the 1960s eventually led to its demise. In the post-World War II era, US yachting expanded away from its traditional centre on Long Island Sound and whilst the number of individual vessels increased dramatically, their dimensions shrank. Responding to the expansion in small boat and dinghy racing small specialised lofts emerged throughout America; Murphy & Nye, Ulmer, Hood, North, Rice, Hard and many others. Competition amongst these drove prices down and these relatively small lofts had comparatively low overheads. Ratsey & Lapthorn were no longer catering to a relatively small number of very wealthy yachtsmen but to a new breed who preferred the personal contact they could have with their local loft. The company's skill base remained enormous but the introduction of synthetic cloth eroded the value of this. Once good low stretch synthetic cloth became widely available the years of experience required to build cotton sails that could stretch evenly without loss of shape were redundant.

The overhead-intensive, centralised New York loft was a victim of the technological and managerial expertise of smaller lofts like Lowell North's. North was an engineering graduate and Star boat champion who pioneered a far more technically advanced approach to sail design and manufacture. To expand his market he established a net work of franchises, all a far cry from Ratsey & Lapthorn's traditional approach. The firm made some attempt to mirror this pattern of growth establishing a loft in Largo, Florida in 1977 but it remained irretrievably rooted to relatively big yachts based in New England. It's final link with the America's Cup was during the joint *Enterprise* and *Freedom* America's Cup defence campaign when Jack Sutphen left to join Dennis Conner as sail co-ordinator for a one and a half year programme of sail development and testing. *Freedom's* 1980 victory with high tech Kevlar and Mylar sails coincided with the final demise of the New York loft which passed briefly into the hands of Horizon Sailmakers before re-emerging as UK Sailmakers in the mid-1980s. Management disagreements had prompted G. Colin Ratsey's retirement in 1974 but far from putting his feet up, he immediately became vice president of Yardarm Sailmakers in Needham, Massachusetts adding the weight of his 50 years of experience to yet another small and ambitious loft.

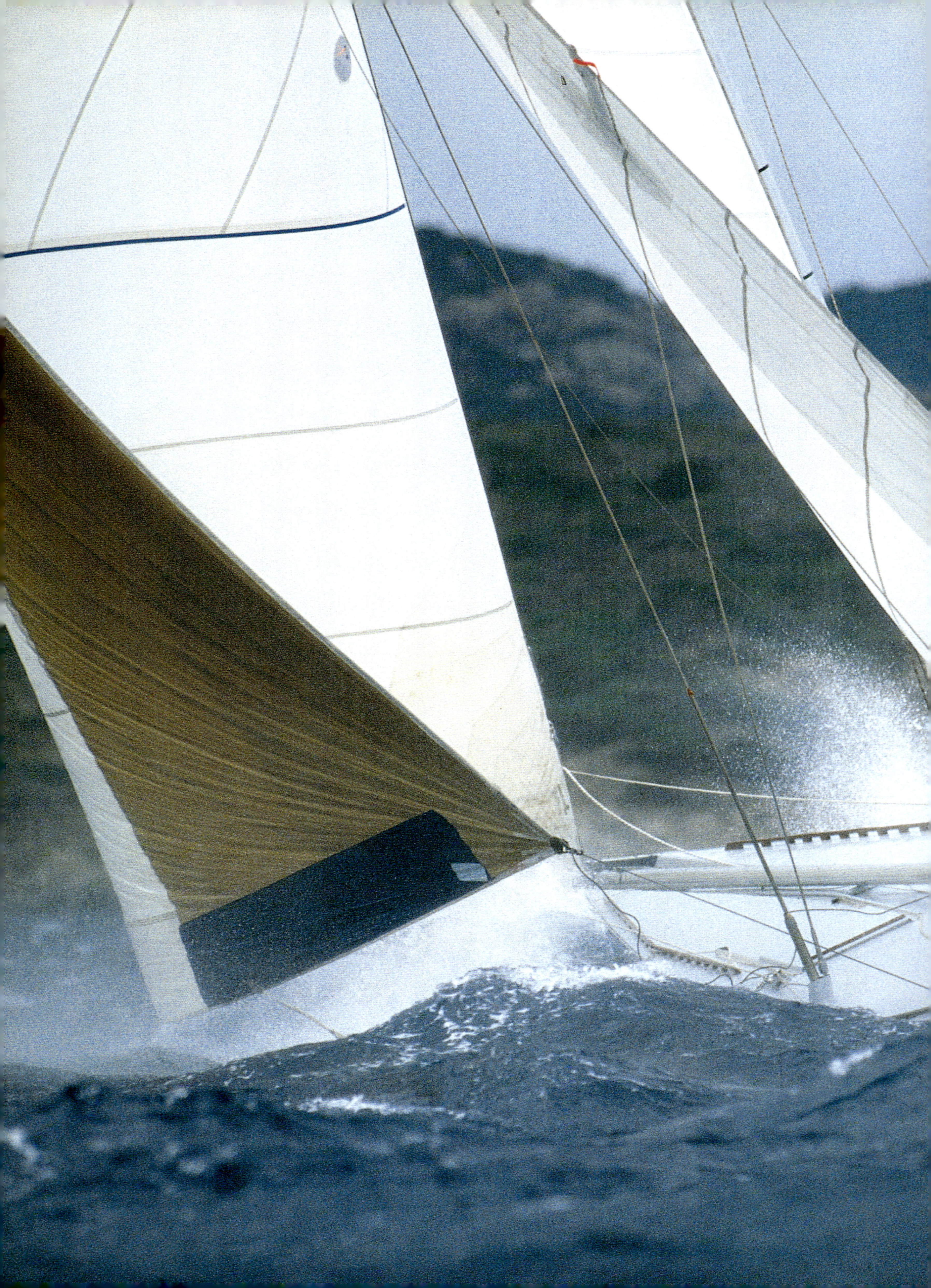

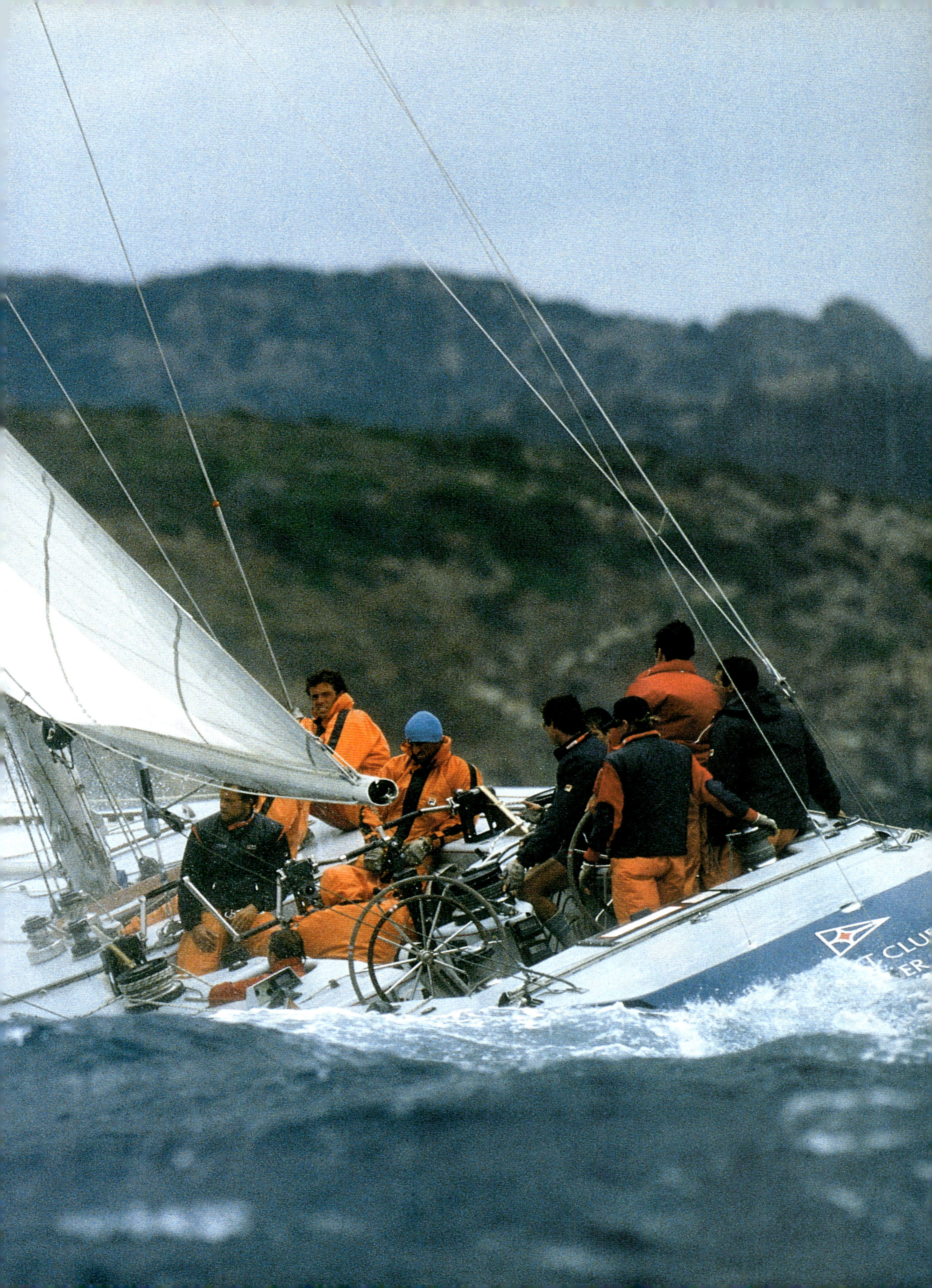

Based in the traditional centre of British yachting, Ratsey & Lapthorn's British lofts faced a very similar challenge to that of their American counterpart. The only significant difference was in-house weaving and the firm's Vectis cloth proved extremely successful, so much so that the Australian owners of the 1967 America's Cup challenger *Dame Pattie* sought and obtained dispensation to use this non-Australian fabric. The sale of Ratsey & Lapthorn cloth to other sail lofts was in stark contrast to the exclusivity the firm had imposed on Haywards but it quenched a long-felt need throughout British sailmaking. Despite the inability to export to New York on account of duties, weaving became the firm's main activity as it sold material to up to 74 other sailmakers in 22 countries. In the early 1970s the weaving division of Ratsey & Lapthorn was generating up to 85 per cent of the firm's turnover as its sailmaking operation contracted. In a bid to increase the viability of its sailmaking activities the over-sized Gosport loft was sold in 1971 with the employees being transferred to Cowes, and sailmaking, although a minority operation, remained viable.

Below: In 1966 the first of Ratsey & Lapthorn's highly successful Vectis cloth came off the company's looms finally providing it with the cloth it needed to excel in the post-cotton age of sailmaking. / *Beken of Cowes*

Opposite: The training ship *Shebab Oman* setting her Ratsey & Lapthorn square sails off Cadiz during the 1992 Columbus Regatta. Ratsey & Lapthorn's skills always remained in great demand on traditional ships. / *Franco Pace*

Over Left: Castles at sea, a Ratsey & Lapthorn suit of sails on four masted training ship *Esmeralda* seen off Puerto Rico during the 1992 Columbus Regatta. / *Franco Pace*

Over Right: For the replica of *HMS Bounty* two suits of sails were made; one of modern synthetic fabrics, the other of hand stitched hemp. With South Manhattan in the background, *Bounty* is setting out to salute the Statue of Liberty on its 100th birthday in 1986. / *Franco Pace*

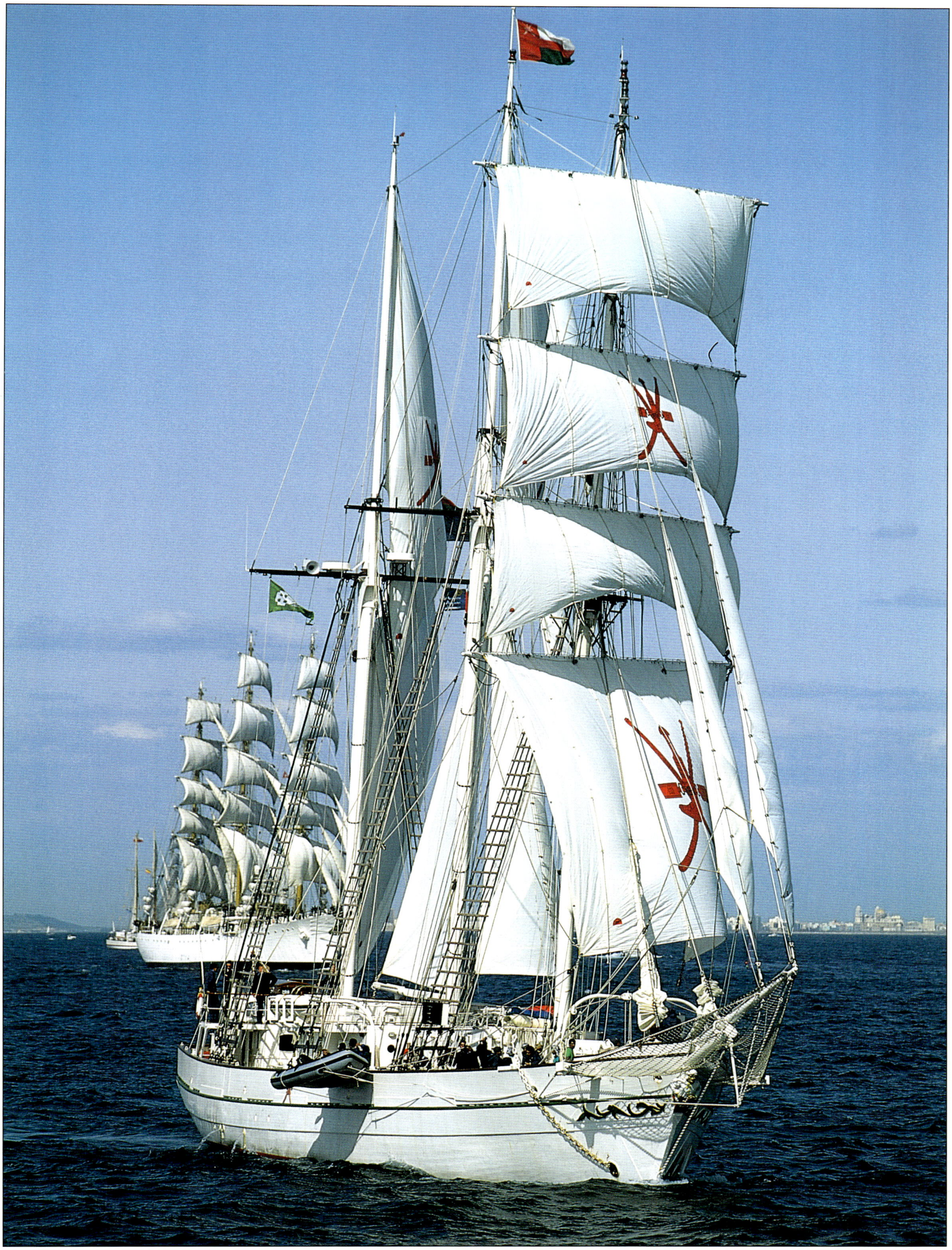

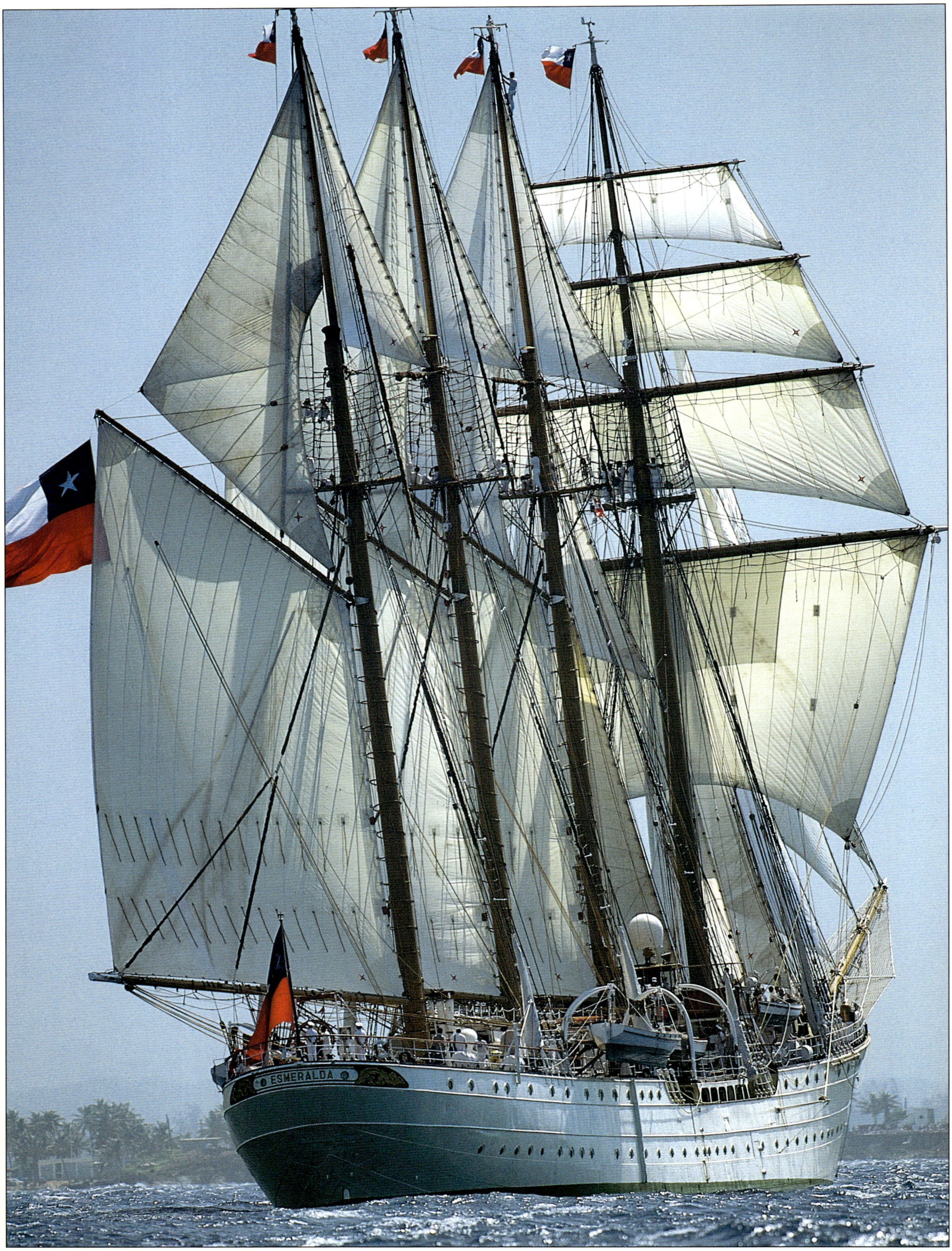
ESMERALDA

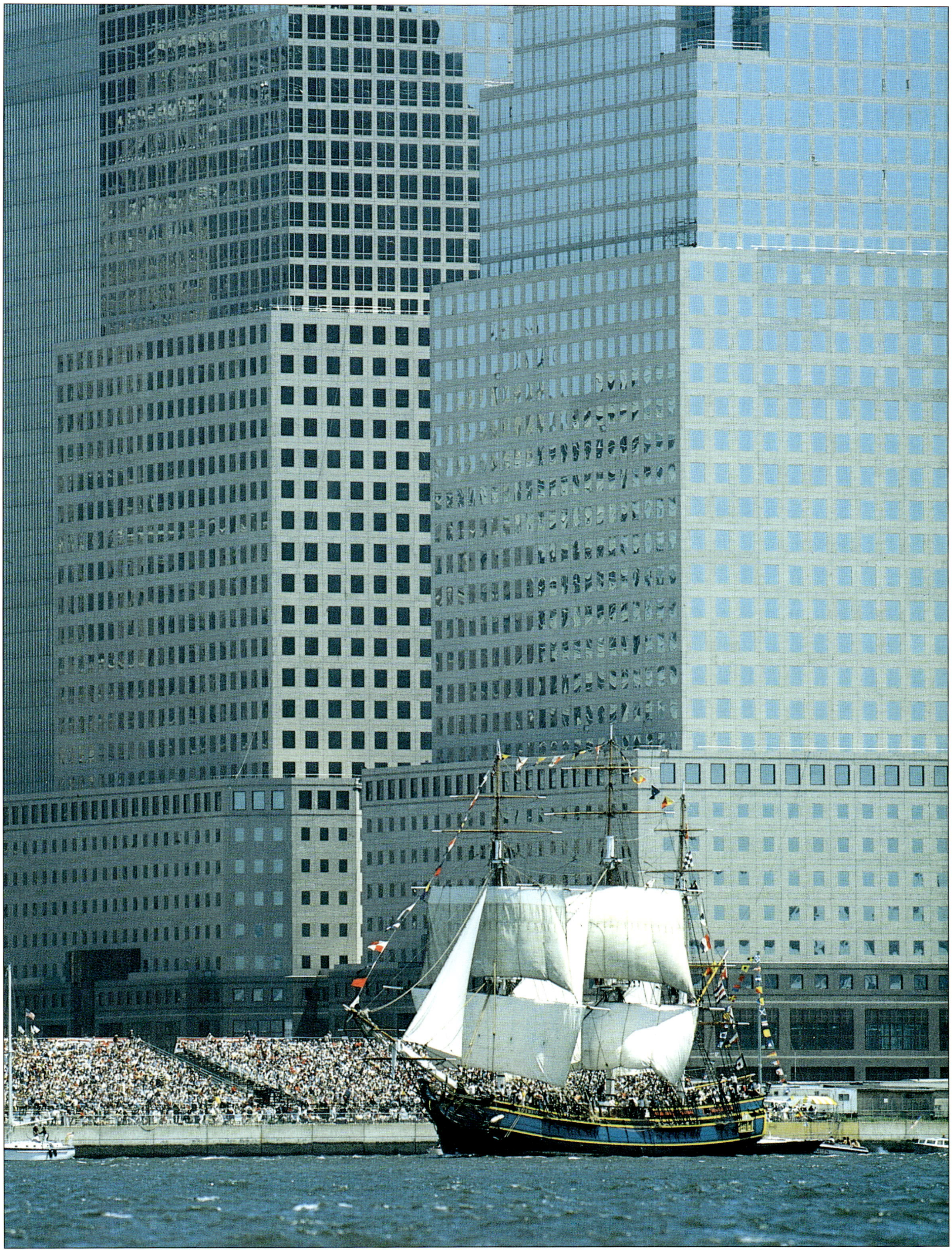

With an eye on its balance sheet the firm invested heavily in new looms in both 1973 and 1978. It was anticipated that these would increase efficiency, quality and profits but the profit never materialised. After endlessly blaming themselves, the firm finally realised that it was the victim of the enormous differential in the cost of Dacron yarn in Britain as compared to the United States. With reduced profits and heavily in debt as a result of its investment in new plant, the firm was particularly vulnerable when problems with yarn quality led to a serious downturn in orders for the firm's cloth. Mark Ratsey-Woodroffe, managing director since 1979 and fully responsible for the firm since the retirement of his step-father in 1983, responded by instituting a new strategy for the firm.

Ratsey and Lapthorn had recently secured the order for the sails for 200' three masted schooner *Jessica* (now *Adix*) and this reinforced Mark Ratsey-Woodroffe's conviction that the firm's future lay in a return to traditional sailmaking. Abandoning weaving altogether, the firm's core of experienced staff were soon working on sails for replica vessels such as David Lean's *HMS Bounty* and the tall ships *Shebab Oman*, *Esmeralda*, *Malcolm Miller* and *Winston Churchill*. These orders were supplemented by increased demand for classic yacht sails as the rebirth of interest in classic yachts gathered pace from the mid-1980s onwards. For owners motivated by a desire to restore the rare survivors of earlier periods in yachting the Ratsey & Lapthorn hallmark was an essential requirement. In the vanguard of this movement, Albert Obrist's restoration of the 1931 Fife-designed and built schooner *Altair* set the standard for subsequent restorations. For 15 years now Ratsey & Lapthorn have been the tailors of choice for the growing fleet of restored classic yachts.

Above: Mark Ratsey-Woodroffe at the helm of three masted schooner *Jessica* during trials off Cowes in 1984. / *Mark Ratsey-Woodroffe*
Right: Andy Cassell of Ratsey & Lapthorn, gold medal winner in the Sonar class at the 1996 Paralympics. / *Mark Ratsey-Woodroffe*
Over Left: Ten years after being launched as *Jessica*, *Adix* arrived at the Nioulargue to challenge *Altair's* domination of the classic fleet. / *Franco Pace*
Over Right: *Jessica* as originally rigged with square sail on the foremast. / *Franco Pace*
Over 2: *Adix*, the remodelled *Jessica* with her stretched out counter, simpler rig and deck structures. / *Franco Pace*

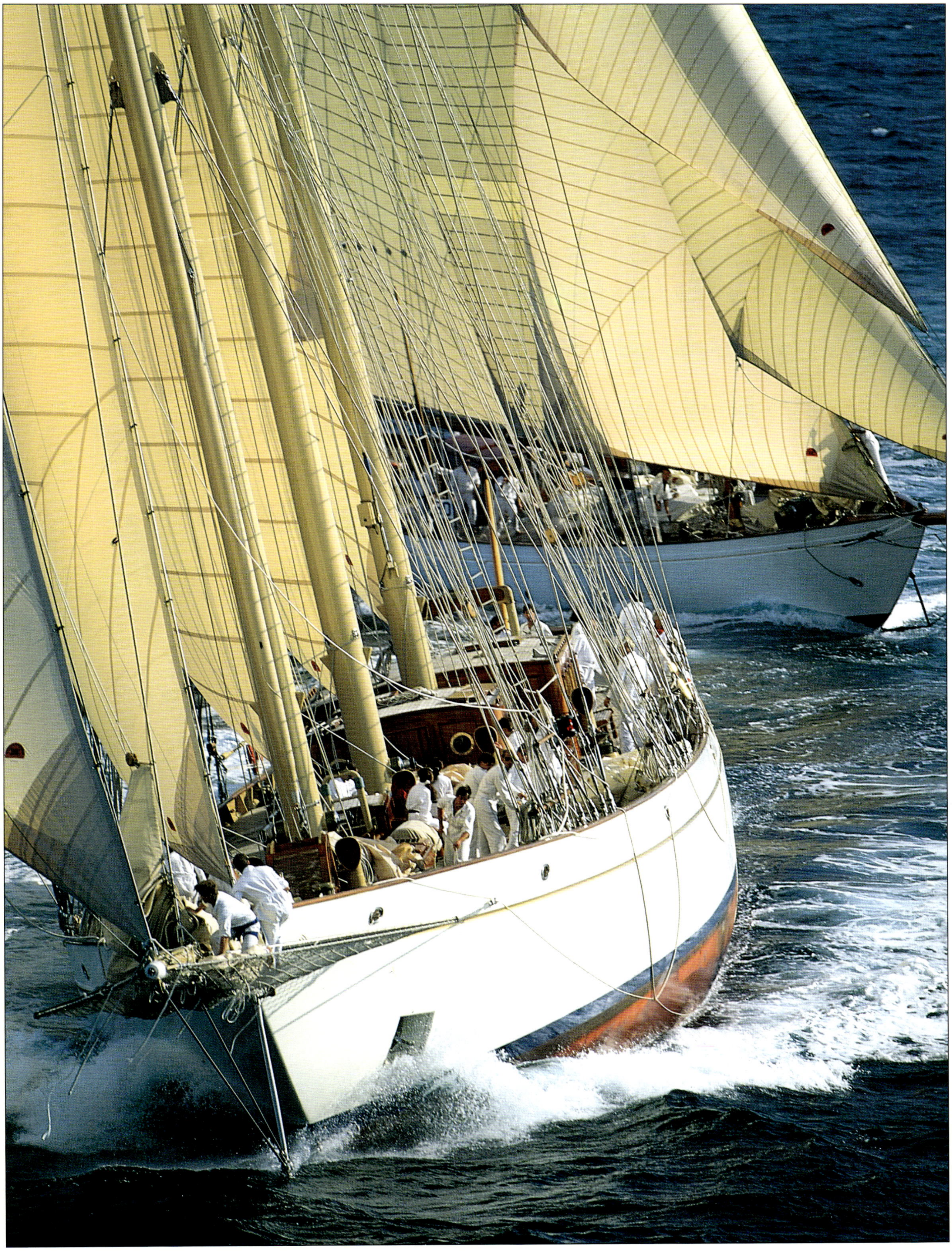

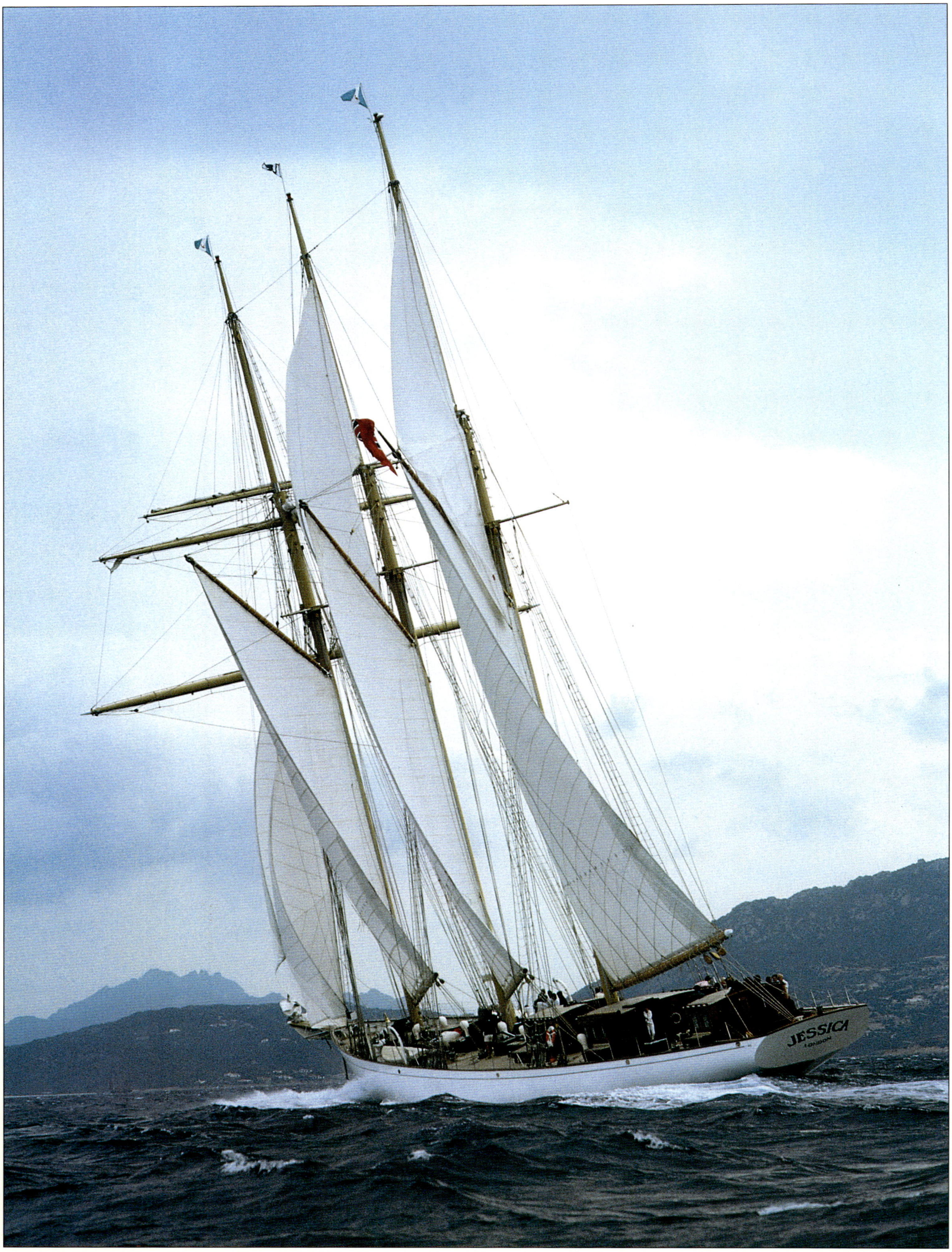
JESSICA
LONDON

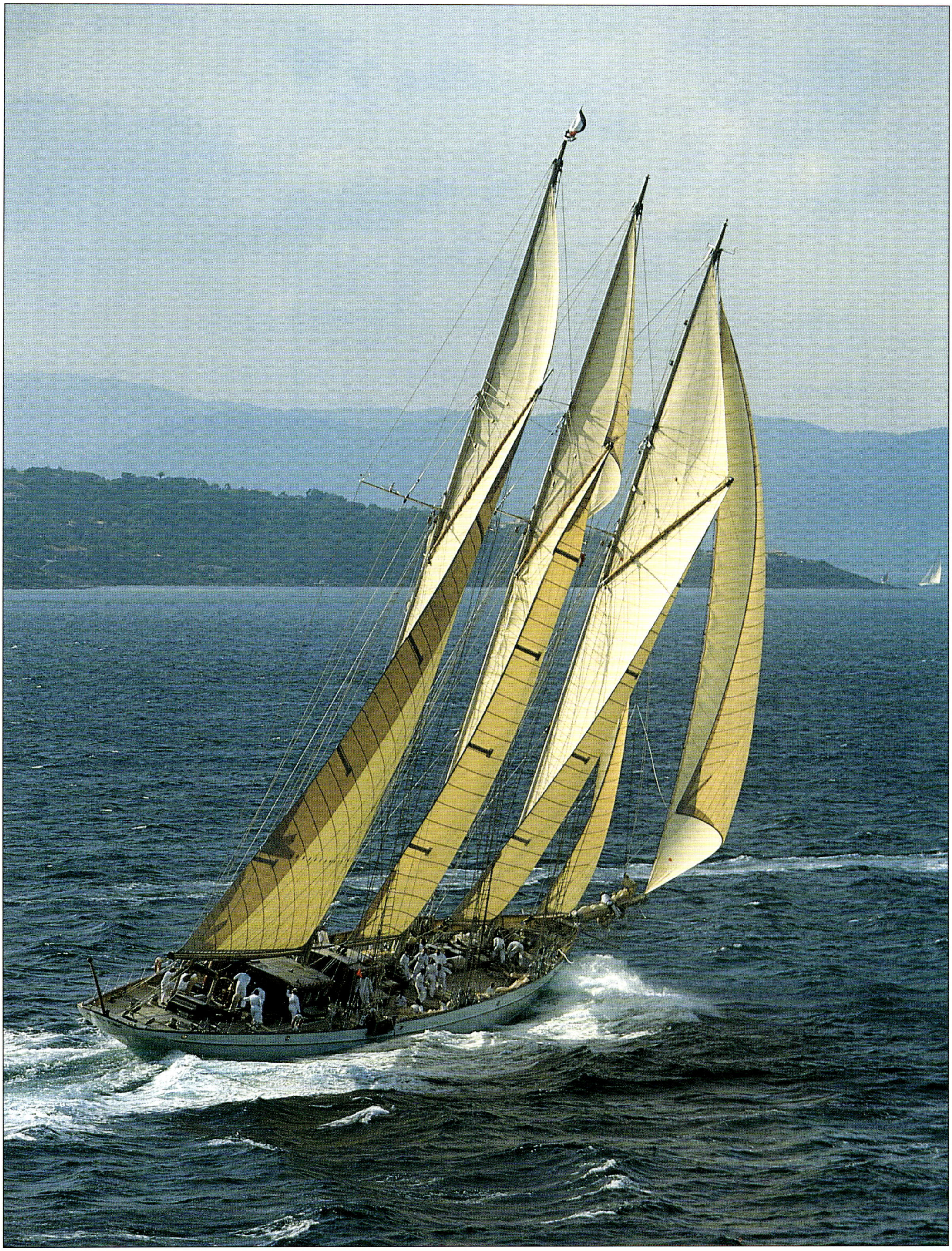

Notes

1. Mystic Seaport Museum, 236/1/2, George Rogers Ratsey Letter Book, 1814.
2. Dixon Kemp, Yacht Racing Calendar and Review for 1888, (London: Field, 1888), p. 113.
3. Mystic Seaport , op. cit.
4. Mystic Seaport Museum, Coll 236/1/1, Ratsey Waste Book 1813.
5. Southampton Town and County Herald, 12 August 1826.
6. Brooke Heckstall-Smith, Yachts & Yachting, (London: Studio, 1925), pp 17-19.
7. Brooke Heckstall-Smith, op. cit., pp. 20-1.
8. The Times, 1 October 1832.
9. Brooke Heckstall-Smith, op. cit., pp. 22.
10. Hampshire Telegraph, 1 June 1888.
11. Vanderdecken, Yachts & Yachting, (London: Hunt's, 1873), p. 86.
12. Mystic Seaport Museum, Coll 91/6/16, T. W. Ratsey to W. P. Stephens, 23 February 1921
13. Vanderdecken, op. cit., p. 90.
14. Hunt's Yachting Magazine, September 1852, p. 114.
15. G. L. Watson, *Progress in Yachting and Yacht Building*, in, Lectures on Naval Architecture and Engineering, (Glasgow: Collins, 1881), p. 122.
16. MS, James Stanley Lapthorn, *History of the Lapthorn's.*`
17. Hunts Yachting Magazine, April 1884, p. 192.
18. Thomas W. Ratsey, Lecture on *Sail Cloth and Sail Making*, 18 March 1924, p. 6.
19. Mystic Seaport Museum, Coll 236/1/11, T. W. Ratsey, *Improved Diagonal Sails*.
20. H. Horn, *Yacht Racing in 1893*, in, Duke of Beaufort, Yachting, (London: Longmans, 1894), p. 435.
21. The Yachtsman, 10 March 1892, p. 966.
22. The Yachtsman, 26 July 1894, p. 343.
23. Uffa Fox, Uffa Fox's Second Book, London: Davies, 1935), p.144.
24. Mystic Seaport Museum, Coll 236, Vol. 51, p. 24, T. W. Ratsey to W. G. Jameson, letter dated 25 April 1902.
25. Ibid.
26. Mystic Seaport Museum, Coll. 236, Vol. 51, p. 321, T. W. Ratsey to Ratseys & Lapthorn Cowes, letter dated 15 July 1902.
27. Mystic Seaport Museum, Coll. 236, Vol. 51, p. 70, Thomas W. Ratsey to Ratseys & Lapthorn Cowes, letter dated 22 April 1902.
28. Mystic Seaport Museum, Coll 236, Vol. 50, pp. 137 & 167
29. Mystic Seaport Museum, Coll 236, Vol. 50, p. 54, Edwin W. Lapthorn to Ratseys & Lapthorn, Cowes, letter dated 3 September 1902.
30. Mystic Seaport Museum, Coll. 236, Vol. 50, pp. 213 & 232.
31. Mystic Seaport Museum, Coll 236, Vol. 50., p. 19, E. W. Lapthorn to Ratseys & Lapthorn Cowes, letter dated 19 September 1902.
32. Mystic Seaport Museum, Coll 236, Vol. 50, p. 232.
33. Mystic Seaport Museum, Coll 236, Vol. 50, p.377.
34. John W. Nicholson, Great Years in Yachting, (Warsash: Nautical, 1970), pp. 169-70.
35. Hampshire Record Office, uncatalogued C. E. Nicholson letters, C. E. Nicholson to W. P. Burton, letter dated 20 August 1914.
36. D. J. Quigley, The Isle of Wight Rifles, (Cowes, Quigley, ND).
37. G. Colin Ratsey Interview, Tape 3, p. 5.
38. Thomas W. Ratsey, *Lecture on Sail Cloth and Sail-Making*, 18 March 1924, p. 7.
39. Thomas W. Ratsey, *The Story of the Sock*, transcript of speech made on 28 November 1929.
40. de Paula Log, Vol. 1, p. 29, 25 July 1928,
41. de Paula Log Vol. 1, p. 198, 7 July 1930
42. de Paula Log Vol. 1, p. 202-3, 15 July 1930
43. de Paula Log, Vol. 2, p. 166, 26 August 1931.
44. de Paula Log, Vol. 1, p. 86, 13 April 1929.
45. de Paula Log, Vol. 2, p. 70, 3 October 1931.
46. G. Colin Ratsey, interview tape 1, p. 20.
47. The Times, 12 March 1935.
48. G. Colin Ratsey, interview, tape 1, p. 16.`
49. G. Colin Ratsey, interview, tape 1, p. 16.
50. Mystic Seaport Museum, Coll. 236/3/3, James Stanley Lapthorn to George Ernest Ratsey, letter dated 15 February 1937.
51. Mystic Seaport Museum, Coll. 236/3/4, Peter Ross Lapthorn to Ernest Atkey Ratsey, letter dated 15 August 1940.
52. G. Colin Ratsey, interview, tape 2, p. 9.
53. G. Colin Ratsey, interview, tape 1, p. 13.